For T.H.E.

LOVE CHILD

LOVE CHILD

A True Story of Love, Loss and
Reunion

Sue Elliott

WINDSOR
PARAGON

First published 2012
by Vermilion, an imprint of Ebury Publishing
This Large Print edition published 2013
by AudioGO Ltd
by arrangement with
Ebury Publishing

Hardcover   ISBN: 978 1 4713 5803 6
Softcover   ISBN: 978 1 4713 5804 3

British Library Cataloguing in Publication Data available

Printed and bound in Great Britain by TJ International Limited

PREFACE TO THE SECOND EDITION

Of the many fascinating things I learnt from researching and writing this book perhaps the most profound is that adoption stories—my own included—don't usually have endings, happy or otherwise. They continue to unfold, rather like life itself. So it is unsurprising that *Love Child*, written in 2004, was only 'the story so far'. This new edition brings that story up to date with a Postscript and gives a snapshot of the UK adoption picture now.

Sadly, some of my original interviewees have since died. I feel privileged to have been able to tell their stories alongside my own. The letters I received after the book first appeared show most movingly that reading about the 20th-century experience of adoption can help others understand and cope with their own lives now. This also gives every reader an insight into previously hidden aspects of everyday life in our recent past. I hope it continues to do so.

Sue Elliott
Spring 2012

BEFORE

18 November 1951
Dear Mrs Wilson,

Could I have news of my Baby, Gillian? I have been longing to write before but thought it would be wiser to wait a week or so. I do hope she is settled now, and that she is happy with her new Mummy and Daddy, and that they like her too. She was such a Darling, and you can well imagine how very difficult it has been to give her up, but I can overcome all that if you can assure me her adopters are nice people. I would also like to know if she now has a different Christian name as I had rather hoped it would not be changed. I would greatly treasure a photograph of her, would that be possible, in a month or two?

I must now thank you for all your great kindness, and in making this decision I know I have done the right thing for the future happiness of my Baby.
Yours sincerely,
Miss . . .

20 November 1951
Dear Miss . . . ,

Thank you so much for your letter.

We have very happy news of your little girl. We had a letter from her adopters quite recently and they say 'I know that you will be pleased to know that baby has settled with us and completely taken charge of our hearts. She is the sweetest little baby, so contented and happy. We are both so happy with her, she is like a gift from heaven.'

1

I am sure you will gather from this that your baby is in good and loving hands and that you need have no fears for her future happiness. We shall hope to send you a photograph of her later on.
Yours sincerely,
General Secretary
National Children Adoption Association

*   *   *

The rain eased off. She brushed little balls of wet from her coat as she waited for the trolley bus. A memorable purchase, that coat, because it was her first without coupons for as long as she could remember. A week's wages. Five-and-a-half days of sitting at that switchboard under the staircase in that terrible draught. *Connecting you now.* It was a nondescript colour, like everything else that winter, but it had some semblance of style and looked more than passable with the Jacqmar scarf. Style was important to her. She could never bear to work far from nice shops. She never had—Piccadilly, Great Titchfield Street, Wigmore Street. Apart from during the war of course. Not much shopping then. That's when the rot set in, she thought.

And now here she was, looking smart for a telephonist in her high-heeled court shoes, matching bag and little felt hat, on the way to the Town Hall to sign the papers. She was keeping up appearances because Mum would have expected it and because it helped. Thirty-one and come to this. The bus hummed and rattled into the stop. She stepped back quickly to avoid the splashes from the swollen gutter. Grey suede—what had she been thinking of?

She sat down under the posters for trips into the country by Green Line. *Lucozade, the glucose drink for the Sick & Exhausted.* It's just sugar whizzed up in a bit of water, Mum always said. Shocking waste of money. Despite kept-up appearances, she was sick and exhausted. Pale beneath the Max Factor, thin under the imitation silk and the seven-guinea coat. Sick at heart. She was going to give her baby away.

'Hello! You look nice. Where are you off to?' She'd forgotten Betty lived on this route. For once she wasn't glad to see her old friend as she sat down in the seat in front.

'Oh, just into town. There's some new bags in Kennards I've got my eye on.'

'You and your bags. How are you keeping?'

Keeping. Barely keeping body and soul together, she thought, even as she said, 'You know. Not too bad really.' Betty knew about it of course. Not everything, but enough to be a comfort when everyone else looked at her with pity, superiority.

'I know,' she said. It was enough. They fell into silence until Betty got up for her stop. 'Come round after tea and we'll have a chinwag.'

Dear Betty. Apart from her father, whom she'd rather not have seen, Betty had been her only visitor at the home on Sydenham Hill. The Princess Alice Emergency Hostel. She expected it to be as grim as it sounded; you heard terrible things about these places. But she found help and humanity there. They were all sorts but they were all in the same boat: as young as 14 and as old as her or older, Scots and Irish and from Australia and South Africa. Mostly not religious—the

3

religious went to other places that sounded much worse. But they had to scrub and polish. The big mahogany central staircase was her job. She didn't enjoy it exactly, but it was satisfying in a way the switchboard wasn't and the days were long without proper work. And at the end of the summer, how those girls had loved and fussed over her beautiful baby. She saw it pass by, the ugly Victorian house called Castlebar with the highly polished staircase, a mirage in the steamy window.

She blamed the Fire Service and the war. She'd loved the work, the usefulness, being near to danger but not consumed by it. And the men. Just her and another girl in the station with all those men, sometimes all day and all night. It frightened her at first—the practical jokes, the remarks and the looks. Any 20-year-old would feel daunted. But she got used to it, then she quite liked it, then she embraced it. That intoxicating mixture of danger and fun and not knowing or caring about tomorrow. Not that she was a good-time girl. No, she liked to think she chose carefully, kept the worst of them at bay. But she did have her favourites and London was full of cheeky men who might not be there for a second date. The feeling of time passing too quickly gripped everyone. Her life then, as now, was about succumbing to the moment, exercising just the right amount of self-control and self-denial for decency, so that you could still look your mother in the eye. But there was too much pain and uncertainty in the world not to seize the chance of love among the chaos.

George had been there at the station and through it all with her. Not quite old enough to be her father but just the father she would have

4

wanted: a strong shoulder to cry on, a handsome enough face to be seen with, wise but never disapproving. His little girl. He looked after her as the men came and went. Through the tears, the scares, the excitements, he was there. Of course his motives can't have been entirely selfless, she realised that. Best not to delve too deeply into the true nature of their attachment, in case it revealed something unworthy in them both. He'd never asked more of her than she was prepared to give, and that was just as well.

At Katherine Street, she got off the bus and walked through the gardens towards the Town Hall. In her handbag were her father's fountain pen and two hankies among the ration books, letters and other jumble. Just before the entrance, the grey suede courts faltered and she turned away down the High Street instead, through Surrey Street market with its sodden crowds and cabbage leaves underfoot. Past the old woman who sold only brown paper carrier bags and pots of Brylcreem, until she came to a small shop on Crown Hill. *Treasure Cot*. A rather expensive shop that had done better before the war. She stood for a long time at the window, the sheets of cellophane casting a yellow pall over the tiny white smocked dresses, teething rattles and satin-tied booties. *For Your Treasured Tot*. She went in.

*   *   *

'You understand, don't you dear, that the Association wants to make sure that Gillian can remain with the parents who now have her and who will love and look after her in future? We

5

asked you here today to sign the documents that will allow an Adoption Order to be made. After this she will be theirs and you will have no further claim to her.'

'Yes. I'm sorry for being a bit late.'

The office was very warm and smelled of stale tobacco. She loosened her scarf and opened her bag for the pen. It felt heavy in her hand; her fingers fumbled with the top. She worried about it not working, then saw an image of floods of ink inundating the papers and drowning her, the woman from the Association and the Justice of the Peace. But her name flowed out just the same.

'You mustn't worry. The little girl will have a happy home life with two loving parents and everything you're not able to give her.'

The tone was sympathetic but the words sounded worn out. She didn't know what to say so she said nothing, returned the pen to her bag and did up her coat. 'Thank you Miss . . . Don't forget your shopping.'

She was by the door. She found her voice.

'No. Those things are for my baby. I want her to look nice for her adopters and I want them to know . . .'

What was it she wanted them to know? That their joy had been cruelly bought at her expense? That she'd fought with her father to keep the child, looked at vile live-in jobs in service rather than give her up?

'. . . I want them to know that I think they must be very wonderful people. Because only wonderful people deserve to have my Gillian.'

She felt proud, hot, slightly ridiculous in her coat. The man and woman in the room looked back at her.

'Of course dear, yes,' the woman said.

1

GROWING

One glorious day in October 1951, we were called upon to attend the offices of the Society. I say glorious day; it may have been raining with howling wind. Who cared, for it was our glorious day anyway. On the completion of formalities and the exchange of relevant information, we were left in a side room on our own. It seemed hours before the door opened and someone placed a bundle into Anne's awaiting arms, and then retreated from the room. Unbelievable. Our baby daughter to be known as Susan Margaret, born on 30 August, had arrived to enrich our lives. The sheer joy of holding our 'bundle'—fast asleep, sound and beautiful. Family life—the real family life—had begun.

You sometimes have to wait a long time to find out what really happened. After my mother died in 1996, my father found great comfort in writing the story of his life. I'd offered to transcribe his two-finger typed manuscript into something more permanent for the family. I learnt a great deal from it and was often moved by his memories.

But when I came to his description of the first moments of my life as their child, I had an extraordinarily emotional flash of revelation. Glowing rosily and short on facts as it was, I realised that this was the first reliable account I'd ever had of the most significant event of my life. And though the facts, such as they were, were no surprise, I still found myself trying to reconcile his story with that other one I'd grown up with. The one so many adopted people grow up with; the story about being chosen.

'Where did I come from?'

'You were chosen.'

'What's "chosen"?'

'Well, we went to London in Uncle's car and we chose you from a room full of tiny babies because you were pretty and good. We took you home and later we went to Court to promise that we would love and look after you forever. And so you became ours.'

My picture of this scene was always the same: a hall of Dickensian proportions with rows of cots, each containing a bawling infant, overseen by a navy blue matron in a pleated cap. In the middle was me, smiling, possibly with a little halo like in the picture of Mary and the baby Jesus in my bedroom. How could they have chosen anyone else?

For those of us who grew up as the subject of this comforting fairy tale, there comes a point, perhaps years later, when we realise that of course we weren't chosen at all. Some nameless person, undoubtedly a woman, probably in an adoption agency, put us together with our parents. We were matched, not chosen. But this doesn't really matter. As long as we feel loved by our parents, they have come to mean much the same thing. But seeing it written down more than 40 years after the event in a first-hand account by someone else who was there still produces a tingle akin to shock.

*   *   *

William Morris had his print works at Merton Abbey Mills by the River Wandle and it inspired one of his loveliest fabric designs. This unassuming watercourse—it barely qualifies as a river—meanders through the badlands of south London on its way up to meet the Thames at Wandsworth. Upstream in Beddington, where once the Wandle powered dozens of mills, raced over weirs and paused long enough to feed lush watercress beds, it still creates a flowing ribbon of green through undistinguished outer suburbia.

I grew up there, near some of those watercress beds in a cul-de-sac of modest 1930s semis called Wandle Court Gardens. Though the beds were choked with weeds by then, the Wandle was still just about clean enough to play in. My friends were Monica Viner and Susie Moulder. We put on puppet shows for a penny in aid of the Sunshine Homes for Blind Babies and made ourselves adventures based on what we'd read in Enid Blyton books. Sometimes we played with Jill Glass. I secretly wished I'd been called Jill and not Susan; there were so many Susans then. I went to Sunday School with Monica at the Baptist church in Wallington. To break the 30-minute walk there, we'd stop in a small woodland park halfway where Monica's father would tell us stories he made up about Black Jake the pirate.

The baby Jesus picture in my bedroom notwithstanding, my parents weren't churchgoers. They had married in 1942 when my mother was 22 and my father barely 20, propelled into union by the uncertainties of war. I loved looking at the few wedding photos they had: my mother petite, dark

11

and pretty with her huge bouquet; my father young and thin in an ill-fitting RAF uniform; pageboy and bridesmaid as satin Boy Blue and Bo Peep. The hand-coloured story they told seemed to come from another time, 'the olden days' I called them. I asked my mother over and over again to tell me about how they'd had to beg and borrow ration coupons for the outfits and the ingredients for the wedding cake. How my father caught influenza and the wedding had to be called off at the last minute. How they could only afford to have a handful of guests at the reception.

After the war, my father had returned to the Public Assistance Board in Croydon where he'd started as a 16-year-old junior clerk in 1938. He saw at first hand the Beveridge Welfare State reforms of 1948 that finally put paid to the old Poor Law and spent the rest of his working life in social services trying to solve other people's problems. 'Maybe we were still soldiers of a sort,' he wrote, 'only in civilian clothes—not seeking victory but seeking to heal. Maybe. Who knows?' He certainly hadn't come from a family imbued with a sense of public service; his father managed a jeweller's shop.

I have a precious pencil drawing taken from a photograph of my mother about the time of their engagement. She is beautiful. They met in the United Dairies shop where she was assistant manageress and were married for more than 50 years. My first birthday was marked by her setting fire to the kitchen curtains by leaving the candle burning on my cake and having to call out the fire brigade. She was there at home as I grew up and I loved her.

My mother made my clothes. After work my father sometimes took me for walks beyond the watercress beds to the allotments where I remember big piles of soot. It was a very sooty place then. Everyone burned coal in the grate, gas came from the sulphurous gasworks on the Purley Way, and smoke from thousands of domestic and industrial chimneys smothered everything with vile yellow smogs every winter. When we first had a television in 1957, I wondered why the Lone Ranger didn't cough. Everyone I knew coughed.

To ward off germs we had viscous National Health orange juice in medicine bottles that we took by the spoonful, and disgusting-tasting cod liver oil capsules. I must have been bandy because I had to go to an old house in a park and do exercises that 'made windows' with my legs. Upstairs in the same house (I can see the oak panelling and the carved banisters of the staircase now) I went for 'sunray treatment'. This meant joining other toddlers in knickers and goggles in an eerily lit room where we played with toy cars around a big humming machine that transmitted ultraviolet rays.

The scarcity of natural sunlight and the absence of central heating at home failed to chill my warm and comfortable life. My parents weren't well off but I knew they loved me.

*   *   *

I knew I was adopted long before I went to school, at least I assume I did. I can't really remember a

13

time before I knew. As soon as I started asking where I came from, my mother must have told me the 'chosen' story. It was a story I liked to hear often. Very little was added in the telling though I remember hearing that my first mother wasn't able to look after me. And I was told there had been another baby Susan before me who had died, and that's why I'd been chosen. I was fascinated by this other baby Susan and wanted to know more about her but I saw that this upset my mother, so I stopped asking.

I learnt much later that Susan Mary had died suddenly at four months in 1948 from a previously undiagnosed heart condition. My mother had a history of miscarriage and high blood pressure, which must have made the death of their first child all the more devastating. I could never talk to her about it; it stayed raw all those years.

When I was five, my mother gave birth to my brother Simon. This was a revelation. So babies came from two places: Mummy's tummy and 'chosen'. Right. And they obviously happened alternately because there was the first baby Susan (tummy), then me (chosen), then Simon (tummy again). It all seemed perfectly plausible. Thrilled by my cleverness at working this out, I told all my friends who were second-borns that this was how families were planned and that they must therefore be adopted. Embarrassment, confusion and distress to children and adults alike ensued and I got a ticking off. But this was my first attempt to figure out how adopted people fit in to the world.

I went to the local primary school where the post-war teacher shortage was still much in evidence and classes were often large. At one point there were 56 in my class. We crammed three to a desk and did a lot of something called 'shredding'. The class teacher was a handicrafts specialist and in every spare moment she had us pulling scraps of fabric apart into their constituent threads to make stuffing for her soft toys. This was an excellent method of crowd control but it didn't teach us much. Singing in the choir ('Rolling Down to Rio' and 'Pedro the Fisherman' are still there in my head after 45 years) and writing compositions allowed me to go to another place that was altogether more exciting and uplifting than 1950s Beddington.

The 11-plus exam was a big deal then; it determined whether you got a half-decent education in a grammar school or were consigned to a future in a paper bag factory via the local secondary modern. I neither passed nor failed my 11-plus. I was 'borderline' and told to expect an interview to see whether I would go to one of the delicious-sounding grammar schools—Coloma, Old Palace or Wallington High—where there were only girls and you got to wear hats and braided blazers. Or to the secondary modern by Hackbridge sewage works, which was full of rough boys.

For reasons my disappointed parents never got to the bottom of, the promised interview was never offered and so I went to Hackbridge. I never expected life to be fair after that.

*   *   *

The first thing I learnt about my life before I was adopted came about quite by chance as we were on

15

a bus going round Hyde Park Corner. My mother, apropos of nothing, suddenly volunteered the information that I had been born at St George's Hospital, a grand building dominating London's busiest roundabout, now the Lanesborough Hotel. This made me feel very excited and proud, to think I had come from the epicentre of this world capital, from this wonderful building. Its position, its importance lent me a prestige uncommon in Beddington. It was about the best thing I'd heard since I was told I was chosen. Only many years later did I discover it was completely wrong.

I never thought very much about my 'life before' until adolescence, when I judged it safe to venture some further questions. I had already assumed and unquestioningly accepted a great deal, whether by failure of imagination or sense of self-preservation. I knew I had a mother who had given birth to me. I knew she couldn't look after me so she had given me up. Only married people could have babies, couldn't they? Adoption was just something that happened; it was part of the natural order of things. There was no doubt in my mind that everything had followed its appointed course; there was nothing unusual or suspect about what had happened to me. But there was a woman out there who had a large part in determining the person I was, and I knew nothing at all about her.

It usually happened at the sink as my mother washed and I dried.

'You know before you had me?'

'Mmm.'

'Did you know anything about my other mother?'

'Not very much really. She was the same age as

16

me, and she was a telephonist. And she wasn't married, which was why she couldn't look after you. I think your father was a Company Secretary where she worked.'

'Did you know her name?'

'Mmm? An old-fashioned name I think. Might have been a Yorkshire name.'

'What, like Braithwaite or something?'

'Mmm, something like that.'

I knew she knew. But she was about to distract me with something much more intriguing.

'You arrived with lovely baby clothes that came from a very expensive shop. I think I've still got them somewhere.'

I wove a story from these few facts. My mother was a country girl from the North who came to London to seek her fortune. She was pretty, lively and successful and had glamorous affairs with rich men. I was the product of a long affair with her boss at work; they were in love but he was already married, possibly to a madwoman in an attic like Mr Rochester in *Jane Eyre*. She had me in the poshest hospital in London and bought me clothes from the most expensive shops. She must have loved me, mustn't she?

I entirely accepted that this was all the information I was going to get. The subject of my adoption was still inextricably linked to the tragedy of the other baby Susan and was therefore far too sensitive for idle enquiry. It wasn't that my mother (it didn't occur to me to ask my father) withheld information, but she imparted it with such caution, such obvious unease, that I feel uncomfortable writing about these exchanges even now. So my questions, such as they were, remained unasked.

17

It wasn't difficult growing up adopted. No one called me a bastard—though I was called a stinking polecat once at Guides—but on the other hand it was quite possible that hardly anyone knew. Obviously the family knew, though it was never referred to, and though my best friends knew, it wasn't cause for either interest or sympathy. I harboured my chosen-ness and my special-ness to myself. I knew my parents loved me. They didn't say so. Parents didn't then. But I knew anyway.

*   *   *

'How would you like to live at the seaside?'

Well of course we would. In 1964 we moved to Bognor where we all began a new life. My mother stopped using her first name Lily, which she'd always disliked. 'Lilies remind me of death,' she said, and adopted her second name, Anne, which sounded much more modern. My father started a new social work job in rural West Sussex, which he loved. My mother got a job as a school secretary, and we lived in a brand new bungalow near the sea, the height of 1960s' modernity. My father painted my room purple and I listened to Wonderful Radio London in the 'homework cupboard' he fitted out for me.

I went to another secondary modern and made friends with a quiet girl called Linda. Linda and I grew raucous together, cackling over endless private jokes. We played at being Mods' molls on Bognor seafront and wrote our book 'The Cabbage Flowers'. *'We do not profess to have produced a conventional thesis on the pchycological (sic) aspects of being sixteen,'* it began portentously, *'but a*

18

truthful, unserious, unabridged narrative on life as we now see it.' This was 1967 and we were actually 15, but we were always in the business of making things sound better than they were. There was a great deal in it about boys ('talent'), and very little about sex, though in a section titled 'Philosophical Gems' we regurgitated the received schoolgirl wisdom of the time:

If you give boys what they want they laugh at you behind your back and call you a tart, if you don't they don't take any notice of you. You're a failure either way—so what do you do?

At school we were the odd couple, different from the girls called Laramie and Lorraine who did Child Care, Typing or Retail, some of whom mysteriously disappeared for months on end and then came back older and sadder. We were going to pass our O levels and make something of ourselves.

We weren't thought university material. I'd always loved being in school plays and fantasised about drama school. The careers teacher was doubtful: 'Drama school? Ooh no, I shouldn't think so. I suppose we could try and get you on a drama course at teacher training college.'

This was when I first encountered my birth certificate. You had to send it, together with proof of your exam results, to get in. I'd never seen mine before. It was disappointingly short. I don't think I expected it to give me any information about my other life, but this flimsy bit of toilet paper was brief to the point of insult. On it was my name, my sex, my date of birth and my country of birth,

19

England, and that was all. Other people had much bigger and more self-important birth certificates stacked with interesting facts about occupations and places of birth. This deliberately uninformative piece of paper seemed to prove that there was something about me worth hiding.

The other thing you had to do to get in to teacher training college was have a medical. This also raised adoption questions.

'Any family history of TB, heart disease or mental illness?'

I didn't think so, but I had absolutely no idea. It didn't worry me much, as apart from the cough I'd never been ill. I instinctively felt there wasn't anything, but over the years I still found myself drawn to depressing television documentaries about Huntington's chorea and other inheritable fatal conditions.

Despite my blank family medical history and a bare pass at O level maths, they let me in to Trent Park College in Cockfosters, at the northernmost tip of the Piccadilly Line. The three women I met on my first day in the hall of residence are, after 35 years, still my closest friends.

'We're just off to the library!'

And, to much winking and giggling, they went. There was a lot in the papers about women's liberation as the 1960s turned into the 1970s, but contraception was still officially only available to the married or the formally engaged. Getting your hands on the Pill involved cunning and subterfuge. The Family Planning Association had just set up shop in the same building as the public library in Enfield. Jenny was about to be married to Nigel 'in carpets', and had her engagement ring as proof;

Alyson didn't but she was in a steady relationship with David. I envied them.

I left Trent Park with an undistinguished BEd, and four of us rented a grim flat with orange swirly carpets and turquoise paint on Wood Green High Road. My first and last teaching job was in a Catholic comprehensive school off the North Circular in Finchley where threats of eternal damnation were tempered by a caring pastoral system. At the end of my probationary year the Head called me into his office where he always kept a well-stocked bar.

'Well Susan, you've had a good probationary year. Joe O'Boyle says your lesson plans are exemplary.'

He winked. We all knew his deputy tended to fuss a bit and thought things like lesson plans were vitally important.

'But seriously, with hard work, there's a good chance you could be our first Head of Drama in five years' time.'

Five years. I didn't want to look that far ahead. More immediately attractive prospects were being offered by the Head of Creative Arts, a smooth-talker who had asked me to move to Bristol and live with him. It was my first serious relationship and I would have followed him anywhere. I wanted to share how I felt about him with my mother but she struggled to understand, and my handwriting didn't help:

Dear Sue,
Many thanks for your letter. It has taken me a couple of days to read some of the words & to read between the lines! I'm still not quite sure what you're

21

getting at but as you are going to the F.P.A. I gather that John is persuading you to form a 'relationship' or get married! When you say was Daddy as persistent or convincing at this stage (what stage?)— well that sort of thing was unheard of in those days, at least as far as we were concerned. Anyway dear, you make the decision if you feel you don't want to wait and you're sure you are in love. I wouldn't like a Sandra situation to develop or you could be left high and dry. All is well. Daddy has finished the kitchen. The Renault didn't pass its MOT, shaft has gone . . .

The 'Sandra situation' my mother feared so much referred to a friend whose engagement had foundered when she became pregnant; she'd had a distressing abortion.

I gave a term's notice and went for job interviews in Bristol.

That summer we lived love's young dream between his flat in Hampstead, and Dartington in Devon, where we walked and went for wild drives in his Triumph Spitfire. I'd just gone on the Pill and thought I'd cracked it. Here I was with this witty, artistic and attractive man who paid court and bought me impulsive presents. Miffy the white rabbit, a children's book character, was our love symbol. One day he turned up with a live white Miffy for me. It cost me a fortune for the hutch and the poor thing died of cold the following January.

As I was about to go back to school for my final term, I was waiting anxiously for my period to come. Even before going on the Pill I'd always been regular. I panicked. He didn't seem to take it at all seriously, joking about not having room in the Spitfire for the pushchair, and what lovely parents we'd make. I was flattered into half-believing he was pleased at the thought of having children with me, but rather than being excited at the prospect myself, I was horrified and afraid. I knew this wasn't what I wanted at all. An exciting and glamorous affair, such as those I'd fantasised my birth mother having, was one thing. Having a child right at what felt like the start of my adult life seemed appalling bad management and too much like horrible reality. I got a glimpse into her life, her dilemma, then.

And I realised, too, what I really felt about marriage and children. I'd always said that I wouldn't get married 'till at least 28', because I grew up believing that everyone had to get married sooner or later, and that seemed an age far enough into infinity for me not to have to think about it. But now I knew marriage and family life didn't appeal to me. I wasn't interested when others showed off their babies, or when my mother stopped to coo over merchandise in baby shop windows. When you're young you have a picture of yourself grown up. I never had a young womanhood picture; mine went straight to middle age.

'Our Susie will end up writing books in a country cottage surrounded by cats,' my mother would say, rather regretfully, I always thought. But she was right; that was my dream. My early admiration for Enid Blyton had turned my head. How I longed to live her life in 'Green Hedges', the Metroland Tudorbethan mansion where she wrote adventure stories on the loggia, whatever a loggia was. It sounded blissful and I wanted to be like that. And

23

it didn't go with babies.

I discovered my feared pregnancy was a false alarm shortly before I discovered that my lover was married, though living apart from his wife. And soon after that it became clear that I wasn't his only girlfriend either. My first big fling had collapsed in disaster and I'd had a near miss. Before, I'd wondered how people could possibly get themselves into that situation; now I saw how easy it was.

*   *   *

The disaster in my personal life gave me an opportunity to leave teaching. In January 1975 I started work in the Education department of the Independent Broadcasting Authority in Knightsbridge. Meanwhile, Linda had married the man who ran the amusements on Bognor seafront where we'd spent so much time hankering after acned youths on Lambrettas, and was back at our old school, teaching. Here, she reported that life among the Laramies had changed since our time:

Feel a little aggrieved because no one told me the 'true' facts of life. 'Things a girl ought to know' are usually things she knew and put into practice long before. This state of mind has developed slowly but surely since Monday when I had to take Joyce Hobbs' Social Education lesson. Tackling such horrendous topics as abortion, the Pill, the Pill for men, other people's Pills, pills in general, pill or cure and that old favourite 'The only contraceptive 100% safe is No', I was struck with the thought of how inadequate and, more to the point, how irrelevant it all was. The 'gals' weren't worried about whether or not to, just if they were getting it enough and of a sufficiently good quality. Perhaps instead we should give teach-ins on 'How to tell your mother you aren't pregnant' and 'Coitus interruptus for a fag—can it damage your health?'

I'd been in my new job a little while when I saw a personal ad in the *Guardian*. A television documentary about adoption was looking for interviewees. I felt I had something to say so I wrote off:

My own experience as an adopted child has been quite unspectacular and so, in its own way, may be of interest to you . . . I suppose I did fantasise about being the unacknowledged daughter of royalty or something, and I was aware of being 'special', though in a rather nice way I thought. Friends were always rather surprised when (if it seemed appropriate) I told them. 'But you're so like your Dad . . .' etc., as if adoption was a bit like lunacy in the family. I often, too, heard others excuse someone with problems with 'Well, she's adopted you know.' It didn't worry me at all, knowing how lucky and happy I was . . .

. . . The provisions of the new Children's Act (can't remember its proper name) I suppose do make a difference. I could find out more if I wanted to. I could even try to find my mother, though it's a thought I'd prefer to keep in the back of my mind rather than act on in any way. It's an option I'd rather leave open. My Mum and Dad may not be my natural parents, but they are my real ones.

25

I was interviewed for the programme and said much the same thing. I was defiant in my defence of adopted people and their adoptive parents, dismissive of those who agonised about their origins, unsympathetic to those with unhappy adoption experiences, and I made a terrible throwaway joke about my conception probably taking place after the office Christmas party.

It was a performance I'm ashamed of now, but one based on what I knew and believed at the time. It was also probably the first small watershed in my long journey to reaching a better understanding of what adoption means. I had part of the picture then, the part provided by loving adoptive parents, to whom my natural instinct was fierce loyalty. And I had me, a young woman struggling between self-confidence and self-doubt. Having to think about what I would say on the programme, and the possibilities that new legislation opened up, started a process. I began to acknowledge that there were other parts to the story I always knew were there but which I had, consciously or not, suppressed.

I was on the phone to my mother shortly after this, talking about the preparations for my brother Simon's 21st birthday.

'I can't believe he's going to be 21. Seems like only weeks ago we were having fights over his Scalextric.'

'Car mad, that boy. By the way, do you know when your programme's going to be on?'

'Not yet, but I should soon.'

'I suppose we'd better tell him.'

'Tell him what? About the programme?'

'Well yes, that. But first we'd better tell him you were adopted.'

I laughed in disbelief. It had never for a moment occurred to me that he didn't know. The reasons for not telling him seemed completely understandable: I was already five by the time he came along and by then my parents didn't think of me as anything other than their own. As my father said then and since, 'You were ours, Ducks.'

*   *   *

Like other legislation, adoption law sometimes takes years to have an effect. It wasn't till the early 1980s that reunion stories started to appear in the press and on television. The 1975 Children Act allowed adoptees in England and Wales access to their birth records for the first time. This resulted not in the immediate flood of applications social workers expected and tried to prepare for, but a slow-growing awareness that the search for origins was now not only legal but practical too. There was an increasing number of reunions between adopted people, their birth parents and siblings. This also provided a platform for the player whose voice had not been heard before. The forgotten birth mother.

She was supposed to have put past indiscretions and misfortunes behind her and started afresh, but instead these women's stories told of lifetimes of loss and regret. They never forgot the child given up for adoption. Even over the course of intervening decades, the scar of separation never properly healed.

Throughout the 1980s I was transfixed by stories of how mothers of illegitimate children had been treated—not only earlier in the century, but much more recently. As the old mental asylums closed in the wake of new 'care in the community' policies, they relinquished their oldest and saddest inmates, institutionalised beyond repair. Among them were women in their seventies and eighties, incarcerated in the 1920s as moral defectives for having a child out of wedlock. They were biddable, poor and not very bright, and they paid doubly for their disadvantage by being locked away for much of their adult lives for violating someone else's idea of respectability. It seemed inconceivable that this could happen in 20th-century Britain and I was fired by the injustice of it.

But there was more, and more recently, about the mothers of children given up for adoption. There were stories of unfeeling social workers, mercenary adoption societies, cruel policies that denied natural mothers any rights, even the right to exist. Hogarthian images of babies ripped from the breast and outraged tales of anguish and loss regularly made the feature pages and colour supplements of the quality newspapers; and television discovered the visceral pull of on-screen mother-and-child reunions. It was all high-octane emotion. I was at once enthralled and sceptical.

About the same time, I was dealing with television programmes about child abuse. I worked for the commercial television regulator and by then part of my job was to vet programmes likely to 'offend public taste or decency' before they went out. We didn't think of ourselves as censors but we were still making decisions about what could and could not be shown. Some of the abuse allegations were so shocking and extreme we found them hard to believe. Because we didn't want to think about the possibility that babies could be raped, it was much easier to believe that the stories were the products of disturbed imaginations. We were soon convinced that they weren't. It was entirely possible that the testimonies of birth mothers weren't either.

Adoption, till then a well-kept secret with inexplicably grubby edges, became in a matter of years a hot topic for every other daytime problem programme, peaktime documentary and entertainment 'people show'. The media were fixated on the reunion as the spectacular centrepiece and denouement of every adoption story. This new interest and openness at last gave everyone involved, adopted people and birth parents in particular, permission to discuss something that had long been unmentionable. This must have horrified many adoptive parents who didn't expect their private business to be so brutally exposed, but the process couldn't be halted. The genie was out.

For my part, I was trying to reconcile all my naive prejudices about adoption being a neat and humane solution to surplus babies and childless homes with an explosion of troubling new information. It was all much more complex and disturbing than I'd thought. And for me personally, this was when the open option to search for my birth mother became a slow-burning probability. My love and loyalty to my parents were unshakeable, but there was now a new and uncomfortable possibility to be considered. My security, and the enrichment of their lives, could well have been bought at someone else's expense. I needed to know whether this was the case and, if so, what I could do about it.

But I had very little to go on, not even a name.

2

THE VICTORIAN LEGACY

Before I thought about it very much, I assumed that adoption in the 20th century must always have happened the way it happened to me in 1951. But history isn't like that and the history of adoption is no different. It had as many twists, convolutions and subtle evolutionary changes in the past 100 years as the social attitudes and developments that helped shape it.

One of my favourite Ladybird books as a small child was the story of Moses in the bulrushes. I loved the illustrations of exotic Egyptian palaces and the romantic story of the princess finding Moses in his basket. I didn't make the connection then, but this was the first adoption story, apart from my own, that I'd come across. Adoption is at least as old as Moses and happened in many different cultures throughout history, but it wasn't until well into the 20th century that it really took off in Britain. It wasn't even legally recognised in England and Wales until the first Adoption Act of 1926 (1929 in Northern Ireland and 1930 in Scotland). This was some way behind the American state of Massachusetts which formalised adoption in 1851, with Western Australia and part of New Zealand following at the turn of the century.

As I discovered, the development of adoption in Western countries closely mirrors fluctuations in the social, economic and moral climate. In Britain, this means the history of adoption is all about poverty, class and attitudes to what makes a family. Above all, it is about bastards.

For anyone under 80 a bastard is just a crude name for a horrible man. But for centuries, and certainly until the 1960s, it meant something more serious and much more real. It wasn't a name you casually attached to someone you didn't like; you either were a bastard or you weren't. If you were, you were one for life and there wasn't much you could do about it. It meant you were born out of wedlock, your mother and father weren't married, you were the shameful product of sin, unwanted and unacknowledged. You were a non-person. You couldn't take your father's name or inherit his money or his title if he had one. In the Middle Ages, bastards were *filii nullius*—the children of no one. You had no rights and no legal identity.

Through the Internet, I found an intriguing book, *Orphans of the Living, A Study of Bastardy*, in a second-hand bookshop. Published in 1968 (incidentally the peak year for adoptions in Britain), it is a powerful polemic by Diana Dewar about, as the jacket blurb puts it, 'one of society's perennial and most painful diseases'. Dewar produces strong research and stronger opinions about the possible solutions to the disease— including adoption—but for me she puts her finger on where it all started:

The British particularly suffer from ancestor worship and reveal extraordinary snobbery about family tradition. The Latin tags on many a family coat of arms proclaim purity and virtue while the lineage records bastardy.

I'm suddenly back in the art room at my secondary modern in 1962. We're having a lesson on heraldry, constructing coats of arms for our families. My Dad is a local government Welfare Officer, so the teacher suggests a quill pen and a few coins to symbolise, I suppose, his idea of my father as a pen-pusher who hands out money to the undeserving poor. But in that lesson we learn about something I find fascinating: the *bend sinister*. This is a band that crosses diagonally from bottom left to top right of a heraldic shield. It is the 'wrong' way round from the usual top left to bottom right and it signifies that the holder is a bastard son. How I love the language of heraldry— the chevrons, lozenges and unicorns rampant—but the bend sinister seems to say so much about family relationships, about bastards being different, set apart and, well, sinister.

I think after that I developed a rather romanticised idea about bastards from 16th- and 17th-century English history, where Charles II put it about a bit and rewarded his mistresses and illegitimate offspring with land and titles. But now I learnt from Diana Dewar and histories of child welfare that the reality of bastardy for the rest of the country over the next three centuries was anything but romantic.

In Britain at the start of the 20th century, Victoria was still on the throne, class distinctions and moral codes were absolute, and life among the working classes was cheap. The lives of children were the cheapest. The Welfare State was nearly 50 years away, children were considered the chattels of their parents and had no rights of their own. Those unfortunate enough to be born into extreme poverty or outside marriage—the two often went hand in hand—were lucky to survive at all. In the early decades of the century, adoption was the least likely outcome for those who did.

Moving a child from one family to another when the parents had died, were impoverished or rejected their illegitimate offspring, had gone on quietly for centuries in Britain. But these transfers were less likely to be adoptions as we understand them than permanent paid fostering arrangements, sometimes known as 'boarding out'. The parent kept full legal rights over the child and often stayed in contact, if only occasionally.

I met Barbara Norrice in 2000 when I was involved in producing a local history book about the area of west London where I live. She is a reserved but very likeable woman who has devoted her life to teaching, much of it in Africa. There is something gentle and otherworldly about her, as if she finds herself, like a time traveller, several decades ahead of the age in which she feels most comfortable. Barbara was the surprise discovery of the architectural historian we had commissioned to write the history of our estate, a small garden suburb founded by radical Liberal MP and creator of the workers' Co-partnership movement, Henry Vivian. Born in 1921, Barbara was Vivian's only child, the illegitimate daughter of a long relationship with his wife's niece. The three lived in an unconventional ménage in the London suburb of Crouch End. Barbara's mother was sent to her sister in Yorkshire to have the child, and at six weeks Barbara went to live with Jane, a professional foster mother. She spent the next

20 years with Jane, her widowed mother whom Barbara called 'Granny', and Jane's son.

When I was about five or six I had whooping cough and went to Brighton with Jane to recuperate. Aunt Dorothy and my Uncle came to see us. I was very excited, especially when they arrived in a large chauffeur-driven car. I know I didn't behave very well, but my Uncle gave me a lovely ice cream.

The man who bought her the ice cream was her father. She never saw Vivian, who died in 1930, again. She had to wait till she was 21 to learn the truth, from a letter written by the woman she knew as 'Aunt Dorothy'. The revelation did not bring them closer. Dorothy chose not to acknowledge her daughter publicly or even to other members of the family, and they had an uneasy relationship until Dorothy died in 1959. Finally, at her mother's funeral, she was introduced and welcomed into the family. Barbara has suffered from depressive illness during her life, perhaps as a result of her strange upbringing, but she is stoical about her mother's position:

I've come to realise what a price my mother paid for remaining silent all her life about our relationship. It must have been very lonely for her watching me grow up stage by stage, yet not being able to talk about it. My parents could have had me adopted and never seen me again, yet that was not an option they chose. Was it loyalty to my father that led my mother to such secrecy? Perhaps it was because she belonged to a generation that felt silence was the only possible response to such a situation.

Barbara was fortunate to have an affluent and influential father who could afford a long-term private boarding-out arrangement, otherwise she might have found herself in the workhouse like the majority of illegitimate babies and destitute children, enduring a particularly loveless and deprived time. Probably up to 80,000 children were living in workhouses at any one time in the early years of the 20th century. If they were luckier, they found themselves in voluntary institutions like Dr Barnardo's Homes, the Methodist Children's Home, or the homes of the Waifs and Strays Society run by the Church of England.

I learnt a lot about the very first of these institutions, the Foundling Hospital, from Jamila Gavin's powerful novel for children, *Coram Boy*. The hospital was started in London in 1739 by Thomas Coram, a sea captain who'd made his money from shipbuilding. After spending time in the American colonies he returned to London and was outraged by the numbers of babies he saw left for dead on dung heaps and young children abandoned on doorsteps. In a fascinating story of early philanthropy, he set about marshalling his contacts among the gentry and glitterati to finance a home for illegitimate children.

Coram knew all the celebrities of the time: Handel arranged special performances of *The Messiah*, and Hogarth, Reynolds and Gainsborough donated pictures to raise funds. The Foundling Hospital became the fashionable good cause of the day and, incidentally, the first art gallery in Britain. It is a wonderful story, told graphically at the Foundling Museum on the site of the old

36

Hospital in Brunswick Square. This overlooks the playgrounds and open spaces dedicated to children that are now known as Coram Fields. Here you can see the keepsakes the departing mothers left for their children—from expensive jewellery to pathetic ribbons—and their farewell letters (*'Go gentle babe . . . And all thy life be happiness and love'*). We may see them now, centuries later, because they were never passed on to the children they were meant for.

Coram took only the mother's first child—he didn't want to be accused of encouraging immorality—but his Foundling Hospital made sure the children were fed, clothed and sent back out into the world with a solid trade and good Christian values. The boys went into the Navy and the girls went into domestic service. As babies they were boarded out with foster mothers in the country then recalled to London at the age of five for a regimented institutional life. What seems heartless now was believed character-forming then. This pattern continued for the best part of 200 years.

I met John Caldicott, a 'Foundling' as they still call themselves, now retired and living in the Oxfordshire countryside. John was born David Throsell in 1936, the illegitimate son of Daisy Throsell, a domestic servant working in Golders Green. Daisy left her job in disgrace and faced destitution, but rather than leave David in the workhouse (*'she believed I'd be raised as an imbecile as there was no education in those places'*) she took him to the Foundling Hospital. Here, like all Foundlings, his name was changed and he was boarded out with a foster mother in the country.

Then, when he was nearly six, he was taken to the Foundling's boarding school in Berkhamsted where he stayed until 1952.

We were just taken by our foster mothers on a coach to the school and left there. The way it was done was very callous. I landed up in this great big hall and the only thing I can really remember is a load of these blue chairs stacked all over the place, and my mother saying to a very stiff and starchy nurse, 'He wets the bed.' She said, 'He won't any more.' There were no goodbyes. You were taken by the nurse and out. There was no love. We would run around in gangs but we never made close friends.

Although many children developed close ties with their foster mothers during their first five years, adoptions were discouraged. The Foundling Hospital's job was to take responsibility for their charges till they were 21, not hand them over to someone else. In any case, John's life with his foster mother was miserable.

She was a cruel woman. She had four others of us, all boys, she always had boys. But we were brought up to be subservient and grateful to those who had taken us in, so I never liked to criticise her.

Life at Berkhamsted sounded little better.

The Foundling Hospital hadn't changed since Georgian times. When I went there in 1942 I was dressed in the brown serge uniform, the red waistcoat and white Eton collar that the children had been wearing since the 1800s. And the way the school was

38

run hadn't changed either. The boys were segregated from the girls, the girls always on the right, the boys always on the left in the school as you walked in, and the only time you would see the girls was at church on Sundays. At mealtimes the girls were on one side and the boys were on the other. There were glass doors which were never opened, or they weren't opened till 1947. That was the first time we saw the girls eating.

His wife Kay got out an old uniform to show me: unlined chocolate brown serge jacket and breeches and red waistcoat lined with calico, all with brass buttons carrying the Hospital's lamb insignia. Like a little military uniform from the 18th century. Stiff, scratchy and made to last.

Things only started to change at the Foundling Hospital in the 1950s. The school at Berkhamsted was taken over by the local education authority and institutional care gave way to adoption and fostering. The Coram Foundation, as it became— and later, Coram Family—was to play a much more positive role in the adoption story from the 1960s onwards.

But in the early decades of the last century, boarding out and institutional care—often a combination of the two—were the traditional means of dealing with abandoned children. Though social reformers like Barnardo revered the family, he believed children had to be removed from the malign degenerative influence of 'bad' parents, ideally to a disciplined communal setting where Christian values could be instilled and children 'trained' to lead a better life. The National Children's Home, as the Methodist Children's Home became from 1908, took a more

39

proactive approach, allowing its foster parents to adopt their charges, so that by 1920 more than 260 adoptions had taken place. In reality, this meant that the 'adopters' now had permanent care of the child, who was no longer moved on or back to the institution. But as adoption was not yet recognised in law, adopters couldn't assume full parental rights and responsibilities, and the child could be reclaimed by its natural parents at any time.

As an alternative to the institutional approach, private adoption conducted between individuals was a risky and disreputable business. Where it happened, it was an informal arrangement without any legal safeguards for adopter, child or natural parent. Money often changed hands, and it was thought by those who considered themselves superior to be something rather shady that only the working classes indulged in.

We don't know how many such adoptions took place before the 1926 Act, but we know from the experiences of those closely involved that it happened. Lily Bye's story of how her grandmother came to 'adopt' baby Aggie in Liverpool is typical of the casual way in which children found new homes at the turn of the last century when their parents were too poor to cope. Lily wrote to me after I'd appealed in *Saga Magazine* for adoption stories.

I'm 96, so this is going way back to 1900. My grandmother was a widow of 50 with her family all grown up and married, when a young woman nearby asked her to look after her baby for five shilling a week, so she could go out to work. After paying regularly for six weeks (and of course seeing the baby

40

was being well looked after), she did the vanishing trick. She had lived in one room in the house opposite. My grandmother took the baby to the workhouse. 'I wouldn't mind keeping it,' she said. So they said she could. No payment. Well that baby grew up to be a nice young woman, and although she wanted to marry, she looked after my grandmother till she died aged 72. Then she married a man in a good position and of course she was given the family name and just considered one of the family. That was adoption in those days. No fuss.

No fuss indeed. Aggie was lucky, not just to find herself in a good home, but even to survive infancy. The infant mortality rate was already high (nearly one in six in 1900), but up until the Second World War babies born outside marriage were twice as likely to die in the first year of life. Aggie's absconding mother was almost certainly unmarried and desperate. Her wages in a factory or shop would have been low and even 'five shilling a week' was hard to find. She knew she couldn't afford this kind of boarding-out arrangement indefinitely. Throwing herself on the mercy of her widowed neighbour was a calculated risk, and she probably judged it the best option for her and her baby. The alternatives were much worse.

*　　　*　　　*

To understand how and why adoption developed in the way it did during the first half of the last century, we have to look at how single mothers and illegitimate children were treated. The lot of the unmarried mother at the start of the 20th century

41

was a very unhappy one. Unlike our secular society today, religion—a rather Puritan form of Protestantism—permeated public and private life and determined social policy. Marriage was the only acceptable basis for family life, and a cruel double standard operated against women when it came to sexual behaviour: men couldn't help themselves, but women were responsible for the purity of the home and the bloodline. Venereal disease and prostitution, including child prostitution, were rife but the moralists made little distinction between prostitutes and unwed mothers who had perhaps become pregnant as a result of a first sexual encounter with a sweetheart or fiancé. The mother without a marriage certificate and her infant were reviled as abominations against nature and moral law—living proof that fornication had taken place.

Purple phrases that survive from Victorian melodrama that we now use ironically (*pure as the driven snow; a Fate worse than Death; Go! Go! And never darken my door again!*) capture how people then thought of the state of 'purity' as opposed to that of sullied and corrupted womanhood, and the ignominy such 'fallen' women deserved. This was especially true in the booming towns and cities of industrial Britain; attitudes in the countryside, where illegitimacy had traditionally been accommodated more sympathetically within the extended family, were often more relaxed.

The Victorian obsession with 'purity' and 'social hygiene'—an offshoot of the sanitarian movement to improve basic public amenities like a clean water supply and proper drains—influenced thinking and moral standards right up until the

Second World War. The Social Purity and Hygiene Movement had influential allies—the first Labour prime minister Ramsay MacDonald was one—and strong links with evangelical churches and the medical profession. It was a formidable alliance of vested interests. They had the laudable aims of protecting innocent young women from predatory men and preventing the spread of venereal disease, but they also sought to exercise social control over the undisciplined and immoral masses through propaganda and vigilante groups. The voluntary National Vigilance Association pursued women 'in moral danger' in Britain's seaports and big cities in order to 'rescue' them, and their literature is full of dire warnings and moral certainties. *Rescue Work* by Edward Trenholme, published by the Society for Promoting Christian Knowledge, gives a flavour:

'Impurity' is responsible for two hideous things, prostitution and venereal disease. It leads often to the murder of the unborn child by abortion or the newborn by infanticide, or else it may bring into the world an illegitimate child, homeless and miserable in its prospects and perhaps incurably diseased.

At the start of the 20th century, concerns about the breakdown of social order were strongly linked in people's minds to fears about the uncontrolled spread of disease—particularly venereal disease. Controlling the sexual activities of young people, and young women in particular, was seen as paramount to the proper conduct of a decent society. Like other kinds of disease, sin was not only passed down through heredity, but hung as a

43

'miasma' in the air, threatening the stability of the Empire by destroying the family. So unmarried mothers were social pariahs, shunned for fear of infecting others.

Infection meant loss of respectability. Respectability was a priceless commodity for a working class woman: if you lost it you couldn't marry or get a job, and you were very likely to be thrown out by your family. Life in early 20th-century Britain was harsh enough if you were poor but respectable. If you were poor and 'fallen' you were at the bottom of the heap alongside vagrants, common prostitutes and the insane. In fact, the moral scientists were quick to make a link between extra-marital pregnancy, the lower classes and mental infirmity. Edward Trenholme again:

Girls of the waif-and-stray class . . . come to speedy grief. A great number of girls who go wrong have very poor brains and little sense, though may not be certifiable as feeble-minded.

In 1913 the Mental Deficiency Act gave local authorities wide powers to certify destitute pregnant women or those judged as 'immoral', and detain them indefinitely in mental institutions. Some of the victims of this legislation were discovered, decades later, as elderly women in mental hospitals, too institutionalised to be rehabilitated back into society. Rose Crompton, illegitimate herself, became pregnant in 1917 after being raped. The baby went into an institution where it died at the age of two. Rose was certified as a mental defective ('moral imbecile' was another classification in use at the time) and spent the rest of her life in mental institutions. She was 89 when she was finally able to tell her story.

It just came in me mind. I thought I shall never get out into the world now. But I was still happy. I thought, well, I'm safer here than outside. Well, you are, aren't you?

As the pitiable product of adultery and fornication, the illegitimate child had to carry the stigma like a badge throughout life. Not only had it inherited the 'bad blood' of its mother, it was effectively and legally fatherless. It could not take his name or inherit any parental property of right unless named as a beneficiary. It was a burden on its mother, or the parish, or became the object of charity. It had to endure the taunts and name-calling of other children in the street and playground and be forever reminded that it was in the world on sufferance. More than just a mistake, it was the product and embodiment of sin.

What came as a surprise to me, given the hysterical response to children born out of wedlock, was the discovery that illegitimacy rates at the time were, by today's standards, extremely low and remarkably constant—around 4 per cent of live births in England and Wales for much of the 19th and early 20th century. There was a moral outcry at the end of the First World War when the figure rose to over 6 per cent and social hygienists predicted the total breakdown of the family. In 2010, the number of children registered to unmarried parents was 47 per cent of live births, a figure on a steady upward trajectory since the end of the 1960s. The family has not broken down but

45

we now recognise different models of family life that would have been morally objectionable even a generation before.

Despite low illegitimacy figures, people were still having sex before and outside marriage. Behind the official statistics are a very large number of shotgun weddings. For much of the 20th century, one in five brides went up the aisle pregnant. If marriage—however hasty or ill advised—was an option, you took it rather than face the consequences of bringing a bastard into the world.

Quite apart from the oppressive moral climate of the time, punitive economic conditions conspired to make unmarried motherhood as difficult as possible. Getting the father of an illegitimate baby to pay any maintenance needed an affiliation order. Mothers were often reluctant to pursue putative fathers but, even with an order, maximum payments were imposed by law. This was five shillings (25p) a week in 1900 and had been since the Bastardy Laws Amendment Act of 1872. There was little enforcement when fathers could not or would not pay up, so many women didn't bother with affiliation orders. But if a mother couldn't support herself and her baby, and her family wouldn't help, her options were grim.

There was the workhouse, which I was to learn from first-hand accounts was the grimmest option of all. Marginally more comfortable were the few available homes and hostels 'for fallen women' run by religious orders and organisations, many inspired by the social purity movement. The aim was to rescue 'penitents', as they were called, from their wicked past with a routine of hard work and improving texts. Here, mothers and babies could be together for up to two years 'for a period of moral recovery and training'. In the longer term, though, the very best outcome the women in these institutions could hope for was a future as a domestic servant while paying for their children to be boarded out with strangers.

No wonder desperate women resorted to unsavoury and even criminal alternatives, rather than submit to a life of penal servitude or penitence.

Though no figures are available, infanticide undoubtedly contributed to the high mortality rate among illegitimate babies, and mothers weren't always the ones responsible. By 1900, infanticide wasn't as prevalent as in latter decades of the previous century, but there were still lurid newspaper reports of 'baby farming' cases before the courts. This was the practice of farming out illegitimate babies to unscrupulous people who took them in for profit, sold them on, or otherwise disposed of them. A Select Committee report on Protection of Infant Life in 1871 described the practice in precise and upsetting detail:

There are . . . a large number of private houses, used as lying-in establishments, where women are confined. When the infants are born, some few of them may be taken away by their mothers; but if they are to be 'adopted', as is usually the case, the owner of the establishment receives for this adoption a block sum of money . . . The infant is then removed . . . to the worst class of baby-farming houses, under an arrangement with the lying-in establishments, by which the owners . . . are remunerated, either by a small round sum, which is totally inadequate to the

47

permanent maintenance of the child, or by a small weekly payment . . . which is supposed to cover all expenses. In the former case, there is obviously every inducement to get rid of the child, and even in the latter case . . . improper and insufficient food, opiates, drugs, crowded rooms, bad air, want of cleanliness, and wilful neglect, are sure to be followed in a few months by diarrhoea, convulsions and wasting away . . . The children born in the lying-in establishments are usually illegitimate, and so are the children taken from elsewhere to the worst class of baby-farming houses . . . some are buried as still-born, some are secretly disposed of, many are dropped about the streets . . . the number of children found dead in the metropolitan and city police districts during the year 1870 was 276 . . . a very large number of these infants were less than a week old.

It sounds little better than in Thomas Coram's day, nearly 150 years before. Although things had improved by the turn of the century, and two Infant Life Protection Acts had been passed in an effort to control criminal abuse of private fostering and adoption arrangements, the practice continued and three baby farmers were convicted and executed between 1900 and 1907. As a result, adoption remained a shady business in which money invariably changed hands, and it was still resolutely associated with the working classes.

One of the measures of the 1897 Infant Life Protection Act designed to regulate the trade in babies was the '£20 Rule': if you paid more than £20 to adopt a child under two, it didn't have to be notified to the local authority. So if you could afford £20 you were obviously a better class of

48

person and didn't want a baby for other than altruistic reasons. Unsurprisingly, this absurdity didn't work and was repealed in 1908. Adoption continued informally, free of any meaningful legal constraint or safeguard, creating happy solutions for some, but still open to the most appalling abuse.

Not only were children vulnerable in the hands of unsuitable or unscrupulous 'adopters', those who did take in children for the best of motives had no certainty that the natural parents wouldn't turn up unannounced at any time to take the child back or, worse, extort 'protection' money in exchange for not doing so. This must have been a miserable cloud hanging over otherwise happy adoptions.

There are now few survivors with this kind of experience. I was lucky enough to meet one of them. Her story shows us why adoption had such a poor reputation in the early decades of the last century.

3

SEARCHING

My father had an old tin box for family papers and odd bits of jewellery that he kept in the wardrobe. I was with my parents in Bognor one weekend in April 1988 when, just before lunch on Saturday, he brought out the tin and produced from it my Adoption Order.

Handing over the Adoption Order must have been a deliberate decision on my parents' part. Over the years they had gradually parted with precious childhood artefacts that they'd decided I should now take custody of. First the commemorative coins (Festival of Britain, Winston Churchill's death) and my school reports (*'reads with great expression'*) and then those first baby clothes I'd arrived in which my mother had kept in tissue paper (*Treasure Cot. Made in England*). But this was something quite different. It was the first document relating to my adoption that I'd seen. And it was electrifying because it revealed two names—my birth mother's and my own.

She was Marjorie Phyllis Heppelthwaite and I was Gillian Heppelthwaite. I now understood why my mother was so bad at pretending not to remember the name. You'd be unlikely to forget this one.

The Order was made in March 1952, more than six months after I was born, and authorised Thomas Harold and Lily Anne Elliott of 2, Wandle Court Gardens to adopt Gillian Heppelthwaite who, 'it having been proved to the satisfaction of the court', was one and the same person as me.

It's hard to explain the impact of discovering you were someone else before you became you. I was Gillian Heppelthwaite only for a matter of weeks, and hardly sentient, but here was the evidence that this other person was also me. This was both confusing and exciting. What would this Gillian person have grown up like? Would she have had the long straight hair I always wanted? No, of course she wouldn't. I wouldn't. But did I look like a Gillian? I remembered Jill Glass in Beddington and how I'd always wanted to be a Jill. Now this yellowed piece of paper opened up to the light after more than 30 years was telling me I almost was, once.

Heppelthwaite. An odd spelling of an even odder name. A slightly ridiculous, old-fashioned name, from the wolds and warps of Yorkshire and another century. Distant, unfamiliar, foreign almost. But Marjorie and Phyllis were much closer to home. Monica's mother was Phyllis and Jill Glass's mum was Marjorie. They were what the mothers of my generation were called. And here, for the first time, the mysterious woman from an unknown, unknowable past became real to me. Now she had a name, she became a person.

My parents must have realised that this might be the trigger to a search. And so it was. Seeing my Adoption Order was galvanising: here was the starting block I needed, and the name was so unusual that the search was unlikely to be a long one. I'd been thinking about it on and off for years, trying to weigh the potential distress to my mother, in particular, against a conviction that I needed to

51

make contact with my 'mother before' to assure myself she was alright and to assure her that I was. I was strongly motivated by the thought that she would now be approaching her seventies—if she was alive at all—and I needed to get to her before it was too late.

Were there other motives? Of course. I wanted to see where I came from. But I was still very anxious about what I might find. She might be mad, bad or dead. She would almost certainly be married, perhaps to a man unaware of her past. This didn't stop me going straight to the London telephone directory as soon as I got home. I sat on the stairs and dived into the H's. There was only one Heppelthwaite and the initials were M.P. The address was 13 Bungalow Road SE25. It had to be her but I'd read enough about searches to know not to just pick up the phone. I couldn't have done it anyway. My hands were shaking too much.

*   *   *

It wasn't as if I was an 18-year-old embarking on this search. I might have had fewer doubts and inhibitions if I had been. I was well into my thirties, with an absorbing job and a settled and happy relationship with Bevan, whom I'd lived with since 1980. He was intrigued to know more, as partners invariably are, and encouraged me to think that it could be done without causing unnecessary pain to others. Monica from Beddington days was still a great friend; she'd become a probation officer and social worker and had an exceptional empathetic ear. So Bevan's idea to make use of her skills and call on our long friendship was inspired.

52

'Monica, I need to ask a big favour of you.'

'Of course. What?'

'I've decided I want to try and trace my birth mother. Will you be my intermediary—if it comes to it?'

'Wow! That's not a favour, that's an honour. When do we start?'

There was the rub. I had everything necessary to start in earnest. The gift of an uncommon name, and a belief that it was essentially the right thing to do. Even so, it was another 18 months before I felt ready to start the first formal stage of the search, applying for my original birth certificate. I didn't need this for my mother's name, which I now had, but it would give her address at the time and it might even give a father's name. The real significance, though, was that the birth certificate came with a big string attached: if you were adopted before 12 November 1975, counselling was compulsory before you got access to your records. This could be done either at your original adoption agency or your local social services department, or the one where the original Adoption Order was made.

I knew the adoption agency in Knightsbridge was long defunct, and I wasn't going to trek over to south London, so the choice was made for me. It would have to be Ealing Social Services.

The counselling was intended not only to impart basic, but possibly sensitive, information about the adoption, but also to 'help adopted people to understand some of the possible effects of their enquiries'. This sounded ominous and potentially painful; it would be about causing hurt to parents and making contact with someone who might not expect or welcome the intrusion after all these years. It would be about examining my motives for causing all this trouble. I was clear about my main motive which I was sure was a healing one; but there were others lurking there, barely articulated, that were probably much more selfish, and I was about to have to confront them. I had lots of time to not look forward to it in the three months it took to get a first appointment.

In May 1990 my mother's older sister Megs (after whom I took my middle name) died. The two were very close. Their father, a master plasterer who made ornate ceiling roses, had died when my mother was 13, leaving my grandmother to take work in a laundry to keep the family. Nanny had come to live with us at Wandle Court Gardens in her last years and I remembered her as a stout, silent woman with a firm set to her mouth. My mother was petite, but Megs was tiny, always frail and anxious. We often used to go to her house for tea and she cut the thinnest slices of bread I've ever seen.

After the funeral in Elmers End, Bevan and I went to have a look at Bungalow Road, a matter of streets away in the same south London suburbs where my mother's family had all grown up. The immediate area around Bungalow Road was very familiar. My mother's old friend Satchie Clark, whom she'd worked with in the United Dairies shop, lived with her sister Edie round the corner in Holmesdale Road, and we visited them often as I was growing up. Even nearer in Holmesdale Road was the Baptist church where Megs and her husband Norman went and where I was bridesmaid at my cousin Valerie's wedding in 1964. So I knew what to expect, but it was still a shock.

Bungalow Road backed on to Crystal Palace's Selhurst Park home ground and contained no bungalows at all. We crawled past the rows of cheap pattern-book Victorian terraces looking for number 13. It was the most down-at-heel house in the street, the paint was peeling and it looked dark and quiet. It was a dispiriting start.

13 Bungalow Road is mean and dirty-looking. I hope she doesn't live there. Who knows where this will lead? It might be very ill advised, but I feel I must do it now or never. Waiting for counselling from Ealing Social Services. It all takes months. Read Polly Toynbee's Lost Children *which was a wrist-slasher, and have made contact with NORCAP [National Organisation for the Counselling of Adoptees and Parents].*

I hoped she didn't live there, but I felt sure she did.

Shortly before my 39th birthday I went to the local council offices for my first counselling session. The social worker was harassed and distant and I didn't warm to her. It was everything I'd feared and felt more like an interrogation than a chat with a supportive friend. There were a lot of questions about my relationship with my parents that only exacerbated my feelings of guilt and worry about the wisdom of my search. I came out in tears. If this was what it was going to be like, I wasn't sure I could go through with it.

Although it wasn't a pleasant experience, it did make me examine my motives and, especially, my rationalisation for not telling my parents about my decision to search. I'd convinced myself that it would be best to wait and see what I found first. Painful as it was, counselling made me realise I was only putting off what had to be done sooner or later. I knew I needed my parents' approval. It wasn't that I thought this might be withheld. Worse, I feared it would be given haltingly, with extreme reserve, in the way the early information had been given.

A couple of months later my birth certificate arrived in the post, and with it another shock. There was no father's name, and I hadn't expected one. Marjorie's address was given as 217 Gipsy Road, Upper Norwood, just a couple of miles north of Bungalow Road. But my much-cherished belief that I was born in St George's Hospital, Knightsbridge was shattered. In fact I'd been born in St Giles Hospital, Peckham, a short bus ride away but a world apart. I'm sure this was a genuine confusion on my mother's part—they were both sainted Gs, the information had most likely been given fleetingly, verbally, and could easily have been misconstrued or mis-remembered over the years. But I was still disappointed. What else that I held dear would turn out to be completely false?

*   *   *

Fireplaces played a vital role in my strategy to break the news of my search to my parents. We had a hideous 1960s' brick fireplace in our living room that we wanted to replace with a period cast-iron one we'd found that was much more in keeping with the age of our house. My father, who always relished a bit of transformational DIY, was enlisted to help Bevan at home in Ealing while I

56

arranged to spend the day in Bognor for the carefully prepared but much-dreaded 'telling' summit.

My mother had been to the hairdressers.

'I'm not sure I like the way he's done it this week.' She was always seeking reassurance about her appearance.

'No, it looks nice flicked up like that.'

'Mm. Do you think so?'

'Mummy . . .'

Here we were, having one of our kitchen sink conversations again after all these years.

'. . . I've been thinking for some time about the possibility of tracing Marjorie Heppelthwaite.'

There. I'd said it, said her name.

'Mm-mm.'

That slight 'go on' rising inflection at the end.

'Well, I've decided that that's what I want to do.'

'I thought you might.'

I studied her face for signs of distress or accusation. But no, just neutrality.

'But I'm not looking for another mother, because that's you. And it won't ever change what I feel for you and Daddy. It isn't about that, it's about . . . I don't know, it's about me I suppose, wanting to find out about me. I've always wanted to know . . .'

I felt my lips tremble and my voice go up a register. I ploughed on, filling the silence.

'I just don't want you to be upset . . .' I heard myself say, even as the tears started to come.

'I won't be upset dear, but Daddy and I wouldn't want you to be hurt, that's all. You don't know her circumstances now. You don't know what you might find. Just go carefully. We'll help if we can, but we don't know anything more than we've already told you. Shall we ring Father and see how they're getting on with that fireplace?'

My mother had a way of ending difficult conversations. It was a pathetic performance on my part, but I still felt relieved of a huge burden. I was also conscious that I'd passed through a door into a place where our relationship would never be quite the same again. We'd spoken of the unspeakable: my life before I came to them.

*   *   *

Although it might seem as if the search and its revelations were all I could think about, there were other things going on in my life and in the world. Diary entries for the first months of 1991 are dominated by the first Gulf War. Not only was I worried about it, I was by then closely involved in regulating commercial television news and current affairs programmes, so it was my day-to-day work as well.

The only diary respite from either war or work appeared on Easter Sunday:

It's really Spring and everything feels different. Garden greening by the minute, clocks on last night and at last I feel like Doing Things. I do have one or two taskettes. Like decorate the kitchen and go to St Catherine's House to trace my mother.

The diary is sometimes irritatingly flippant about serious things. Ealing Social Services had tracked down my adoption agency file. This was a significant and exciting development; I went back for another session with the social worker, to find out what was in it.

'I've done you a summary of information about your adoption,' she said, passing me a typed sheet, while keeping the file firmly in front of her. Obviously there was such dynamite in this file, it had to be carefully mediated and there was no way it could be shared with me straight away. She talked me through some basic facts. I was a good weight at birth and had gained weight since; I'd been breast-fed for the first month, and so on. But I wasn't taking anything in. All I wanted was to get the file home and look at it. She spent ages photocopying it all before handing over the originals in a cheap brown envelope.

I clutched it for dear life on the way home and fought with Bevan as he tried to wrest it from me when I got there. He didn't understand how proprietorial I felt about it, and neither of us appreciated the impact it would have. I took it straight upstairs to the spare room, shut the door and started reading.

*   *   *

3.10.51. Castlebar
Miss Marjorie Phyllis Heppelthwaite, 217 Gipsy Road, West Norwood, S.E.27.
Father knows about baby.
Girl born 30.8.51 weighed 8 lbs 8 oz now 8 lbs 11 oz.
Age 30.
Occupation. Telephonist.
Religion. C. of E.
Education. Elementary.
Father's occupation. Sanitary Engineer.

Baby's Father. Peter White.
Age. 48.
Occupation. Clerk Cement Co.
Education. Secondary.
Description. 6', broad and dark.
Nationality. British.
Known each other 2 years. Married man. Has not helped at all. Father fond of sport. Mother very fond of music.
Baby really very sweet dark hair and hazel eyes.
A very pleasant girl with dark hair, hazel eyes and good features except for a rather ugly mouth. She seemed a superior type and had a thoughtful attitude towards adoption.
M. Wilson

Rather an ugly mouth. Seemed a superior type. How judgemental, how patronising it sounds. I am appalled and fascinated from the first page. Here is the official foolscap-sized story of my conception, birth and adoption, told through case notes and correspondence between Marjorie Heppelthwaite and the National Children Adoption Association (Incorporated). On yellowing pulpy paper gone brittle and crumbling away at the edges. With carbon copies of correspondence often typed on the back of old fundraising flyers (*Our Chairman, Her Royal Highness Princess Alice, Countess of Athlone, has graciously consented again to be present at our 'June Ball' . . .*). Here is the missing two months of my life. The story it tells must have been replicated hundreds of times in different places all over the country that year, but is no less heartbreaking for that. It bears scant resemblance to my adolescent

60

fantasy.

Marjorie is a single woman of 30 who keeps house for her widower father in Norwood and works as a telephonist at the Portland Tunnel Cement Company in Piccadilly. There she meets Peter White, a clerk, and they have a two-year affair. When she becomes pregnant there is no question of marriage: he is already married with children. As soon as she starts to show, she is obliged to leave 'for health reasons' as it says on her leaving reference. She is referred to the National Children Adoption Association by a moral welfare worker attached to Streatham Congregationalist Church who confirms in writing that she is 'a respectable girl' before they accept her. She goes to 'Castlebar', the Association's mother and baby home on Sydenham Hill, for six weeks before the birth. When I am born she feeds me herself for the first month and then on Cow & Gate Half Cream. We are both tested for syphilis. At six weeks Marjorie gives me up to my new adoptive parents, of whom she knows nothing, and in March the following year signs the final release papers.

It is all fascinating, revealing, chilling. But I am completely unprepared for the letters.

18 November 1951
Dear Mrs Wilson,

Could I have news of my Baby, Gillian? I have been longing to write before but thought it would be wiser to wait a week or so. I do hope she is settled now, and that she is happy with her new Mummy and Daddy, and that they like her too. She was such a Darling, and you can well imagine how very difficult

61

it has been to give her up, but I can overcome all that if you can assure me her adopters are nice people. I would also like to know if she now has a different Christian name as I had rather hoped it would not be changed. I would greatly treasure a photograph of her, would that be possible, in a month or two?

I must now thank you for all your great kindness, and in making this decision I know I have done the right thing for the future happiness of my Baby.
Yours sincerely,
Miss M. Heppelthwaite

There are others. The agency's replies are kind, firm and usually accompanied by a request for a donation. Their last letter to Marjorie is dated 18 September 1952, just after my first birthday, replying to another letter she had written.

14 September 1952
Dear Mrs Plummer,
I would very much like to have news of Gillian, I think of her often. Am sure her Mummy and Daddy love her very much, and she is getting to be very interesting now.

Will you please accept this small donation in remembrance of the help and kindness you have shown me in the past.
Yours sincerely,
Miss M. Heppelthwaite

Dear Miss Heppelthwaite,
We very greatly appreciate your kind donation of 10/- towards the funds of this Association and send our official receipt enclosed.
We have quite recently had the very happiest news

of baby Gillian who is progressing rapidly and is the apple of her parents' eye! She has not long returned from a holiday and they say that she is a 'lovely and bonny baby'. She had her first birthday on August 30th, as you know, and 'kept pointing to her pretty cards' and saying little words of her own to them.

You may rest content that she is with parents who love her very much and who will do their utmost for her happiness always.
Yours sincerely,
D C Plummer
General Secretary

So final. *You may rest content.*

I feel sick and sad and angry but I can't articulate any of it, to Bevan or anyone. The letters give me an all-consuming insight into her pain. I can think of nothing and no one else for days afterwards. I keep imagining I see her on the Tube, even though I don't know what she looks like. She is with me, following me, like a ghost.

It was hard, harder than I thought. I felt defenceless, weighed down, bereaved almost—such a heavy sadness. It was terrible at work; I couldn't stop crying, wanted to die on the Tube, to think of her pain, those letters, those trusting sad terrible letters.

*   *   *

So those searing stories of loss were true. And it hadn't just happened to other people, it had happened to Marjorie Phyllis, a woman who had apparently nurtured me like a proper mother for the first six weeks of my life, not dumped me

63

without a thought at the first opportunity. Then, because she seemed to have no other option available to her, she gave me up so that I could have the 'normal home life with two parents and a good education' that she was unable to provide, as it said in another letter on my file.

Her *acceptance* of the inevitability of it all was terrifying. What made it so inevitable? This wasn't the age of the Poor Law; how could anyone in 20th-century Britain have so little choice when only a couple of decades later *Daily Mail* editorials were ranting about feckless single mums shooting straight to the top of housing queues?

I'd studied John Bowlby in Child Development lectures at college. His famous theory of maternal attachment was first published the year I was born. Children deprived of a mother's love and care in the first months of life never recover. He was careful to say that 'substitute' mothers could do the job just as well; it was the quality and consistency of care that mattered. But why should substitution be necessary when it seemed most of these women longed for the chance just to do their maternal duty? How could anyone think it was the right thing to do to separate the best part of a million babies from their mothers and keep on doing it until the supply of those babies ran out in the 1970s?

At best it seemed a gross piece of social engineering—putting bastards into respectable two-parent homes to make them better people. At worst a human tragedy of undiscovered proportions. And yet, and yet. For the majority of those at the other two points of the adoption triangle, it brought security, love and the chance of a family life where none existed before. And adoption was still providing the only hope of a home some children could expect. It was impossible to condemn outright, and I couldn't. It had worked for me and it was still working for many children who otherwise faced a life of being 'cared for' by local authorities. But it hadn't worked for Marjorie and the many, many like her.

Now I'd been granted this insight into her experience, I not only had to find her, I needed to know much more about why it happened this way.

*   *   *

A few weeks later I went to St Catherine's House in the Aldwych with a friend, to check what I instinctively knew, that the Bungalow Road Heppelthwaite was indeed Marjorie Phyllis. Unlike the majority of adopted people who spend hours and days at St Cath's, we weren't campaign-hardened researchers. We had a one-in-a-million name. We didn't have to scour the thousands of volumes of births, marriages and deaths. The local electoral roll confirmed that Marjorie Phyllis Heppelthwaite lived alone at 13 Bungalow Road, SE25.

We sat in a coffee shop opposite Bush House and took stock. Some people's searches take years; mine had taken 15 minutes. I knew her from the day I got my Adoption Order, which was the day I found her in the phone book. It may have all stretched out over a long period, but the final confirmation, when it came, seemed an anticlimax. The search was over but it still felt like the beginning. There were so many questions. She'd never married. Why not? Was she already on the shelf at 30 and then damaged goods after me? The case notes said she was both respectable and respectable looking. Was the experience so devastating she was never able to make relationships again? When did she move out of Gipsy Road? Why didn't her father let her keep me? Did she love Peter White? How did she cope later?

The questions were all about the past, and I still saw in my mind's eye a slight young woman in 1950s' fitted coats and smart little hats. It was much more difficult to imagine a woman of 70.

*   *   *

I'd been keeping Monica informed as things developed; she'd been my alternative counsellor and a far better one than Ealing Social Services had provided. Now it was time to talk about how she would make contact with Marjorie on my behalf. Did I ever consider making direct contact? Not for a minute. I was too much of a coward; I don't think I could have borne a rejection. If all the stories I'd read of searches throughout the preceding decade had taught me anything, it was that making contact is the most sensitive bit of the operation and it needs careful, ideally expert, handling. You don't go crashing in on someone else's sensitive past on an emotional whim. You plot, you prepare, you think through all the 'what ifs?' beforehand. And you don't do it yourself.

We agreed what an initial letter might say and, at the start of the summer, Monica wrote to Marjorie.

Dear Miss Heppelthwaite,

I am doing some family research for a close and longstanding friend of mine. In the course of my researches I have come across some information which leads me to believe you may be related to her. My friend was born on 30 August 1951 in St Giles Hospital, Peckham, and was adopted at the age of three months. She had a very happy and loving family life with her adoptive parents and younger brother, and is now, after much thought, wishing to contact members of her original family, particularly her mother. I have been helping her in this quest, and I am writing to you in the hope you can provide some additional information for her.

I realise that this may be asking you to think back a long time and this might be difficult, or that you may not be able to help at all. However, I would very much appreciate it if you would contact me in any event, so that I will know the position. This, of course, would be in the strictest confidence ...
I very much look forward to hearing from you.
Yours sincerely,
Monica Viner

About 10 days later, Monica had a call from her. Who knows what went through her mind during those 10 days. She had obviously hesitated before responding. Was she fearful? Confused? Guilty?

Monica said she knew straight away what it was about. They had an easy conversation, and the two salient facts that emerged were that she had a dog and she belonged to the Mothers' Union. Putting to one side the sad irony of the latter, I was cheered by both bits of information. She obviously wasn't a reclusive madwoman if she had a dog and went to the Mothers' Union. On the other hand she might be a religious maniac, but it seemed unlikely. I'd met women from the MU and they were perfectly normal.

This all sounded reassuring. But it was still unclear whether she wanted to meet me, and I knew we might have to take things slowly to get to that point. The only way I could cope with the enormity of what was happening was to throw myself into work and focus on the possibility of a meeting. The simple goal of a reunion is the fixed point for everyone who traces. To protect yourself, you don't think about what might lie beyond.

It was high summer. Monica went on holiday; Marjorie had promised to ring again on her return at the end of August.

6 October 1991
Dear Miss Heppelthwaite,

It is some time since we spoke on the telephone and I am wondering how you are. From our conversation in July, I realise that I left you with much to think about. I can only hope that both the memories and the current situation where I am asking for your help, have not been too distressing or difficult for you.

My friend, whom I have always known as Sue, would like to send you some photographs and information about herself, and I am wondering if this would be acceptable to you . . .

I did so enjoy our last conversation. I hope I can look forward to speaking to you again.
Best wishes,
Monica

Had she had second thoughts? Changed her mind? Forgotten?

4

BEFORE THE FIRST ADOPTION ACT

Vera Butterworth's extraordinary story shows how precarious informal adoptions were before the 1926 Adoption of Children Act first introduced legal and binding arrangements. I met Vera at her small bungalow north of Rochdale, in the area she'd lived all her life. The place was like Piccadilly Circus. As soon as I arrived a friend dropped in to do some tidying up for her and a neighbour called by to see if she wanted anything from the market (*'If they're giving stuff away, I'll have a half. If they're charging, I'll have a quarter'*). She'd just come back from the doctor and was worried about her hearing: she'd suddenly gone very deaf in both ears but that didn't stop her telling me her story.

After an early life of grinding poverty, Vera found a loving adoptive home when she was six, but she lived in fear of being taken back by her parents to a life on the road. She was born Rachel Robinson in 1923 into an itinerant, destitute family with five children who tramped the countryside of north-west England in search of work, staying in workhouses and cheap lodgings.

I were born at Jericho, this workhouse. My Mum and Dad had no home. They lived in these doss-houses, so if they were having a baby they went to the workhouse. They had to work for their keep afterwards so, of course, the baby and the mother would be in until they'd paid off their debt. You were

70

poor and that's how they treated you. This is how it used to happen; we was in and out, in and out, and in between that we lived in these lodging houses. There were no beds, we used to lie on the floor.

We used to do Ratcliffe, Bury, Haslingden and walk as the crow flies, over the fields, climb the hedges over, backwards and forwards. I guess when Dad did have a bit of work it were the handcart going out for rags you know, rags and bones.

I don't remember sitting down to a proper meal. We would knock at doors and ask for food, walking from one place to another. This went on and on for quite some time and I don't think we ever thought anything about it because it were just our way of life. That's how I met the Hodgkinsons, through travelling about and travelling down to their cake shop and looking in. I fancy it looked like Aladdin's cave, all these cakes. I guess to us it looked lovely and, you see, they started taking notice of us and sort of giving us stuff, you know, helping us along till we got very, very familiar. They used to buy us shoes.

I was the oldest of them that were looking through the window, maybe the cheekiest of them, and we looked in this window and saw these cakes and then this lovely face of Mrs Hodgkinson as we peered through, and maybe she felt sorry for us but she were like an angel looking out and then she called you in the shop and give you something. I think they could see that I were out in all sorts of weather, and they felt sorry and that's how I came to be taken in with them and it didn't matter to me Mum and Dad. They could probably see that I were being looked after better than any of 'em and I were off their hands, so I went to live with the Hodgkinsons.

71

Vera settled well and started going to school, where she was anxious to lose her name and her past.

I didn't want the schoolchildren I were with to know what sort of life I'd been living, so I changed me name to Vera Hodgkinson. It wasn't Hodgkinsons that changed it, it were me. I were that adamant that I didn't want to carry this Rachel Robinson name. I wanted to change me whole life.

But, unknown to Vera, money was changing hands and her parents were blackmailing the Hodgkinsons. She brought out a small selection of letters that were starting to crumble with age.

They'll burn these when I'm gone I expect.
    'Dear Mr and Mrs Hodgkinson, I write these few lines hoping this letter finds you in the best of health as it leaves me and my wife at present. Excuse me for not writing before now as we have not been in the best of circumstances and we have had our baby in hospital with his face. How is our Rachel going on? Is she not bothering about us? Or is she content? If she's all right we want to know if you will settle up with us. As you know Mr Hodgkinson we have nothing and we would not like to fetch our Rachel into a lodging house again, which you know, and I am doing nothing at all here for things are so bad . . . Yours truly.'

They wrote again when they found out she'd been on a day's outing to Southport.

'Just a few lines but I think you have a cheek to send

72

our Rachel to Southport without our permission. You all have a good cheek. You'll have your own road with that child but we warn you for it. I'll be coming to Haslingden and we'll let her stop a few more weeks, it won't do her any harm and then it will be our turn . . .'

They did come and take Vera back and she spent a miserable time in a lodging house. But money was always tight and she found herself back at the Hodgkinsons again. This time, they attempted to formalise the adoption but Vera's father was having none of it:

'Mr and Mrs Hodgkinson, I was very mad about the way you have our child but it is not yours and we will never sign. We have been to a solicitor and if she is not here before Saturday there will be further trouble. He has told us to write and tell you and I will take further proceedings. In the first I did not ask you to take the child, you asked us while such time we got settled down. You don't think for one minute we've forgot her because you're mistaken. You had a cheek to have her name changed when you know what terms we were on. Well, no more at the present . . . Mother and Father.'

The uncertainty, with occasional threatening letters and visits from the Robinsons, continued.

I was always frightened of me Mum and Dad coming to take me back again because I knew really that I hadn't been properly adopted and I thought they would have every right to take me back. I were frightened of going back. As I got older they stopped

73

coming any more. They must have got tired, and I think the Hodgkinsons said they couldn't have any more money for me so they signed a form so that after I lived with them all the time.

The 'form' they signed was among the letters. In quasi-legal language (*'Re: Adoption of Rachel Robinson'*) it stated that the Robinsons relinquished care of and responsibility for Vera to the Hodgkinsons and had no further claim to her. The parties who signed the document may both have believed it was legally binding, but it wasn't. Legal adoption was already possible by the time Vera first went to live with the Hodgkinsons, so why didn't they take this option? Didn't they know about the 1926 Adoption Act? Did they think a legal adoption would be too expensive? All Vera knows is that they gave her love, a proper bed to sleep in and decent food to eat. She lived with them till she married. Though she never saw her natural parents again, she was reunited with her brothers and sisters when she was in her seventies.

One of the things I learnt from Vera's story was that the history of adoption doesn't fit into a neat chronology. Informal and 'quasi-legal' arrangements like this continued for years after the 1926 Act was passed. Acts of Parliament don't change things overnight; they sometimes take years to seep into people's consciousness and alter attitudes and behaviour. The full impact of such legislation often isn't felt until much later. Vera's experience in the 1920s and early 1930s has all the hallmarks of a pre-1926 adoption and shows us why legislation was needed. The illegitimate and the children of the very poor who were most

74

likely to be the subject of informal adoption arrangements were vulnerable, and decent adopters had no rights or legal safeguards.

But getting to this first landmark took time, intense lobbying and a horrific war that altered attitudes to life itself. By the end of the first decade of the century, the term 'illegitimacy' may have replaced 'bastardy' for the purposes of polite conversation, but the condition was still a lifelong handicap and unmarried mothers continued to be reviled. However, some new voices on the matter were starting to speak up against the dead weight of moral consensus.

The First World War changed many things in Britain, including the lot of women. Even before then, however, the fight for women's suffrage and the growing feminist movement gave a platform for influential women to promote a less judgemental line on unmarried motherhood. In a 1912 pamphlet, *Whose Children Are These?*, Ethel Naish, a Newnham Scholar, puts forward a political and economic case for improving facilities for unmarried mothers and their babies, while deliberately avoiding the moral questions that seemed to obsess everyone else:

Of even greater importance to the State than the provision of Dreadnoughts is the physical, mental and moral calibre of its citizens . . . these weak and young mothers, with babies seriously handicapped at the outset of life, are becoming not only a material weakness, but a very real source of national danger.

She called for more voluntary Homes for mothers and babies where they could stay together for at least nine months after the birth, State and parental contributions towards their welfare, and enforceable affiliation orders. Though her demands weren't nearly as radical as those of the National Council for the Unmarried Mother and Her Child, established in 1918, Ethel Naish voiced a view that gained currency through the war as the human carnage mounted: that all human life was valuable and indeed essential to the security and prosperity of Britain. And, unlike the social purists, she didn't believe bastards and their mothers had to be rescued and reformed before their lives could be valued.

Another voice of reason was Josephine Butler, a Victorian pioneer of women's rights, who died in 1906. She was intensely religious and had close associations with the social purity movement, but she was also a feminist by instinct and by intellect and believed in universal suffrage. Best known for her work with prostitutes—she campaigned to repeal the draconian Contagious Diseases Acts which effectively removed their civil rights—she was also involved in other women's issues such as employment, education, child welfare and the plight of unmarried mothers. Her name lived on until the early 1970s in Josephine Butler House, a training college established in Liverpool in 1920 for the moral welfare workers who were later to play such a key role in the adoption story.

So, even before the upheavals of the Great War, there were chinks in the wall of blanket disapproval and some efforts to rehabilitate mothers and babies in a practical as well as a moral sense. The presumption was that mother and child should, if at all possible, stay together for their physical and moral wellbeing. Adoption was not yet a legal or reputable alternative, but the 1914–18 war was about to change that.

Two facts of wartime life and death prompted the push to legalise adoption. First, the movement of troops and military and civilian casualties meant increasing numbers of illegitimate babies and destitute orphans. At the other end, the horrific slaughter of so many young men on the battlefields of France made those at home fear for the future of the nation. The Mothers' League, a voluntary body, urged the childless rich *'to come forward and help to save and rear the babies we want so badly'*. The letters pages of popular newspapers debated what could and should be done, and whether giving assistance to unwed mothers and their children, or taking their children for adoption, wouldn't just encourage further immorality. Meanwhile, some were taking matters into their own hands.

*   *   *

For someone who was obviously such a formidable self-publicist, very little information has survived about the life and work of Clara Andrew, founder of the National Children Adoption Association, one of Britain's first adoption societies and the one that arranged my own adoption. In surviving newspaper reports and official records, she leaps from the page, a determined and opinionated woman who liked nothing better than battling with bureaucracy on behalf of 'our suffering children'.

Like Thomas Coram, Clara Andrew was an activist and propagandist who shamelessly exploited her titled and influential connections to create a voluntary, non-denominational institution that was to have a profound effect on later adoption policy and practice. She first became aware of adoption while working with Belgian refugees in the early part of the war, when '. . . *many persons applied to Miss Andrew for Belgian children to be adopted into English homes, but national and religious reasons made such adoptions undesirable'*. An interesting foretaste of much later discussions about cross-cultural and international adoptions.

By 1916 Clara was back in Britain, 'associated with war work' in government factories in the big cities. I doubt she was filling munition shells herself; more likely she was engaged in some voluntary welfare effort with women workers. Either way, here she '. . . *had personal knowledge of many children, not only homeless, but whose future seemed hopeless. The effort to lend a hand soon proved that all the existing institutions could not grapple with such a problem, and driven to action by the pathetic stories, an experiment was tried, and an appeal made to those who would give homes to our suffering children. Some five or six adopters responded to the appeal, and on their happy stories that they had found the "one child" for them, was laid the foundation of the association, which henceforth grew rapidly with little influence and less funds behind it, simply because it fulfilled a need'*.

Voluntary committees were set up to 'carry on the propaganda', and to handle appeals and potential adopters, first in her native Exeter, then Salisbury, the Isle of Wight, Plymouth, Liverpool and Bristol. So this evolving federation of 'associates' arranging adoptions became the first national adoption 'association' in 1917.

The propaganda worked, because by 1918 what became the National Children Adoption Association had a national headquarters in Sloane Street, London. The following year its new patron, HRH Princess Alice, a granddaughter of Queen Victoria, opened the first hostel for babies awaiting adoption at Tower Cressy, a splendid house in Kensington. Its services were much in demand: 448 adoptions were completed between April 1919 and October 1920, 2,310 children passed for adoption and 1,653 adopters approved.

Though the stated targets were 'orphans' and illegitimacy dared not speak its name (bad for fundraising), it is clear bastards were covered by the euphemism 'those whose future seemed hopeless'. Even just after the war, three-quarters of the NCAA's adoptions were of illegitimate children. It was among the first to advocate adoption as the preferred alternative to institutional care and, by implication, care of the mother:

The policy of the association has been to advise adoption, which was primarily intended for orphan children only as a last resort. But where a child cannot be maintained by one or both parents they believe that normal home and family life are better than the limitations of an institution and they therefore recommend complete adoption.

The old spectre of baby farming still exerted a powerful influence on policy and the NCAA's efforts to make adoption respectable:

No premium or weekly payments are allowed to the adopters and it is felt that with this safeguard, only those who can afford to take a child will apply and that the fight against 'baby farming', which was one of the main reasons for starting the work, is greatly strengthened by the rule forbidding financial help either from the association or friends of the adopted child.

The war had other effects that contributed to the new interest in adoption: boarding out became more difficult as women who may have fostered went to work in offices, shops and factories; mothers were looking to replace sons lost in the war; and young spinsters with no prospect of marriage looked to adoption as a way of having a child. The flu pandemic of 1918 contributed to the already low birth rate, and babies—any babies— were in demand.

The immediate success of the NCAA and the other main agency, the National Adoption Society also established at the end of the war, proved a new and growing acceptance of adoption as a neat solution to childless homes and homeless children. But there was still no such thing as a legally binding adoption. Adopters faced the possibility that their child could be removed by the natural parent, and adopted children lacked the security of a permanent family from whom they could inherit.

The NCAA attempted to resolve this by getting the two parties to sign Indentures—between the association and the adopting parent, and between the adopting parent and the relinquishing mother. These legal contracts, more common for binding apprentices to their masters, set out the ground rules for the adoption:

> *... the mother hereby assigns to and relinquishes in favour of the adopting parent ... the right ... to have the permanent care and custody of the infant ... The mother hereby covenants that she will not nor will any other person or persons on her behalf at any time or times during the minority of the infant molest, disturb or in any way interfere with the adopting parent ... or any other person or persons in the upbringing, maintenance, education or otherwise in respect of the infant, nor will she ... make any claim whatever against the adopting parent ... nor contest the right of them to have the permanent care, custody and guardianship of the infant.*

She also had to agree to the child's name being changed *'as the adopting parent may think fit and proper'*.

For her part, *'the adopting parent hereby undertakes during her lifetime properly to maintain, clothe, educate and otherwise provide for the infant'*.

The formula for the 'closed', or secret, adoption that was to be the norm for the next 50 years was set.

The need for legal recognition and protection was now pressing, but campaigners found it hard to interest politicians and policy-makers. This may have been because the ruling class, as it then was, strongly resisted the idea of inherited wealth passing outside the bloodline to adopted children. But this wasn't an issue for the vast majority of the population who didn't own any property. Though the NCAA was achieving success in persuading the propertied middle classes to adopt (Clara Andrew

81

reported that over half of her adopters were from 'the professional classes, tradespeople, clerks and sergeants in the police'), the main concern of adopters was not inheritance, but whether they were legally entitled to keep the child and bring it up as if it were their own.

The new adoption societies were joined in the campaign by Dr Barnardo's Homes and the National Society for the Prevention of Cruelty to Children (NSPCC), founded in 1889. These institutions didn't particularly favour adoption but were concerned that it would continue to be open to abuse—including the dreaded baby farming—as long as there was no law to regulate it. In fact, apart from the adoption societies, there was no real body of support for adoption as a solution to unwanted children.

The National Council for the Unmarried Mother and Her Child (NCUMC), established in 1918 as a response to the large rise in illegitimate births, was a staunch campaigner for financial support for mothers, repeal of the Bastardy Acts that so discriminated against those born out of wedlock, and change to the punitive public attitudes of the time. Unlike the NCAA, NCUMC didn't see adoption as a solution to illegitimacy, believing that if at all possible, mother and child should be kept together. The NCUMC wanted to see an Act that would allow a mother to legitimate her child by adopting it, and for no other reason. Many other organisations that gave evidence to the first Parliamentary Committee set up under the chairmanship of Sir Alfred Hopkinson to consider the possibility of legislation in 1920, including the Salvation Army and the National Council of

82

Women, also took the view that adoption was very much a final resort. The National Children's Home, which of all the voluntary institutions had the most experience of arranging adoptions, was the only one to voice positive support.

Clara Andrew also gave evidence to the Hopkinson Committee. She may have been outnumbered, but she wasn't to be outgunned. Her sights were firmly set on the needs, not of unmarried mothers, but of childless couples and deserving infants. She believed they should have the right to be united as a family without anyone knowing that the child had been born illegitimately elsewhere. Secrecy was vital to keeping the stigma of bastardy at bay and therefore making adoption 'respectable': '. . . *in all illegitimacy cases the best thing that can happen is that the child's identity should be hidden*'. She was supported in this by the police magistrate, W. Clarke Hall, who believed '*at the point of adoption the whole past history of the child should be shut down . . . when a child is adopted, its life from that time should begin* de novo'.

The perceived need for secrecy in order to protect adopting families' respectability had an all-consuming impact on adoption policy and practice for the next 50 years. It may have been well-intentioned and understandable at the time, but it was to cause heartache for many of those involved in the adoption triangle for generations to come.

Getting to the first Adoption Act was a tortuous business. After the Hopkinson Committee strongly recommended legislation in 1921, the government, who didn't believe it was necessary, declined to introduce a Bill or even publish the Committee's findings. There were eight unsuccessful Private Members' Bills and another Parliamentary Committee in 1924, which took a more equivocal line on the need for legislation, before the rather rudimentary Adoption of Children Act was finally passed in 1926.

Rudimentary because it laid down the basics, but little more. Adoption had to be a judicial procedure and, once made, an Adoption Order was irrevocable. An Order had to have the consent of the natural parent (in effect the mother) but the courts could override this if the parents could not be found, or had abandoned or neglected the child. The Act also introduced the idea of the *guardian ad litem,* an official who would represent the child's interests in court.

Adoptions would now be recorded in an Adopted Children's Register by the Registrar General. To preserve confidentiality, access to information that revealed a child's original parentage would not be available except by court order. This was intended to protect the child from the intruding eyes of third parties as well as from relinquishing parents who might want to 'interfere' with the adoption once granted. But of course it meant that the adopted child was also denied access to this information. In a curious anomaly, the Scottish Adoption Act of 1930 gave adopted children access to birth records from the age of 17, making searches much easier in Scotland than elsewhere in Britain till the law was changed in 1975.

There was a lot missing: there was no attempt to set minimum standards for adoption practice or to regulate the many adoption agencies that had sprung up to follow the post-war success of the NCAA and the National Adoption Society. And it fudged the tricky issue of inheritance: it wasn't until 1949 in England and 1964 in Scotland that adopted people could inherit as of right from their adoptive parents. Even today, hereditary titles cannot pass to adopted children; the ruling classes had the last word.

The 1926 Act was hard won and far from perfect, but adoption was now legal and on the road to respectability. But it still had a way to go.

5

FINDING

I celebrated my 40th birthday not knowing whether the woman responsible for my being in the world would want to meet me, or whether she would decide that the past was best kept in a box.

On 13 October, after she had responded to Monica's second letter to say she would like to hear from me, I settled down to write the most difficult letter of my life.

Dear Marjorie,

I hope I can call you Marjorie—that's how I've been thinking of you for some time now; if you would rather I call you something different, I'm sure you'll tell me!

As you can imagine, I sit down to write this letter with very mixed feelings—of great happiness and of apprehension. I should apologise for the fact that it's typed and not handwritten. When you see how awful and illegible my handwriting is you will understand that I could not risk using it for this important letter—you'd never have been able to decipher it!!

Nevertheless, I hope it will say all the things I want it to . . .

How do you describe yourself and how you feel to a mother who parted with you when you were three months old? In the only way you can—by putting yourself in the best possible light and in terms that reassure and don't reproach. At least, that's what I had in mind. I was writing about 40 missing years. What to put in, what to leave out? There was a self-conscious reference to meeting the Archbishop of Canterbury in the corridor at work, which I thought might impress a member of the Mothers' Union. I wrote about my year working in Australia, my job, how much I loved Bevan and my house and garden in Ealing. Three close-typed pages later, I was only just getting round to feelings.

. . . My Mum and Dad are coming to stay with us next weekend and I will tell them that it now looks as if I will have an opportunity to meet you. They have been very understanding about my wish to trace you and to try and make contact with you. Obviously I didn't want them to feel that this was in any way a rejection of their love over the years. I love them very much and they will always be my Mum and Dad. I believe they understand that I had a need to try to find out more about you and about the circumstances of my birth. Now I know a bit more I feel more at rest. I realise it is a terrible imposition on you to appear suddenly and unannounced in your life and I hope this hasn't caused you too much upset. Monica is a very old and valued friend who has helped me tremendously in my search; I do hope you feel you can talk openly with her . . .

. . . This has not been an easy letter to write, and I know I haven't said some of the things I wanted to say, but I very much wanted you to know that whatever happens in the future, I am very, very glad that I started the search for you, thrilled that I have found you and to discover that you thought about me over the years—as I have so often thought and

wondered about you.

Whatever your circumstances now and however you feel about events in the past, I hope we can meet as friends.

It didn't say so explicitly, but I hoped the letter conveyed the message I'd wanted to send since I first started thinking about finding her: that I was fine and happy and, rather than blame her, I felt only sadness and sympathy for her predicament in having to give me up.

Soon after that, I ring her for the first time.

'Is that Marjorie?'

'And is that Sue?'

We laugh. A dog barks in the background.

'Oh shut up Benny! Just a minute Sue, I'll put him next door.'

Sounds of woman speaking reprovingly to dog. Door shuts.

'That's better, now we can have a bit of peace. I got your lovely long letter. I'm sorry I haven't replied. I'm not really one for writing.'

No, I thought, I don't suppose you are, after those letters 40 years ago.

'That's OK, I didn't really expect a reply. It's just great to be speaking to you at last.'

'I knew as soon as I got that first letter from Monica it was you. Isn't Monica a lovely girl? She says she's known you a long time . . .'

And so we're off. Her voice is strong and unhesitating in the south London tones of my childhood. We talk easily.

Marjorie sounds bright, calm and jolly and I don't feel any qualms about meeting her—perhaps I

88

should. She's very south London, very capable and didn't pull back from talking about the details, the pain of parting, her relationship with her father—and the amazing revelation that Monica was the first person she had ever spoken to about it. She could be forgiven for being bitter and twisted. She appears not to be at all.

But I still had doubts.

I don't feel at all prepared for this. What will we talk about? How will it develop? Where do we go from there? It's very peculiar. Surely I should feel more excitement, apprehension. Everyone around me— including my parents—seems very excited for me, and fascinated by it all. Shanta [my secretary] is uncontainable; it's as much as I can do to keep her from crying every time she comes in to talk to me about her own wayward family. She keeps talking about 'a mother's love' conquering all. I'm sure she's right.

*　　　*　　　*

Nearly 40 years to the day after we were last together, Marjorie and I meet again. She has made the journey to my house in Ealing. I come out into the front garden to meet her and we stand there, hugging each other for several minutes, not saying anything. She is warm and spontaneous, that's the first thing I notice. The second thing is that she is small, white-haired, and doesn't look like me at all. And—they were right—she does have rather an ugly mouth.

She looks smart in jade trousers and matching

top and wears a crucifix on a chain, something I never see again after that day. Perhaps it is her equivalent of my mentioning the Archbishop of Canterbury. We sit on the sofa holding hands; hers are delicate and well kept, with polished nails. We talk about ourselves, looking for points in common: no serious illnesses or operations but a terrible squeamishness about blood; similar body shapes—slim arms and legs and tubby bodies; a fondness for egg on toast and television. She has a ready sense of humour and seems positive about life, though it sounds as if she struggles financially.

'Champagne ideas and beer money, that's me.'

She talks about her beloved dog, Benny. 'He loves his rabbit and chicken, Benny, and I love him. I'm sure I wouldn't get out of bed sometimes if he wasn't there looking up at me, asking me to take him out for a walk.' She has a friend, Edie. 'I go to Mothers' Union with her, but I can't stand the woman really. She always wants to know the ins and outs of a pig's ear. Far too interested in other people's business. I never tell her anything.' She has no living relatives. Benny is her one true friend.

She says again how hard it was to part with me; she doesn't remember anything about getting home after going to give me up. And how her father held me in his arms in the hospital but refused to countenance her bringing me home to Gipsy Road. ' "You've made your bed," he said, and I hated him for that.' She talks about the mother and baby home. I am surprised that she says she was happy there. 'It was a lovely old house, high up, with views over the country, far away. I was glad to get away from my father, and the girls all helped each other out. We all had our little jobs to do. Mine was the stairs, I polished the stairs. It was a very grand staircase, lovely it was.'

She looks at photos of me growing up and I look at her few photos of her mother and father, herself as a teenager, as a young woman, and in the Fire Service in the war. I wonder how she feels looking at my baby pictures, seeing evidence of the years she forfeited, but she is very composed. We talk and talk until it is time to take her to Victoria to get the train back to Selhurst. I can't imagine such a smart, personable woman going back to a dump like 13 Bungalow Road. We hug again.

'This has been our red-letter day, Sue.'

'And there'll be more to come, I'm sure.'

*   *   *

There is so much emotional investment in reunions, they're bound to seem anticlimactic or disappointing in retrospect. I felt enormous relief and some disappointment. I warmed to her as a person, but there was no lightning bolt of recognition or inescapable bond. I'd read about adopted people experiencing such overwhelming emotions on being reunited with birth parents or siblings that they compared the experience to falling in love. I couldn't imagine anything like that. When I thought about it, my disappointment lay in not being able to see any physical resemblance between us. But a 40-year-old and a 71-year-old rarely look alike and I wasn't in a position to see the much subtler things others saw. Bevan, who immediately liked Marjorie and seemed positively enchanted at the prospect of another mother-in-law, had no doubt he saw them:

'It's amazing, you hold your heads in exactly the same way, and you make the same faces!'

Maybe it had something to do with how our bones fitted together.

Over the next weeks, as we chatted on the phone, I learnt more about her. She'd grown up an only child a few streets north of Bungalow Road in Sydenham. She was still in touch with an old school friend, Betty, whom she saw occasionally. Her much-loved mother died of a weak heart when Marjorie was in her twenties; without her, she 'went off the rails'. Her relationship with her father, a plumber more out of work than in, had always been poor. 'He was a very jealous man. My mother's doctor begged her not to marry him.' She kept house for him, as was customary for unmarried daughters then, until she left for Bungalow Road. She was a GPO-trained telephonist and had at one time worked for the publishers Faber & Faber. 'I met that Graham Greene once.' But what she enjoyed most was working in showrooms in the West End's rag-trade district as a receptionist/telephonist. 'I just loved being with all those clothes.'

She often spoke of her time in the Auxiliary Fire Service during the war, in Streatham Fire Station with all the men, where she had a good time. They always seemed to be older men and most of them were married. 'If only I'd met someone nice like Bevan,' she'd say. Even in her seventies she was an outrageous flirt. Men liked her.

The agency had done an uncannily good matching job. Marjorie and my mother were both born in 1920, six months to the day apart. They grew up and lived in the same south London suburbs and came from similar working-class stock. Their fathers were skilled tradesmen but both families struggled: Marjorie's because of her father's fecklessness; my mother's because her father died when she was 13. The big difference between them was that Marjorie never found the partner and family she craved and her life gradually disintegrated. Streets away, the people who came to be my Mum and Dad, despite starting with very little and having their share of tragedy and hardship, worked hard to achieve their dream of a comfortable, stable family life.

*　　　*　　　*

We were regularly in touch by phone, and just before Christmas we took her out to lunch at a pub in Dulwich. We went back to Bungalow Road afterwards and, after we'd battled our way past Benny's ferocious defence of the front door, we saw for the first time what we'd taken on. Marjorie may have looked smart and sounded capable, but she was living a Miss Havisham life at Bungalow Road. If possible, it was worse inside than it looked on the outside.

'You'll have to excuse the mess. I haven't had much time to tidy up.'

It was obvious she was a stranger to housework, but this was something else. Piles of neatly folded clothes, dozens of them, old Littlewoods catalogues and copies of the *TV Times* covered every bit of floor space downstairs, all coated in a fine blanket of dust and dog hair. An ancient gas fire in the back living room was the only heating in the house and candles the only light in a room where the bulb had gone. 'I can't get up steps any more, it makes me go all dizzy.' Upstairs in the bathroom there was no hot water but a bath full of dead flies. 'I wash in the kitchen,' she said, but we didn't dare venture in there.

She appears to live in organised squalor. Quite shocking really, not at all how I would want to live. She resents the house that is falling around her and lives as she pleases. My instinct is to want to help her change it, move somewhere better; Monica advises me wisely that she must ask for help if she really wants it. Have I taken on a liability or met a friend or been reunited with my mother? Too early to tell. But I do seem to have made her happy and it has been worth it so far.

*   *   *

How had she got herself into this state? She told the story of how she first came to Bungalow Road in 1960 when she was nearly 40. 'There was this ad in the *Croydon Advertiser* for a live-in housekeeper.' To William Russell, a single man with a small landscaping business (although on his death certificate it says he was a retired clerk), and nearly 20 years her senior. 'And you know how it is, Sue, one thing led to another.'

They lived as man and wife until his death in 1973. Much good it did her. It seems he had no other relatives but he didn't leave her the house. He left her £100. The house was left to Dr Barnardo's Homes (as it was then) and the Salvation Army *'in equal shares absolutely'* as his will says, allowing her to continue living there '*until her death, marriage or her ceasing to live therein*'.

Just to be quite sure she wouldn't presume on his generosity beyond the grave, he added a codicil shortly after signing his will with his wish that '*Miss Heppelthwaite does not take a man to live with her at No. 13 Bungalow Rd.*'. I discovered all this much later. All I heard at the time was Marjorie's sad and bitter regret that he had not seen fit to marry her or to leave her the house they'd shared for the past 13 years. 'Bill was mean, that's all there is to it.'

She had her old age pension and a small civil service pension from her last job as a counter clerk with the Inland Revenue in Croydon. 'I hated that counter—they were so *rude* to you. Sometimes violent too. I was glad when they said I could retire.' The house wasn't hers to sell, and she couldn't afford to keep it in good repair. Barnardo's and the Salvation Army had taken over as trustees of Bill's estate and she was in touch from time to time with Barnardo's Legacy Department—'that nice Mr Runchman'—who organised buildings insurance and provided occasional small income payments from the residue of Bill's estate. She had little money and less incentive to keep the place in good order. As if to spite Bill Russell and his mean-spiritedness, she'd long since given up on it.

I thought of my parents' immaculate G Plan-filled bungalow and my mother's exacting housekeeping standards; I thought of my own less pristine but nonetheless clean and comfortable terrace which we were gradually furnishing in Arts and Crafts style. Bevan was tidy, like me. I couldn't

95

live in dirt and disorder; it would be a sign that I'd lost control. And that's what had happened; Marjorie had lost control. Worse, I could see how it might have happened, and that it could happen to anyone.

Who knows what her relationship with Bill was really like? She never said she loved him; it sounded like a marriage of convenience but without the marriage and with rather more convenience for Bill than Marjorie. Her relationship with her father had always been poor and she needed somewhere else to live. Bill needed someone to keep house for him, and within a short space of time he got that, and the rest, without having to pay. Marjorie even earned her keep by going out to work. Bungalow Road was meant to be a refuge, but it soon turned into another dead end with another jealous and domineering man. As she would readily admit, a pattern in Marjorie's relationships with men was already clear.

'Men! I've had enough of them,' she'd say frequently and with feeling.

*   *   *

I wasn't as shocked as I could have been. My father, whose social work caseload brought him into contact with some pretty unsavoury premises, often came home with tales of old ladies in horrible houses far worse than Bungalow Road. But despite Marjorie's calm and cheerful exterior, it seemed to me that the state of the place reflected not only her feelings about her past with Bill (and who knew what else) but was also a sign

96

that she was probably in a long and intractable state of depression. If I didn't do something about it, no one else would.

When I was there one day, I noticed among the many letters stacked on the mantelpiece some with different names.

'Mrs. M. Russell. Miss Marge Ashdown. Who are these people, Marjorie?'

As if I didn't know.

She smiled, embarrassed.

'Oh Sue, I get fed up with Heppelthwaite. I never liked it in the first place, and no one ever spells it properly anyway.'

'Yes, but where did Ashdown come from?'

'Well, it's Paddy you see. Paddy Ashdown. I've always liked him. And his name.'

Poor Marjorie. She wanted to be someone else. Someone better.

As our relationship developed over the next months, I broached the possibility of a move. The progression from 'I don't think I could face it' to 'Yes, I must get away from here' was precipitated by the arrival of a riotous family of six with two Rottweilers next door. Bevan helped her fill in the forms for local council sheltered housing, but the response was swift and brutal. She wasn't homeless so she wasn't a priority of any kind. And they weren't prepared to nominate her to another council or housing association either. So I took up the cudgels in the way that middle-aged, middle-class women are supposed to and wrote begging letters to every housing association in south and west London.

Dear Madam or Sir,

I attach an application form on behalf of Miss Marjorie Phyllis Heppelthwaite for sheltered housing.

She is my natural mother and I have recently been reunited with her after 40 years. She is 72 in October and has never married nor had other children. She lives alone in a small house in south Norwood which she does not own. She is in generally good health apart from blood pressure and breathlessness using stairs, but there are other problems with her current housing situation. She has 'lost heart' in looking after the house and has no money for repairs or improvements which are sorely needed; she lives effectively in squalor although she takes great pride in her personal appearance. She has been unhappy in the house for some time but this has become acute since harassment from a family of five children under 16 next door—she got on well with previous neighbours who moved to the US and let the house to Croydon Council. After a number of rows and taunts from the children, she now avoids going out—even into the back garden. She gets very depressed about this and has few people other than me to talk to about it. She has no other living relatives . . .

. . . I realise that there may be many others in greater housing need, but I believe a home visit may establish her circumstances, which are hard to illustrate here. As an example, she was last winter using candles in her living room as she could not reach to replace the light bulb and 'didn't like to ask' a neighbour for help . . .

She has lived in this area of south London all her life, but no longer feels any ties there—she says there are only unhappy memories. She would very much like to be nearer me and my partner in Ealing, and we would welcome this. She is a lovely lady, bright and sparky despite all her past unhappiness and she deserves better. I have written to about 20 housing associations, but most of them as you know only entertain nominations from council lists. However, I am determined to do my best to try and get her re-housed in suitable and more pleasant accommodation for the remaining years of what has been for her a rather unhappy and unfulfilled life . . .

After many months of drawing blanks, Notting Hill Housing Association offered a home visit. This was the breakthrough we needed. I knew that once they saw her living conditions, they would be much more likely to offer her a place, and so it turned out. To my huge relief, they said they would make her an offer—but only one—of a flat in one of their four west London sheltered housing developments.

One louring autumn Sunday afternoon, Bevan and I cycled round some grim estates from Acton to West Ealing to recce them all. The best by far was Walker Close, recently opened by Glenys Kinnock, and set in a bit of greenery by the River Brent in Hanwell within sight of Brunel's magnificent railway viaduct. I could see Marjorie there.

In the meantime, I'd also established contact with 'that nice Mr Runchman' in the Legacy Department at Barnardo's. When I introduced myself I could almost hear his relief over the phone. 'I've been worried about your Mum for some time, but it wasn't right to put any pressure on her. The house is in a bit of a state. Now we can help her.'

The news that I'd turned up from her past and was now trying to re-house her was obviously welcome from Barnardo's point of view. Martin, as he insisted I call him, came over to Bungalow Road from Barkingside and we talked through the situation and the implications of a move. As a trustee of Bill's estate, he was going to be key to the success of a move and any future financial arrangements. He was sympathetic but guarded: his job was to protect Barnardo's interests, not Marjorie's. But he turned out to be the best ally we could have hoped for.

Towards the end of 1992, Notting Hill offered Marjorie a ground floor flat at Walker Close. I'd never been lucky in raffles and Ernie never picked my Premium Bond numbers but here I felt I'd won the biggest, most fabulous lottery in the world. There was never any doubt that we'd accept the offer.

'Oh, look at this! French doors and everything. And a nice little cooker!'

Marjorie loved it from the moment she saw it. There was another good omen: the next-door neighbours, Syd and Eileen Eustace, came out to introduce themselves. 'Don't worry love, we'll look after her,' they said. And they kept their word.

*   *   *

The day after Boxing Day 1992, we moved Marjorie out of Bungalow Road. It was half *Carry On* caper, half horror story. In the preceding weeks, I'd ask her how the packing was going. 'I'm doing a little bit at a time,' she said. Jolly good, I thought.

100

Marjorie looked panic-stricken as Bevan and I, together with a courageous friend, arrived at 9 a.m.: she'd done no packing and the house was in exactly the same state as when we last saw it. I felt so sorry for her. Her life was about to be put in a skip; no wonder she looked confused and frightened.

So the three of us cleared more than 30 years of debris over the next five hours. The cry 'Chuck!' was much used, and not as a term of endearment. God knows what we threw out, but we salvaged very little. A few sticks of furniture, personal papers, a bit of jewellery—enough to fill a hired Transit. The rest went to the dump. It took four trips.

On top of the wardrobe the dust was so thick you could pick it up in *rolls*. Even Quentin Crisp would have been impressed. In the back bedroom we discovered a bed hidden under piles of clothes that had spilled out to engulf most of the room. A small walk-in cupboard on the landing was filled floor to ceiling with empty Parazone bleach bottles. 'I've been meaning to get the money back on those.'

No one else had the stomach for the kitchen so I put on heavy-duty rubber gloves and big overalls I'd taken the precaution of bringing along, and took a deep breath. In cupboards the contents of ancient tins had exploded to form a solid union with the woodwork. Cartons of eggs dating back several years were stacked in neat piles. Saucepans filled with old fat stood guard around a cooker that you could just about make out for burnt-on grease. In the fridge unfamiliar organisms grew on unrecognisable forms that once were food. And under the sink were dozens of balls of different

101

sizes, thrown into the garden over many years, their disappointed owners long grown up. I was steeling myself for vermin, but there were only some very large spiders. I didn't have time to feel sick or to think about it; there was too much to do. It was a Bank Holiday and the dump shut at one o'clock.

When the house was finally clear and the van packed, we all went to the pub at the end of the road for stiff drinks and a few laughs. It was as hilarious as it was pitiful. Then we set off for Hanwell, waving the problem family and Bungalow Road goodbye forever. By then, Marjorie was positively cheerful.

*   *   *

The only downside, apart from having to shift 30 years' worth of accumulated detritus, was that Benny couldn't go with her. It's hard enough re-housing an old lady, but it is virtually impossible to find a new home for an old dog. Battersea Dogs Home, contrary to my confident expectations, wouldn't take him, and I finally got him into an animal shelter in Huntingdon.

'He'll have a lovely time in the country,' I enthused, but it didn't wash. We both knew we were condemning him to a lonely exile where love and chicken would be in very short supply.

When I rang up a few weeks later to find out how he was, they told me he fought the other dogs and had to be put down. I couldn't bring myself to tell her; she kept saying how she missed 'her Ben'. After some months, I broke it gently that her true companion and friend had pined away without her.

She cried. I bought her a lifelike plaster Labrador puppy that sat under the TV and smiled at everyone, but it wasn't the same. Benny, unlovely mongrel that he was, had saved her from isolation, loneliness and probably much worse.

* * *

Marjorie was settling well into her new life in Hanwell and keeping the place nice. She had a well-designed one-bedroom flat with a neat kitchen and bathroom. A door from the living room opened on to a small patio facing some scrubby woodland that fell away to the River Brent and the sound of squabbling ducks below. It was very pleasant in an urban kind of way. On the other side of the river were the grounds of Ealing Hospital. That's handy, I remember thinking.

With an advance from Martin Runchman we'd furnished the flat cheaply from sales and, together with some good cast-offs, it looked smart and comfortable. Even the bits salvaged from Bungalow Road looked good. She got on famously with Syd and Eileen next door and she loved feeding the birds and squirrels outside her living room. She blossomed and we were even confident of persuading her to start using the bath again.

She'd been at Walker Close about three months and we were in the process of planning a housewarming party for everyone who'd helped with the move. Bevan and I had just got back from taking a party of his students to Edinburgh for the weekend and there was a letter waiting from Martin Runchman:

103

Dear Sue,

Out of the blue and the reasons that lay behind it I cannot guess at, we received a telephone call into the office a few days ago when I was away on business, from the Kent County Council Social Services Department.

My secretary did no more, quite rightly, than to ask the caller to kindly write to us and as you will see this has now happened. I enclose herewith a letter from Tess Munday, Senior Social Worker. I do not know what this letter is about and as you will see from my letter of reply I have been very guarded in my response. May I leave you to take what action you feel is appropriate?

I didn't need to read the attached letter. As soon as I saw the words 'Social Services Department' I knew there was another child. Marjorie had had another child and she hadn't told me.

6

SECRETS AND LIES

Ma and da didn't have a lot of love to give. Why, I don't know. I was never nursed, I was never kissed, never cuddled. If I got into trouble with friends outside school and came home crying, Ma always used to say to me, 'What are you crying for? Go out, stand up for yourself. If you can't hit 'em with your fists, kick 'em, and if you come back in, I'll give you a punch and you'll have something to cry about.'

Doreen Larsen is a smart, tiny woman in her early seventies (*'I'm far too young to be living in this old people's bungalow. I hate it, there's no space'*). She insists on showing us the sights in the north Yorkshire country town where she now lives, keeping up an entertaining commentary in her broad north-east accent. I find it hard to believe that she spent almost 30 years in Denmark. She says she still writes and sometimes even thinks in Danish. She looks back at her time there with her Danish second husband as the happiest of her life. By comparison, her childhood, young womanhood and widowhood in the north of England have been full of hardship and bitter memories.

Though she called them Ma and Da, the couple who brought Doreen up were her maternal grandparents. Doreen was her mother's second illegitimate child. She and her brother John Henry were put in the Hartlepool workhouse after she was born in 1932, when they threw her mother out.

The experience of being an unmarried mother or an illegitimate child in the 1920s and 1930s was harsh, and fear of the workhouse was still acute. In fact, workhouses had been renamed 'institutions' in 1913 and the old Poor Law finally gave way to Public Assistance and local authority control in 1929, but 'the workhouse' remained a vivid and horrible spectre for many. Conditions and staffing had improved and some institutions now provided basic hospital care, but their bleak buildings and 100-year-old reputation for punishing the poor, the feeble-minded and the unmarried mother were harder to overcome. Informal adoption within the family was often seen as the only alternative to leaving illegitimate offspring in the workhouse, but this didn't always result in a happy experience for the child.

Doreen's mother subsequently married and asked her parents to take the children out of the workhouse and look after them until she was settled and could take them back. But she never reclaimed them, so they stayed with their grandparents, believing them to be their parents. It was a tough and loveless experience.

Ma was an old fishwife. Da didn't work, he was an arthritic with two walking sticks. Da would stand me out in the back yard—I'd be about six—and he'd get me to hold this big sandbag till he could see my little legs starting to buckle, and that's how he trained me up to carry the sacks of sea coal. [Small pieces of coal rejected during the washing process, flushed out to sea and brought back in by the tide. Sea coal was valuable salvage for the poor in coastal mining areas.] *We used to have to go down on to the beach to collect sea coal. This was for the home; if there was any extra it would be sold. When the tide was up we went round the shipyards and bus stations collecting cigarette ends for me Da's pipe. I had an Oxo tin and it had to be filled up. If it wasn't filled up, Da never used to be happy about it. I'd been dilly-dallying instead of collecting.*

We worked, we came home and we went back to school. We had what we thought was a normal, rough childhood—plenty of smacks, plenty of knocks. Da couldn't walk quickly on his legs but his walking stick used to come in very handy because he'd hook it round your leg or round your neck and he'd get you to him one way or the other. But I will say this: Da's hand wasn't as heavy as Ma's.

Doreen's mother went on to have other marriages and eight more children (*'My mother liked tail ends and I don't mean fish'*). Growing up, she became aware from odd things said by a relative that the woman she knew as Auntie May was in fact her mother, but she soon discovered the penalty for revealing this knowledge.

The summer holidays we'd go to my Auntie May and Uncle Leslie's farm. Auntie May used to have a big zinc bath you used to put in front of the fire on the stone floor. Uncle Leslie was sat at the window behind me and I was in the bath and me Auntie May had this big tin mug and she'd filled it with water and put some crystal soda in it to soften my hair because it was very long and plaited, and she told me, 'The water's coming, keep your eyes closed.' I didn't and of course the soda went in my eyes and I started making a fuss. Uncle Leslie said, 'Stop being such a

107

babbie and let your Auntie wash your hair.' And I stood up and I said, 'She's not my Auntie, she's my Mam.' Well, Ma got hold of me, pulled me out of the bath by my hair, shot me into the parlour and said, 'You little flamer, now get out there and tell your Uncle Leslie you're sorry.' 'What for? She is me Mam.' 'Yes, you little bastard, I know that, you know that, she knows that but he doesn't bloody know that. Now get out there and say you're sorry.' And that was the last time. I never ever saw my Mam again. We never ever went back to the farm, never. And that was just before I was 12.

She sees now that her grandparents were taking out their fury with their errant daughter on her and her brother. Though she hated it, she can't bring herself to blame them because she believes they saved her from an even worse fate.

We suffered for her wrongdoings, and it was wrong. But at the same time, if it hadn't been for them, where would I be? The workhouse.

Despite the advent of the first Adoption Act in 1926, informal adoptions like Doreen's within the family, and Vera Butterworth's with compassionate strangers (see Chapter 4), were still the norm. At least, I think they were. One of the difficulties of tracking the history of adoption is the unreliability of official figures. Available statistics, especially before 1950, don't give a full or accurate picture of what was happening. After 1926, records of legal adoptions collected by the Registrar General don't distinguish between those granted to members of the child's family and to non-relatives. And those like Doreen's and Vera's are not recorded at all. Estimates of non-relative legal adoptions immediately following the 1926 Act are low— about 1,500 in 1927 against total illegitimate births of over 29,000—and they creep up only slowly until after the Second World War. It is also likely that in the early years following the Act, many adoptions were those legalising existing informal arrangements, so the figures are far from the full story. But two things are clear: the continued existence of *de facto* arrangements meant there were many more 'adoptions' than official figures suggest; and legal adoption gained ground only slowly until the Second World War heralded the boom years of the 1950s and 1960s.

In common with many sad stories, Doreen's is one of history repeated. Like May, she became an unmarried mother while still a teenager. When her son was born in 1951 she saw adoption from another, no less painful, angle. Her experience then shows that even 'proper' adoptions could involve deception and coercion. But that comes later in the story.

May's flighty behaviour and casual attitude to her first two children seems not to have been typical. As a first resort, young women in her position were more likely to try and find a workable arrangement with their families to pass a child off as their parents', or that of a married sister or aunt. Because of the stigma of illegitimacy, the secret was often kept for decades, sometimes till death, with heartbreaking consequences for the mother.

*   *   *

109

Someone who experienced informal adoption within the family from a mother's perspective was Ada Haskins. Born in 1911, Ada had an illegitimate son in 1930 after her first sexual experience, and gave birth to him in what she knew as the workhouse. Her mother brought the child up as her own while Ada got a job in domestic service in London to provide for him. He grew up believing Ada was his older sister. It wasn't until 1988 that she confided in a researcher.

I've been up there three or four times to try and tell him before I die that I'm his mother but I just can't go through with it. He's 57 now himself and it would be such a shock for him, I don't know if he would accept it. Sometimes I think it's God punishing me for the sin of having an illegitimate child. I married afterwards, a very happy marriage and we desperately wanted children but couldn't have any. My only son doesn't know I'm his mother.

Hiding illegitimate children within the family was probably much more common in the first half of the last century than is usually acknowledged. When I was talking to one of my oldest friends about plans for this book, I was amazed to learn that her mother, Betty, whom I remember as a formidable woman—a teacher of speech and drama with a strong Methodist and Salvationist background—was one of illegitimate twins, born to the woman my friend knew as 'Auntie Beth'. They had been separated at birth and brought up in different branches of the family, with little or no contact over the years. Though it wasn't exactly a secret, it wasn't discussed either. Betty herself refused to talk about it with her daughters. For people of my parents' generation, the stain of illegitimacy still needed to be covered up.

Even closer to home, my father recently revealed that he'd always wondered whether his elder brother William, always known in the family as Son, was illegitimate. This was the only reason he could think of for Son being brought up by his paternal grandparents rather than in the family home with him and his sister Vera. Did his mother have an extramarital affair? Had his father taken responsibility for an illegitimate child? My father and Son have been estranged for more than 40 years; we'll probably never know.

*　　　*　　　*

Though adoption—legal or informal—within the family was far from ideal, it was the option of choice for many unmarried mothers. But if they were rejected by their parents and couldn't support themselves, the alternatives were stark and few.

Abortion was illegal, though amateur and 'back-street' abortions were common, with all the miserable consequences of infection, infertility and sometimes death that followed. Once born, children could be left in the workhouse (or council-run children's homes after 1929) or placed in a voluntary children's home like Dr Barnardo's.

The mass export of 'parentless' children from voluntary homes to help populate and farm the distant dominions of Canada, South Africa and Australia (and at a stroke create more places in homes) started in earnest in the late 19th century

111

and continued well into the second half of the 20th. Child migration met Britain's economic and imperial needs admirably for over six decades, and was no doubt defended as character-building for the children. Their experience tells a different story of hardship, exploitation and cruelty. They were invariably told they were orphans, when the majority were in fact illegitimate with living relatives, and their natural parents were rarely informed they had been sent abroad. The scale of the project and the story of the thousands of child migrants—many still scattered and separated from their original families—only emerged in the 1980s. What was considered an ideal solution to the twin problems of homeless children and an underpopulated Empire now seems to us cynical and inhumane.

By the 1920s there were new alternatives to handing children over to institutions (see Chapter 4). The campaigning National Council for the Unmarried Mother and Her Child had set up 14 homes and hostels in London, nine in the rest of England and one in Scotland to provide a supportive environment while mothers went out to work. There was also a new breed of 'moral welfare' workers being trained at Josephine Butler House, established in Liverpool in 1920, linked to a growing network of Church mother and baby homes. By the late 1920s, the Church of England had 25 long- and short-stay homes. They had some Ministry of Health funding and aimed to rehabilitate women morally and place them in jobs in domestic service so they could continue to support their children. But they sounded grim places. The women, often known as 'penitents', lived for up to two years in institutions with names like The House of Mercy, where they were engaged in *'happy and healthy work'*. This 1927 description of one home tries valiantly to be upbeat:

In the needlework room, girls sit cutting and stitching at long tables while a Sister at a high desk reads aloud from an interesting book.

Laundry work is undertaken but the writer hastens to tell us that this is *'only a little Church washing of altar linen and the like'*. Unlike those terrible Roman Catholic Magdalene places, he seems to be saying.

Mary Magdalene, the penitent fallen woman who washed Christ's feet with her tears and became a saint. The notorious Magdalene laundries were probably the most extreme manifestation of the Catholic Church's efforts to punish sex outside marriage and keep women in their place. Next to the workhouse, they were most women's idea of hell, or they would have been if conditions in them had been widely known. At least you had a good chance of getting out of the workhouse and talking about what went on there; once you were inside a Magdalene laundry it was often for life. They were common in Ireland but there were some in the UK too, even one of a kind in London. Here, until as late as the 1970s, unmarried mothers and girls considered at moral risk were virtually imprisoned and used as slave labour in regimes that were sometimes cruel and sadistic. Babies were removed at birth and placed immediately for adoption, or brought up in

113

residential nurseries apart from their mothers.

Bevan and I first saw Peter Mullan's brilliant piece of polemic, *The Magdalene Sisters*, in a small cinema in a run-down arts centre in Brentford, a working-class area of west London. The film was so shocking, moving and infuriating that I wanted to go out afterwards and kill a nun. As the credits rolled, no one left, and when the lights went up we realised we were in the company of a large number of late middle-aged and elderly women, some nodding and whispering in small groups, many in tears. I wanted to ask them, 'Did this happen to you? How did you bear it?' But of course I didn't.

Doubtless the Church of England and the other denominational mother and baby homes weren't anything like as oppressive as the Magdalene laundries, though plenty of unmarried mothers tell of hard work, harsh regimes and insensitive treatment. Washing and scrubbing is a common theme in their testimony. You don't hear 'scrubber' used for women of loose morals much these days. Was this where it came from? According to Partridge, the authority on slang, it's Australian in origin after wild mares that mate indiscriminately in the Outback scrub. But the image of women trying to scrub the stain of their sin away is somehow much more compelling.

*   *   *

Dot Stephenson, born in 1929, tells an extraordinary story of her time in a Church of Scotland home just after the Second World War. She was 16 and in love with a Polish soldier she'd met at a YMCA dance. Her father wouldn't let her marry a 'foreigner' so she decided to get pregnant to force his hand. But she misjudged her father, who threw her out.

The time that I'm talking about there was nowhere to go. The only social services you had was to have kids put in homes or for people like me that were expecting babies and shouldn't be, put in an asylum. They would do that and say there was something wrong with them. You were looked down on, you were frowned on, you were more or less ostracised, you were a loose woman. But I wasn't a loose woman, I planned what I did. I did it for a reason: I wanted to get married, but I just didn't know the depth of me father's hate. He would rather me suffer; he would rather get rid of the baby than let us stay at home.

Six months pregnant, she hitched lifts in lorries to an aunt in Dundee, who persuaded her to have the baby in a local church mother and baby home.

When you walked in the door, it was like walking from the 20th century into the 15th century. The girls are all walking in formation with their hands down real prim, you know, grey frocks and white pinnies, black shoes. And Sister Lucy says, 'Oh yes, you can stay and we'll look after you, but you have to work.' I said, 'Oh, I'm not frightened of work.' Work! You had to scrub all the linen for the place, their linen, our linen, the babies' stuff, the bedding all had to be scrubbed by you. There was no laundry taken out, and you did it all with like a lye soap, it was a real hard soap, and cold water. You didn't have any hot water. Couldn't get a lather, your hands used to crack

115

with the cold.

She returned to the home after having her baby in Dundee Royal Infirmary. One day when she was bathing him a Sister came with some beautiful baby clothes and told her to get him dressed.

I had him all nicely dressed and she went, 'Give him to me.' So you know I says, 'What do you mean give him to you? What for?' 'Oh,' she says, 'he's being adopted today.' Well it was like somebody stopped me breath. There is no way I can describe how I felt because I felt about six or seven different ways at once. I felt breathless, betrayed, because no one when I went there had said the baby had to be adopted, that was never ever mentioned. All they said was that they'll take care of you and the baby; they don't mention what's going to happen afterwards. The other feeling was you go like ice, as though all the blood's drained from you, you're rigid, and then you sort of come to life and rage. Well, as she went to get him, I punched her. I hit her, I really did belt her one. I thought I'd decapitated her, but me hand slipped and went right through this pane of glass and there was blood everywhere. I didn't realise what I'd done, I just grabbed him and ran. I ran to me Aunt's and when I got to the door she just looked at me and said, 'What on earth have you done?' She thought the bairn had been injured, it was the blood. I was just screaming, you know, I was hysterical.

It was the girls under 21—then the age of majority—and those with spirit like Dot who answered back, who seemed to attract the harshest treatment and the most determined efforts to get

116

them to part with their babies for adoption. Whatever the practice in Church homes themselves, the public policy—particularly before the war—was to keep the baby within the family rather than persuade the mother to have it legally adopted by strangers. Best of all, the mother should if possible work to keep the baby, because this protected her from future mischief. In his 1927 booklet for SPCK—*Rescue Work*—Edward Trenholme is unequivocal about adoption, even within the family:

It not seldom happens that a girl's parents, aunt or married sister compassionately take charge of an illegitimate child. If an adoption can be arranged a child can be taken permanently off the mother's hands, but rescue workers do not favour this course except sometimes for special reasons. Mothers, even unmarried mothers, love their babies and are themselves steadied, purified, ennobled by that mother-love in their hearts. It may be the saving of a girl to have her own baby to love and support.

It didn't work for Dot Stephenson. Her baby was finally adopted by her mother and father but they insisted on bringing him up in ignorance of his real origins, and she was told she wasn't welcome in their home.

Women have got a tie that binds, an invisible tie that binds, and even though you've given [the baby] up, you're still tied. You can't cut it no matter; it's there, it's invisible, it binds you to your child. I don't care how hard-hearted or callous you are, you miss them every day and every minute of every day. You might be doing things and people think, oh she's not bothered, but they're wrong, because it's always at the back of your mind. Birthdays are the worst, because you can't be there. You can send a card, you can send presents but all the presents in the world can't fill the gap that you've got inside you. I don't know how to explain this—me, lost for words, I never thought it would happen! You're going through life as an automaton because your life stopped when the adoption process went through. Your life actually stops.

I was anxious to find Sisters or moral welfare workers with experience in these homes more than 50 years ago, to hear how they saw their work. Of the dozens of replies I received from former social workers and adoption workers in response to an appeal in *Saga Magazine*, only a couple were from women with this experience before 1950. One was from a 90-year-old former Church Army [An evangelical wing of the Church of England, run on militaristic lines.] Sister:

After my shortened Church Army training due to the Second World War, I was commissioned as a Church Army Sister on 24 April 1942. I was sent to be a nursing sister in a home for unmarried mothers and their babies at Weston-super-Mare. These young mothers aged 14 to 20-plus cared for their babies and helped in the general running of the home. The mothers all kept their children. After a year or so they went into domestic service, taking the children with them. I did not choose to be a Moral Welfare Worker, but I do not regret having been involved in this caring ministry. A couple of young women who came to me for help are still in touch. I have not encouraged

118

them to do so. However, I am glad that I am still available for them.

Dot and my correspondent live on different planets, but that is not to devalue the work of the dedicated Christian women who saw it as their duty and vocation to help and guide pregnant girls. Though Dot and others would disagree, they believed they were doing the right thing and some young women were grateful for it.

*   *   *

Meanwhile, what of Clara Andrew and the nascent adoption societies? In 1933 she was busy escorting Queen Mary on a tour of the newly opened NCAA nursery training centre and hostel for children in Sydenham, south London. The *Kentish Mercury* reported:

A beautiful and commodious modern residence, standing in fairly extensive grounds with magnificent views over Kent and Surrey, has been placed at the disposal of the National Children Adoption Association for the purposes of the hostel. It is called Castlebar.

The national agencies such as the NCAA and the NAS were doing good business, but so were dozens of smaller regional and local agencies set up in the years following the First World War and the Adoption Act to meet increasing demand from the childless. Many were based on dioceses and took babies from the local church mother and baby home; many had a moral or philanthropic purpose;

119

some were plain businesses.

The 1926 Act had set no minimum standards or regulations for adoption, and there was increasing concern after 1926 that many agencies were little better than baby farming operations. Money continued to change hands, either through fees or compulsory 'donations', standards of vetting prospective adopters were variable at best and many adoptions were inappropriate or poorly arranged. 'Casework', the social work term for proper investigation and assessment, was still in its infancy, and social work had yet to be professionalised. Social workers were largely voluntary or paid by the churches. Training for the moral welfare workers had begun at places like Josephine Butler House but courses were as theological as they were practical, and adoption theory did not yet exist.

The old spectre of baby farming was raised again, and in 1936 a committee was set up under the chairmanship of Lady Horsburgh MP to *enquire into the methods of adoption agencies and societies and report whether any, and if so what, measures should be taken in the public interest to supervise or control their activities'.*

The Horsburgh Committee found cause for concern: some children had been placed with blind, deaf or mentally unstable people or those who sought to exploit them for financial gain. Some societies assessed adopters via letter rather than face-to-face. The Committee also uncovered widespread *de facto* adoptions and discovered that less than a third of the adoptions carried out by one of the largest societies (unnamed) in 1935 were legalised.

However, there was some good news: the Committee was glad to report that they found no evidence of baby farming. The 'third party' adoption—an arrangement that had probably been going on for years—was, however, recognised officially for the first time:

It is often the case that the mother of an illegitimate child asks the matron of the maternity home for assistance in finding an adopter for the child and such persons are able to introduce her to such adopters. No money passes hands and there is no reason to doubt the good intentions of the introducers. On the other hand it does not necessarily follow that the adoption has been wisely arranged.

This observation was prescient: there was to be much angst in the following decades about third party adoptions.

Horsburgh made a number of important recommendations that resulted in the Adoption of Children (Regulation) Act in 1939. All agencies were to be licensed by local authorities and obliged to have Case Committees with qualified people to consider the suitability of adopters. The personal suitability of adopters was to be assessed as well as their economic and social position, and every applicant was to be interviewed personally by the Committee or its appointed representative. Children could not be advertised for adoption and no payment demanded. These regulations remained in force for much of the 20th century.

The Second World War created another peak in the number of illegitimate births—63,420 or 9.3 per cent of live births in England and Wales in

1945. Like the First World War, this brought about a sea change in the nature and scale of adoption.

One of the 55,173 babies born out of wedlock in 1944 was Bernard Cornwell, author of the internationally successful *Sharpe* novels. I first heard the story of his adoption and bizarre upbringing when he was a guest on *Desert Island Discs*. Bernard lives in Cape Cod, USA, but he generously agreed to answer my questions and introduced me to his birth mother, Dorothy. I met her at her Basingstoke flat where the living room bookshelves are packed with historical novels and biographies. 'I'm a wannabe writer,' she confessed. She reminded me strongly of Marjorie (also coincidentally the name of his adoptive mother) and looked nowhere near her 83 years. In 1944 she was in the WAAF and her affair with a Canadian airman began in a Swanage pub.

It was a typical wartime romance. We never talked about things like sex; everything was glossed over. All servicemen were issued with condoms before they went out, so there was no need for them to impregnate anybody, but men being men . . . It sounds stupid to say how innocent I was; it never really occurred to me. I didn't even know what to do or how to do it. It was more like a fumble in the dark than anything else.

By the time she discovered she was pregnant, she had been posted to Wales.

I was in my Officer's office one day doing some filing and she got a sideways view of me and that was that. That was goodbye to my life. I loved the Air Force, the freedom, but I had to go home, there was nowhere else to go. My father was upset and told me I wouldn't be able to keep the baby and stay there. But I'd already made arrangements through a doctor who didn't have any connections with my family. I knew there was no way I could keep a baby. I had no money and my family wouldn't support me. How would I have lived? Where would I have lived? There was no choice. Adoption seemed to be the best hope for Bernard's future.

Dorothy went to a private nursing home in London, where the matron told her she had the perfect couple to adopt her baby, a Joseph and Margery Wiggins.

They were wonderful people and quite well off, so she said. It all sounded great. You don't want to think of your child going into poverty. They came and stood at the foot of my bed. I don't remember them saying anything to me to be honest. I know I sat up and I spoke to them and I didn't get any feedback. They just stood there, like avenging angels.

Avenging angels turned out to be right. Bernard looks back on his experience growing up with the Wigginses:

It was not, I think, a successful adoption. Margery plainly disliked me, and I was a disappointment to Joseph, so I cannot say it was a happy experience for any of us. She was a very bitter woman, who was illegitimate herself, and had experienced a difficult childhood. She and I did not get on at all, and while, when I was an adult, I became fonder of Joseph, I

123

have never thought of Margery with anything except dislike. I think she was almost certainly the one who wanted to adopt children, and the more the merrier, because she liked babies. She adopted five, in the end.

Margery and Joseph were members of a Christian sect called the Peculiar People, a group restricted to south-east Essex and excessively strict. They were evangelical fundamentalists, so every word in the Bible was considered to be literally true, and any transgressions from the paths of righteousness were punished brutally. This was not a regimen that suited me, so I found myself in fairly constant conflict, and the fact that I was adopted helped me to understand why I disliked my parents. So truly it was a help, indeed a blessing. I knew I did not belong, and I felt very strongly that there was a private part of me, utterly separate from Margery and Joseph, that neither they nor their religion could touch, and that in time that part would prove to be the real thing. I was never good enough and, try as I did, I still got punished, and in the subsequent misery I retreated into this private area—the one that knew there were different, nicer parents. Film stars, princesses and Spitfire pilots were jointly responsible for my birth and I dreamed that one day a big car would draw up and my imagined parents would take me away. My 'real' mother, I was sure, would be glamorous, would wear cosmetics and high heels—these attributes were solely provoked by the Peculiar People's disapproval of such things.

Bernard's unhappy experience was a classic example of a third party adoption: one arranged privately by the matron of a maternity home, a doctor, solicitor or other respected community figure regularly in touch with unmarried mothers and childless couples wanting to adopt. Depending on your point of view, they performed a valuable public service brokering private adoptions, saving both parties the bother of all those tiresome investigations by do-gooding social workers. Or they were a menace that gave adoption a bad name. Not only did they sometimes result in unwise placements like that of Bernard with the Wigginses, there was also scope for financial deals to be done under the counter. In her 1958 book *The Adopted Child*, Mary Ellison had no doubts:

At their worst, third party adoptions present suspect features of the most dubious kind . . . irregular and sometimes disgraceful arrangements for the placing of many infants and children continue to be made, in spite of the facilities afforded by the law to all mothers who wish to hand over their babies for adoption.

Though the rules were tightened up in a new Adoption Act in 1949, third party arrangements were not outlawed in England and Wales until 1982, despite pressure from agencies and adoption workers. In 1953, Home Office minister Kenneth Younger, addressing the Standing Conference of Adoption Agencies, said he had 'heard more disquiet on this topic than any other' and claimed the proportion of third party adoptions to those arranged through agencies was then five to one.

Despite the inadequacy of the law and the rather ramshackle development of adoption policy and practice, legal adoption was firmly established by the end of the first half of the 20th century. The debate was no longer about whether adoption itself was reputable, but whether some means of arranging it were more reputable than others. Agencies and societies that had sprung up since the First World War were still largely denominational, or at least nominally Christian, and had widely varying standards and practices, despite the best efforts of the Horsburgh Committee. Importantly, the old child welfare institutions were joining in at last: the Church of England Children's Society started to place children for adoption in 1935, with Dr Barnardo's one of the last to register as an adoption agency in 1947, finally abandoning its unwavering preference for institutional and foster care.

The influential Curtis Report of 1946 had a lot to do with Barnardo's change of heart. The Curtis Committee was charged with enquiring into *the care of children deprived of a normal home life*. Its findings were disquieting and its recommendations led to the 1948 Children Act—one of the pillars of the new welfare state introduced that year. It found conditions for children in the old workhouses appalling (*'children were being minded by aged inmates and by cleaners'*) and those in many voluntary and council-run children's homes little better. In many homes it noted *'a lack of personal interest in and affection for the children which we found shocking'*. It concluded that fostering was better for children than institutional care, but that adoption was even better: *'If successful, it is the most completely satisfactory method of providing a substitute home.'*

Curtis provided the gold seal of approval

adoption needed. Together with the availability of many more 'unwanted' babies following the war, the improving reputation of the main agencies and growing acceptability to the middle classes, adoption was poised to enter its boom years. These brought the prospect of family life for thousands of childless couples and the chance of a better start for the babies they adopted. But for the mothers, the experience was one they'd never forget, nor ever fully recover from.

7

KNOWING

Dear Mr Runchman,

I have for the past year been seeking the whereabouts of a Marjorie Phyllis Heppelthwaite who was born on 8 October 1920, and have learnt that recently you have had dealings with a lady by this name who you have assisted in moving to sheltered housing in Ealing. I now have an address and would like to check with you if it is the same before I approach this lady on a personal matter.

Any assistance you can give will be much appreciated.
Yours sincerely,
Tess Munday
Senior Social Worker

The letter gave nothing away, but said everything. There was no doubt in my mind that there had been another child, on whose behalf Tess Munday was now conducting a search.

I was shaken and furious. It felt like a betrayal. This open, likeable woman I thought I'd got to know had chosen not to tell me something as important as this. I couldn't stop the words 'and after all I've done for her' forming on my lips, but righteous indignation was only one of the tangle of feelings I was struggling with. I was hurt and disappointed in myself that I'd obviously made such a poor job of our relationship that she didn't feel able to confide in me. I was angry with her because the concealment felt like a slap in the face. And, of course, the existence of another child meant that she was no longer just mine. This new revelation had changed the whole basis and dynamic of our relationship.

The one thing I couldn't bring myself to do was reproach her for having another illegitimate child. That would have required a distance I didn't have and a moral position I didn't hold. This was much more personal, about her and me.

The following day at work I rang Tess Munday. This isn't the kind of conversation you can have in an open plan office so I was glad of my old-fashioned room with its firmly shut door and solid walls.

'Tess Munday?'

'Yes.'

'I'm Sue Elliott. You wrote to Martin Runchman about Marjorie Phyllis Heppelthwaite.'

'Yes.'

'I'm Marjorie's daughter.'

A pause and the sound of thoughts being gathered.

'I see. And was your mother born on 8 October 1920?'

'Yes.'

Oh for God's sake, get on with it.

'Well, it's possible she might be the same person I'm looking for.'

I kept a small scream to myself.

'Did your mother ever . . . talk to you about . . . events in her past?'

Well yes, but not this one. Infuriatingly, she went on hedging, trying, as I'm sure she thought, to prepare me for something I actually already knew.

I rudely cut her short.

'You're going to tell me Marjorie had another child.'

'Well, if it *is* the same person, then she did have a baby, yes, in 1956. She called her Linda and she was subsequently adopted. Linda is my client and she'd like to establish contact with her mother. Obviously, this will come as quite a shock to you . . .'

Yes and no. I managed to keep my composure for the rest of the conversation. I told her briefly about Marjorie and said that of course I was sure we'd both want to welcome Linda if she wanted contact but that Marjorie and I had only recently been reunited ourselves and she might find it all a bit overwhelming. She wasn't the only one. We agreed to talk again the following day, when she 'might' be able to tell me more. I put the phone down and burst into tears. My secretary, Shanta, sought out brandy and, in her efforts to console me, said those awful words 'and after all you've done for her'.

I cried for the rest of the morning, feeling wretched, pathetic and self-pitying. I couldn't think of anything else. Bevan came to rescue me at lunchtime and we went to a wine bar behind Harrods to talk about it. There, a strange thing happened: the more we talked, the more the anger and distress lifted, to the point where it dawned that this threatening 'other child' who'd arrived to upset my exclusive relationship with Marjorie was in fact my adult sister. This was such a novel thought and held such promise that it overwhelmed all the negative feelings. As we were crossing Brompton Road I said to Bevan, 'I've got a sister!', and by the time I got back to the office I felt quite differently about it all. It was extraordinary. Shanta shook her head and tutted in the way she always did when she was bemused by something.

My second conversation with Tess Munday was altogether less strained. She agreed straight away that it was Marjorie she was looking for and that Linda—now called Fiona—was delighted to know that, not only had Marjorie been located, but that she had a sibling. She would love to talk to me. I gave Tess my number.

'Hello? Is that my big sister?'

'Hello! Is that my little sister?'

We laughed, not nervous laughter but open and easy. It was as easy as talking to Marjorie had been that first time. I sat on the stairs and swapped life stories with my new sister. She was married with a two-year-old daughter and taught dance in a girls' secondary school. We seized on the similarity with my own career start as a drama teacher. 'So Marjorie had two very talented, artistic offspring!' More laughter. We were already speaking the same language.

She had grown up a much-loved but only child and was even more thrilled at the prospect of having a sister than I was.

'I've been so excited since Tess told me, I haven't been able to sit still for what I call "fizzy bottom"—you know that feeling?'

'Sounds more like a bad case of flatulence to me, but yes, I know.'

Ever since my epiphany on the crossing outside Harrods I'd had an entirely pleasant feeling of excitement and anticipation too.

I answered her questions about Marjorie and told her about the horrendous move and her new life in Hanwell, and how we were all Marjorie had in the world. We wondered how the news might best be broken that now *both* her little chickens had come home to roost. And we agreed there was nothing to stop us meeting as soon as possible, so we arranged to meet at her home in Kent that Saturday.

*   *   *

Dear Martin,

Thank you very much for forwarding Tess Munday's enquiry about Marjorie. I am grateful to you for your wariness.

As you may have guessed, I have discovered I have a sister! I'm now getting over the shock, have spoken to her on the phone and am due to meet her tomorrow. Marjorie doesn't know any of this yet; Fiona and I have to discuss how best to break it to her, particularly as she chose not to tell me anything about it.

I'm sorry you have been so involved in our personal affairs, Martin—like me, you must feel you are part of a long-running soap opera sometimes. Or perhaps you will miss the excitement once Bungalow Road is sold! Either way, I am extremely grateful to you for your sympathetic approach through all of this.

I was pleased to hear that Bungalow Road cleaned up OK and has survived the family next door (so far). Marjorie has settled very well and is enjoying her new life. I hope this latest news won't knock her back. Fiona sounds a very nice person and I hope she will

132

become 'part of the family' quickly. How strange that she should decide to trace Marjorie so soon after me. Life is funny.

Understatement. The timing was surely too unnervingly close to be a coincidence. Only a matter of weeks after the comic-horror move from Bungalow Road, Fiona had gone there with her husband Steve in their spring half-term break. She had found the address from the electoral roll. The 'sold' sign was up outside; Fiona immediately jumped to conclusions—Marjorie was dead. But practical as ever, Steve had suggested they go to the estate agent anyway to find out more.

That agent, who must have been a paragon of humanity among his kind, told them that the house was being sold by Barnardo's and gave them Martin Runchman's name. The old lady there had, he thought, moved to Ealing but he had no forwarding address. We deliberately left none. Marjorie had decided she wanted a complete break from her old life and was especially keen to get away from Edie.

Tess's approach to Martin got a dusty response:

Dear Ms Munday,
I do not feel that I am in a position to comment upon your letter and I think in the circumstances it would not be appropriate for us to speak on the telephone. I have, however, arranged to send on your letter to a lady, whom I shall not name, who may choose to contact you further.
Yours faithfully,
Martin Runchman

133

His cloak-and-dagger stuff about the unnamed lady, who of course was me, set hares running. Tess assumed from Martin's careful formality that I must be Marjorie's solicitor. No wonder she was fumbling for words when I revealed myself, not as the cool professional contact she had expected, but as the aggrieved and bolshie daughter.

Timing is all. Had Fiona left her expedition to Bungalow Road till her next school holiday, the trail would almost certainly have gone cold. The timing had been more than fortuitous. We both decided to trace at much the same point in our lives and had found our mother—and each other— within the space of little more than a year.

*   *   *

We knew we liked each other on the phone and our meeting confirmed it. But it was still a shock to see Fiona for the first time as she came out of their cottage to meet us.

'My God, you look just like Marjorie!'

I'm not sure what I expected, but Fiona had Marjorie's fair colouring and similar features, and I felt something of that bond of recognition I didn't experience when I first saw Marjorie.

'And you've got our bedroom curtains!' So what if they were Laura Ashley and common enough; it seemed significant. You look for connections and, when you find them—however prosaic—they confirm that you are inextricably linked to something, someone else. Here was another person who had been a stranger till now but I knew we'd be sure to have a lot more than curtains in common.

134

One thing we didn't have in common was fathers. Fiona seemed to know more about hers than I knew about the shadowy 'Peter White', who I was beginning to think might be a pseudonym (*'tall, broad, fond of sport'*; an Identikit picture if ever I saw one). Fiona's father ran a tobacconists with his brother near, or possibly in, Gipsy Road, and played in a band in the evenings. Like my putative father, he was married, although it was unclear whether Marjorie knew this when she started her relationships with them. We agreed that she must have had a desperate time and that we had no inclination whatever to find out more about these men. We were as interested in them as we assumed they had been in us. 'Bastards!' we chorused, and then laughed when we realised what we'd said. We were the bastards.

We compared upbringings. We had both grown up on the fringes of London in solid middle-class homes, Fiona's rather more comfortable than mine as my father worked in the public sector and hers was something in the City. She was an indulged child and her parents made sacrifices to send her to private schools, including a specialist dance school. When it was clear she wasn't going to be a professional dancer, she went on to Goldsmiths College to train as a dance teacher in the Laban method.

I knew all about the Laban method because at Trent Park, where I'd trained, there was a Laban dance course and all the girls on it—and they were all girls—were uniformly lithe and pretty, unlike us dumpy thesps doing drama. We called them Laban Lovelies and envied them their poise and attractiveness. Another connection.

135

Unlike me, Fiona had stayed in teaching, and now lived a busy life in this overcrowded cottage with Steve, her second husband, who was in the process of retraining for teaching after 20 years as an engineer with BT. 'It was having Katie that made me think, how on earth could Marjorie have given me away?', and so her search began.

We both had loving adoptive homes and particularly strong attachments to our fathers, but Fiona's parents were even more reticent on the subject of her adoption than my own. 'I wasn't told till I was 11, and I didn't really understand then. I accepted it, and then much later I was angry.' She found some difficulty in coming to terms with the idea through adolescence, which caused problems later. Discussion on the subject was never welcomed at home and this meant that she had not told her parents about her search. We were to talk about this a great deal, later. I thought of my own struggles about whether to tell my parents or not; how much more difficult it must have been for Fiona.

So much else to say, but we knew we'd carry on talking. Fiona hugged me in front of the Laura Ashley curtains as we made ready to go.

'Bye for now, big Sis.'

*   *   *

Telling Marjorie would be difficult. It would be a double shock for her: that the daughter she'd given away in 1956 had turned up, and that the daughter given away in 1951 knew before she did.

We were in her living room at Walker Close going through the invitation list for the housewarming party. Marjorie, who loved a party, was really looking forward to it. She saw it as a way of thanking everyone who'd helped her into her new life. 'I want the *good* people,' she had said, leaving hanging the question of who the bad people might be.

On the list were Monica of course, Martin Runchman, half a dozen of my friends who'd been so supportive during my search and after it, my brother Simon and his girlfriend Sarah, Syd and Eileen next door and some other neighbours.

'There's someone else you might want to invite, who I know would love to come.'

'Oh yes, who's that then?'

'Linda.'

'Linda who?'

I didn't reply straight away to let the name sink in, and she repeated it again quietly to herself. Had she made the connection; was she playing for time?

'Linda who was born in 1956 and who very much wants to see you again.'

Another pause, a brief look of pain. I didn't know for a fleeting moment whether she might try and deny it. But then her characteristic crinkly smile.

'Really?'

'Yes. Really. I met her last weekend and she's lovely. I know you'll like her, and she looks just like you.'

She seemed as open and accepting as she was at my arrival in her life and genuinely pleased that Fiona, too, had found her. Why hadn't she told me? 'I thought you'd think the worse of me,' was all she would say. The one thing I *didn't* think. But

137

it was clear she was ashamed: 'I should have known better, especially after you.' And, as she recalled details from the past, I got the impression it wasn't a happy affair. 'I didn't know he was married, Sue, till it was too late.' It had happened all over again, just like before.

I never liked to press her on the details. She'd tell me what she wanted to tell me. And I increasingly wondered whether, in order to cope over the years with the weight of hurt and guilt, she hadn't just pushed all those painful memories away somewhere deep, where they wouldn't trouble her. Maybe she even started to wonder whether they happened at all. My arrival, now Fiona's, reminded her they had, and it must all have come back to the surface in an unwelcome rush. But she came from a generation where sharing emotions was thought weak and embarrassing, and she'd got used to not having anyone except Benny to talk to, so if she felt turmoil she kept it close.

Fiona came over to Walker Close to meet her shortly afterwards and emotions were briefly exposed then; all three of us cried together. She told us how much she'd wanted to keep us, but there was little choice then, no help or benefits. Only shame. 'If your family wouldn't take you with a baby, you were stuck. My father was a pig about it all. If only Mum had still been alive, she wouldn't have let me lose you. I thought about a live-in job in service somewhere so that I could keep you, but that would have been no life for you.' So she gave us up.

We told her she'd done the right thing and that we didn't blame her, and we wondered to ourselves how she could have gone through it all twice. And after the tears there was room for a laugh and a joke.

'Now come on Marjorie, how many more of us are there?'

'Oh, eight!' she said, and we all laughed.

After that, though never in Fiona's presence, she'd always call me 'My Number One Daughter'.

*   *   *

The housewarming party in the spring of 1993 was a very happy day. There were too many people for the flat, so we had it in the communal lounge at Walker Close. As a surprise, Fiona brought a celebration cake she had specially made in the shape of a TV with Marjorie's favourite *EastEnders* on the screen. 'Happy New Beginning,' it said, and it was.

There was a lot to celebrate; not only my reunion with Marjorie and her escape from Bungalow Road, but also the return of her other lost child and the start of our relationship as sisters. No wonder Marjorie looks a bit bewildered in the photos; we must have been carrying her along on a wave of our own elation. For me it felt like the culmination of two years of intense physical and emotional activity that had resolved itself in unexpectedly happy ways. Adoption reunions are fraught with difficulty and danger but this one seemed to have turned out much more positively than I could have hoped for.

*   *   *

It was very important to feel I had the support of

139

my parents through the search and subsequent upheavals. When I told them about Fiona, a few days later a small basket of flowers arrived with 'Love and Happiness Always, Mum and Dad' on the card. Whatever their private thoughts about my decision, they made every appearance of being interested and supportive, and I was very grateful for that. I would have found it impossible had they been hostile or equivocal. It helped that my father had some experience of adoption reunions through his work, and he understood why it was so important to me. My mother didn't have this background and it was much harder for her. Though I told her many times that no one would ever replace her, it is a lasting regret that she was probably never fully reconciled to my need to know about the time before they had me.

I very much wanted them to meet Marjorie, and they agreed to do this. It seemed to put the missing link in the chain somehow. For her part, Marjorie was enthusiastic about meeting them. From those letters she had written to the adoption agency, I knew it helped her greatly to think of them as the 'very wonderful people' who had given me such a good and loving home. This was how she still thought of them and I was glad.

They met at our house just before the move to Hanwell. Bevan went with my father to Victoria to meet Marjorie from the Selhurst train and bring her back to Ealing. We had a pleasant, if slightly formal lunch but I knew it was going to be alright when, in the afternoon, they all felt sufficiently relaxed to doze off in each other's company.

Looking at them having their 40 winks, I was struck again by the similarities—and the differences—between them. They had their first 20 or so years in common, growing up in the same streets with the same hardships. My mothers both left elementary schools at 14. My mother worked in a dairy; Marjorie trained with the GPO as a telephonist. They lived through a London ravaged by bombs and war and death. Then their lives diverged. Now here were my mother and father, comfortably retired, two successful children and grandchildren to come, much achieved to be proud of. Here too was Marjorie, holding her head up, but with nothing to show for her adult life but piles of clothes and bitter memories.

When they'd all gone, Bevan told me what happened at Victoria when my father and Marjorie first met. After a warm greeting, he had put a hand on her arm.

'I've always wanted to meet you, Marjorie.'

'And I've wanted to meet you both. Thank you. I think you've done a wonderful job.'

'Well, let's just say all three of us have done a wonderful job.'

It was so typically generous of my father. Nothing in the world could have made me feel more loved, at that moment or since.

*   *   *

Apart from the positive feelings about finding a sister, I was glad to have some support with Marjorie's ongoing rehabilitation. Though she was always smartly turned out and went to have her hair done regularly, her looks were spoiled by her lack of teeth. She seemed quite happy with the few she had, but I was trying to talk her into having

141

dentures, and now Fiona was here to provide the necessary two-pronged attack. Under this pressure, and with some misgivings, she agreed.

The dentures episode led to more contact with Barnardo's, the Salvation Army and their respective solicitors, as we tried to work out a modus operandi for ensuring that Bill Russell's modest estate could continue to help Marjorie now she had moved from Bungalow Road.

It soon became clear that no dentures would be available on the NHS for someone who hadn't been registered with an NHS dentist for decades, if ever. A private set was going to cost hundreds, so we approached Martin to see if we could get a sub from the small trust set up under Bill's will that he administered jointly with the Salvation Army.

He came to my office to discuss the possibilities with Fiona and me, and in his careful way came up trumps as usual.

Dear Sue,

May I say how very pleased I was to meet up with you again and to meet your sister Fiona for the first time. I hope the pair of you did not feel I was too inquisitive in asking you about your family circumstances but the situation is unusual and the way matters have developed and the interest you have taken on behalf of Miss Heppelthwaite have really proved that you both clearly have your mother's welfare very much at heart and you are both to be commended for that, especially bearing in mind the bad start you both had . . .

(Does he mean us?)

*. . . I hope I can still use your goodself as my main
contact point in dealing with your mother's affairs . . .
We broadly agreed how we would deal with various
aspects of the finances but of course I am clarifying
matters with our own solicitors just to ensure that we
are proceeding in the right direction. I also enclose
for your interest and further information a copy of the
late Mr Russell's will . . .*

I suspect the late Mr Russell didn't intend to
subsidise Marjorie's future dental arrangements
when he drew up his will, or to help give her some
small comforts in the few remaining years of her
life in Walker Close. But with Martin's diligent and
sympathetic support, this is what happened, and
Marjorie got her dentures.

Getting her to wear them was another thing.
She'd got by on four rickety teeth of her own for so
long and her gums were so toughened that it was
torture for her to keep the plates in for any length
of time, and she insisted on removing them
whenever she had to eat anything. Marjorie liked
to please us but there were some things she just
wouldn't do and this was one of them. After all
that effort and expense, they finally went in a
drawer and stayed there. A rehabilitation too far,
obviously.

*   *   *

We settled into a comfortable routine. I would
cycle over to Walker Close every couple of weeks
and we'd talk on the phone often. I cultivated her
little patch of garden and installed some gnomes
and a wooden wheelbarrow Bevan's carpenter

143

friend Spike had made. Bevan took her out for her favourite lunch of egg on toast at the local council golf course, and they enjoyed their chats together.

I managed to wean her off the catalogues, so the piles of clothes were kept under control, but I couldn't stop her sending chunks of her pension to sponsor a mongrel in a dogs' home—Benny's shadow still loomed large. 'I'm a terrible softie when it comes to animals,' she'd say.

We talked about the past often, but there were gaps where she didn't venture and I didn't probe. When she talked about my father she used a different name from Peter White, confirming my suspicions that he was some kind of crude composite, but I never challenged her. She told me he was clever at maths and liked the gee-gees (a rather broad interpretation of 'fond of sport' I thought). Nothing I could relate to at all. She didn't know I had my adoption file with all her letters; they were too upsetting and personal to be shared between us.

Her life had been a catalogue of failed relationships with men, starting with her father. Her mother had always been a semi-invalid and Marjorie would nurse her when she was ill. 'I'd stay with her all night when she was bad. He never did a thing.' She believed her father was jealous of her relationship with her mother, and described him as a waster and a fantasist. Indeed, the few photos she had of him all showed him wearing various uniforms and outfits—the music hall toff Burlington Bertie, a naval uniform, the thick leathers of the First World War Flying Corps. 'He wasn't entitled to wear any of it,' she said with some bitterness. Her attraction to older, usually

144

married, men wasn't hard to understand.

She occasionally talked about someone she knew at Streatham fire station when she was in the Fire Service during the war. He was older but different, much more of a father figure to her, though it wasn't clear whether this was a purely platonic relationship. And about her time in the West End showrooms. Early on she'd worked at Moss Bros where she was relentlessly pursued by one of the managers. 'I had to leave, it was wearing me down.' There was a wealthy furrier who courted her and a Jewish boss who was very good to her. She covered up for his affairs when his wife came into the showroom with her poodle under her arm. 'He's out at golf,' she'd lie as she sat at the switchboard.

She always maintained a haughty disdain for these suitors which wasn't entirely convincing. She liked men and men liked her. I wanted to ask intrusive and tasteless questions about contraception and where they had sex but never felt I had the right. But it wasn't difficult to imagine a young woman looking for love, wanting to please, and men taking advantage of her open, compliant way. I could see it all being played out in 1950s' costume against a background of Players cigarette smoke and big band dance tunes.

She still knew how to flirt at 75. We had a small party for her birthday and one of her favourite men was there. It's quite possible that Marjorie was in love with Stephen Leahy. I'd got to know Stephen, a producer and successful creator of entertainment formats, while I was working on ITV gameshows. Like many gay men in the entertainment business, he knew how to show women a good time with fun and laughs along the

145

way, and he lavished attention on Marjorie such as she'd not experienced for 50 years. You could see her face light up when his name was mentioned.

'Ah, my Stephen! What a lovely man. Do you really think he's, you know . . . ? What a shame . . . If only I was 30 years younger!'

If only. He played up to her and she loved it.

'Marjorie, darling! Let's elope!'

You could see how it might have been.

*   *   *

As my relationship with Marjorie and Fiona developed, there were some major changes and sadnesses elsewhere in our lives. Bevan lost both his parents in the space of 11 months, my father had a severe attack of eczema and my mother's health and hearing rapidly deteriorated. She'd had a major operation to remove a brain tumour in the 1970s and, though she'd made a good recovery, her senses—particularly taste, smell and hearing— were permanently impaired and she relied on high doses of medication for the rest of her life. Her hearing was a real problem; she felt isolated and irritated with everyone because she couldn't join in.

Shortly before my 43rd birthday, I discovered I was pregnant. Initial shock gave way to delight. It was very late in the day and we hadn't planned to have any children, but Bevan was so pleased and I thought it was such an extraordinary thing to have happened that it must be fate. Or something. When I had a miscarriage after 10 weeks, it was desperately disappointing but I nevertheless felt I'd been given something special and for a reason.

Even though there's a terrible sadness and disappointment, I can't help feeling it was still a very positive, enlightening experience for me. It did open up, briefly, lots of new possibilities; it was energising, creative, lovely. I felt both in and out of control but it was exciting, wonderful and entirely unexpected and unsought. A gift that I can't, won't regret.

I don't think I consciously made the link at the time, but it also meant in a small way that I now shared with both my mothers the experience of losing a child.

8

MOTHERS

In 1950 Doreen Larsen was 17, pregnant, and had just discovered that her merchant seaman boyfriend was married with two children.

I daren't say anything to Ma. She'd have broke my back. I knew I was pregnant and there was nothing I could do about it. There was no way back, I couldn't go home. I had to go to Auntie Daisy's at Catterick camp. It was alright till she found out because I was showing, so I was out again. Back to Hartlepool sleeping rough, washing on the railway station out of fire buckets. I didn't have a feeling of fear. I had a feeling of aloneness and not being wanted. I didn't understand fully the consequences of being pregnant and having a baby, because we'd never learnt anything. For all I knew, babies came out of your belly button.

Michael was little more than four pounds at birth, and Doreen lived in the local former workhouse while he was in hospital gaining weight. Then they were both moved to St Monica's, a mother and baby home in Bishop Auckland.

I was called into the matron's office and she said that an army man and his wife who were big in the church were wanting to adopt Michael. I said, 'Michael's not for adoption, I've said he's not getting adopted.' She said, 'The best thing for Michael is to have a mum and dad and somebody who can give him what you can't.' I said, 'But if I was given the chance, then it would be OK.' 'But you'll never be in that position,' she said. 'You're a young girl, you're homeless and we can't let him go under those conditions, so adoption is the best thing.' 'But it's not the best thing for Michael and it's not the best thing for me. I know what it's like not to have a mum and to be treated rough.'

Promised the chance to find work while Michael went to a residential nursery, Doreen left the home hopeful of being able to keep him. Then one day she was picked up by her moral welfare worker in a car and told she was being taken to see Michael. But she found herself in the office of a Justice of the Peace in Middlesbrough.

This old man came in, well, he seemed old to me, and he said, 'Right Doreen, I've got some papers here for you to sign.' I read them and I said, 'No, they're papers giving my consent to adoption and I don't want Michael adopted.' 'But we've got parents that are waiting.' 'I don't want him adopted, they promised me they'd find somewhere for me to go.' He said, 'Sign.' I said, 'No, I won't,' and I threw the pen at the other side of the table. 'Right,' he said, 'you sign that paper and if you do not sign that paper, there's a paper here I'm going to sign.' 'What's that?' I said. 'This is to state that you are going to be committed to an institution and I can't say if you'll be there till you're of age or if you'll be there forever. Either case, you won't see Michael.'

What did I do? I had to sign. I honestly didn't want to, but I had to because it just went through my head, what if I'm put away like some idiot, and I don't come out ever again?

There are enough stories of coercion, particularly of young mothers, to indicate that practices in some church mother and baby homes in the 1950s and 1960s were distressingly unorthodox, if not illegal. Adoption legislation was far from watertight, but it did by then set out a formal procedure intended to ensure that mothers had time to give informed consent. From the 1949 Adoption Act, by law they could not do this until at least six weeks after the birth (*we called it "grieving time"*,' I was told by one 90-year-old former hospital almoner), and they could in theory contest an Adoption Order when it was made three months later. Few mothers did this, perhaps because the courts could in any case ignore her if they believed consent was being unreasonably withheld.

The homes, run by religious organisations and the adoption societies, were an essential component of the 'system' for dealing with unmarried mothers in the middle decades of the last century. They usually took mothers in six weeks before the birth (to hide women from neighbours and relatives while the pregnancy was most obvious) until six weeks after (the statutory minimum time before consent for adoption could be given). Often mothers went to homes far away from where they lived. We know this partly because the illegitimacy rates recorded in London and the seaside towns—favourite destinations—far outstrip the national average. In 1950 this was 5.1 per cent, but in London it was 7 per cent, in

Eastbourne 7.9 per cent and in Brighton 8.9 per cent.

For some, the homes were a genuine sanctuary, as I believe Castlebar was for Marjorie, but for others they were bleak and brutal. Patricia Basquill has made her horrific experience in a Church of England mother and baby home in Newcastle in the early 1960s her life's work. As a result of her experience, she set up Trackers International in 1979, a voluntary organisation that helps bring adopted people and their natural parents together and campaigns for official recognition and redress for the iniquities of bad adoption practice since 1950. More than 40 years later, she's still angry.

I was put into Elswick Lodge. It was 23 December and it was frightening. Every girl was in the late stages of pregnancy and the level of work was horrendous. Some girls were scrubbing floors literally on their hands and knees. I did the staircase with two other girls. It had to be scrubbed down with paraffin from top to bottom, then it had to be dried off with old pieces of rag. When it was dry we reapplied the next lot of polish by hand from top to bottom, and that was every week. Everything was redone and done again and it was so repetitive. It was a punishment. This was all you were fit for.

The one break we had was Sunday, and we were all marched through the streets, heavily pregnant, to church. Everyone knew who you were. They knew exactly what you'd done: you were pregnant, you weren't married and you were being escorted by the staff of the Diocesan unmarried mothers' home. None of them spoke, but they all looked, and the women were the worst because they never looked at

151

your face, they just stared at your stomach. This was supposed to be the Christian church. There was no forgiveness, and by God compassion was missing. On the wall directly opposite my baby's crib was a large biblical, black-edged text, 'When lust hath conceived, it brings forth sin. James 1.15'. That was actually facing my baby's crib.

I wasn't in there very long before the tactics began. It was 'you're not entitled to any benefits, no-one's going to employ you with a baby, no one is going to offer help because they'd be accused of condoning immorality. You won't get accommodation, not when you haven't got a ring on your finger. You don't have a hope in hell'. So I began looking through Lady *magazine and I wrote letter after letter, literally begging. I would have worked for nothing if I could have just taken the baby with me.*

When Elaine arrived after a difficult birth, Patricia was determined to keep her.

A group from the Mothers' Union visited and they walked down the balcony where all the prams were out. Elaine was in one of them and they stopped. A large lady wearing a purple velvet hat with a big feather leaned over and said, 'Oh what a beautiful baby, your Mummy's going to love you to bits.' I was in the nursery window and I said, 'She's got a Mummy. She's my baby and nobody else gets her.'

As the weeks went on, the moral welfare worker upped the pressure. She came in one day and said, 'I've gone to a great deal of trouble and I've found Roman Catholic adoptive parents who are willing to give Elaine a home.' You'd think she was talking about a kitten or an unwanted puppy.

152

Placing a baby with a Catholic adoptive family was considered at the time one of the biggest challenges in adoption work. For a start, the influx of girls from southern Ireland and other Catholic countries coming to England to have their babies meant there was a surplus of Catholic babies over potential adopters. And, according to Margaret Kornitzer, the adoption authority of the time, Catholic teaching stated that the removal of the child by adoption should not be used as a solution to the sin of the mother. She should take time to 'face up to her troubles morally and spiritually, and must not be considered merely as a source of the material for adoption'.

In fact, Patricia was from an Ulster Protestant family but her boyfriend, Sean, the father of her baby, was Catholic. Having a 'Papist's bastard' was about the worst sin she could have committed in her family's eyes.

She was exactly nine weeks old and she was laughing and gurgling. She knew exactly who I was; she knew my voice. I started to breastfeed her and I heard the nursery door open. I didn't look up, and I saw a pair of shoes, very dark brown brogue lace-up shoes there, and I'd heard someone go behind me. The first thing I knew, one put their knee in my back and took hold of my arms and the other one just took her, just grabbed her literally as I was breastfeeding her, and Elaine had her fingers in my hair around my locket. The locket went with her, some of my hair went with her, and she just screamed. I was screaming, I was trying to fight back, and one of them got hold of my hair and jerked my head backwards and it really hurt.

And they were gone. They were gone literally in seconds.

Patricia didn't know it then, but Elaine was taken to adoptive parents in Inverness. Later, after she had found a job and somewhere to live, Patricia was taken by the moral welfare worker to a Justice of the Peace to sign the consent forms. Even at this late stage, she hoped to get Elaine back.

I pushed the paperwork away and I said, 'I'm not signing. I want my baby back.' The moral welfare worker came across and said, 'You need to understand something now. If you don't sign that form your daughter will be taken from this wonderful Catholic couple [it later transpired they were Scottish Episcopalian] and she'll be put into a church children's home. She'll grow up like an orphan, she'll never know who you are, and you'll never see her again.' And that's when I signed.

Patricia believes she was consistently lied to: about the benefits that were available to unmarried mothers at the time, about her legal rights, and about alternatives to adoption like temporary fostering until she could find a home and a job. And, like Doreen Larsen, she believes she was coerced into giving her consent.

She maintains that bad adoption practice was widespread and serious enough to amount to an orchestrated conspiracy to remove healthy white babies from young, working-class, unmarried mothers to meet the increasing demand from childless married couples. It's an extreme claim, but it is a legitimate way of looking at adoption's boom years if you are one of those who relinquished a child against her will. Was she lied to? The 1948 National Assistance Act gave unmarried mothers access for the first time to financial support without having to sign on for work, and Maternity Allowance was payable regardless of marital status. Family Allowance, however, introduced in 1945, excluded the first child and so effectively disqualified the majority of unmarried mothers. At about the time Patricia had Elaine, 26,000 unmarried mothers were getting National Assistance but it came with strings attached. Mothers were expected to get an affiliation order from the putative father and any maintenance was then deducted from the benefit, which was hardly enough to keep body and soul together to start with.

Moral welfare workers undoubtedly knew what was available: the National Council for the Unmarried Mother and Her Child, for example, produced publications for social workers about the legal position of illegitimate children and their parents, and 'the social services, statutory and voluntary, which are available to them'. But other judgements came into play. Housing was a real problem, particularly in the years following the war. Private landlords did discriminate against single women with children and the little council housing available was allocated to families. Work where you could keep a baby was menial and low-paid; women with children were often ruthlessly exploited by employers. In the final analysis, moral judgements probably overrode practical ones: a vulnerable 16-year-old on the streets with a baby was something to be avoided, for the baby's sake as

155

much as the mother's.

But there were alternatives. A number of social workers who contacted me, including some moral welfare workers, mentioned that they had often applied to the Thomas Coram Foundation, as it then was, for grants to help mothers keep their babies, and the Foundation also provided a pioneering foster care scheme until mothers could take their children back. But it seems in Patricia's case the decision had been made that she was unfit to keep her child: her file even describes her as 'morally deficient'. For her, this is a tragedy that has dominated her life.

I vowed, as God is my witness, I will pay those bastards back, and I've been doing that for 25 years to the best of my ability.

What do the social workers have to say? No social worker is going to own up to coercive tactics or to supporting cruel and punitive conditions in mother and baby homes. I imagine some might even justify such behaviour, given the social and moral climate of the time, as firm and necessary discipline with emotional and 'over-sexed' young women when a baby's future was at stake. Certainly, those former adoption workers I met and corresponded with were absolutely sure that what Doreen and Patricia describe so vividly was outside their experience. They were adamant that they did everything possible, despite limited options, to help mothers keep their babies. One, a local authority child care officer in London in the 1950s, wrote:

Far from 'forcing' the mum to give up her baby, my

156

colleagues and I sweated blood to try to help her not to, if that was her wish.

Over the years I interviewed many mothers and not once did I believe her confirmation of consent, either from fear or despair or failure to understand or whatever, was false. Nor do I believe I was too naive or deficient in social work skills to realise the woman was deceiving me. Great tact, sympathy and understanding were necessary. Some were indignant, believing their word had been doubted. Many were relieved to get it all over with. Some were grateful that their child would have a good home. Most were simply resigned.

I suggest some mothers insist, perhaps inadvertently, they were forced to give up their babies because they feel more comfortable projecting guilt on to the adoption workers, rather than acknowledge that, at the time, they truly believed they were doing the best for their babies, let alone admitting they could not face the undoubted hardships of single parenthood.

Ann Haigh, who runs Barnardo's Family Connections service, also suggests that some mothers' memories do not match the official record, and the information they gave at the time, for example the father's name, does not always correspond to what they say now.

When we meet birth mothers [wishing to trace], we hear their story and compare it to what we have on the file. Quite a high proportion don't match. Especially in the early adoptions, women never expected that anyone was going to have later access to their file. And people's memory over time gets blurred. Birth mothers in the fifties and sixties didn't have the practical or moral support they have now. As society has changed, it's actually quite difficult to think, 'I did give my baby up, I did see somebody, I went to the Justice, I signed the papers', but when you meet people they say, 'they took my baby away at birth and I never saw them again'.

The former adoption workers most likely to volunteer their experience are those, like my correspondents, who were highly motivated, thoroughly professional to the standards of the time, and who believed they were doing their best for all concerned—mothers, babies and adopters—in often difficult conditions. They enjoyed their work, were fulfilled by it, and remember it with some affection.

I met Florence Shepherd, who ran a Diocesan mother and baby home in Erith, Kent between 1963 and 1967. Florence, a Baptist, trained at Josephine Butler House after taking a sociology diploma at London University. 'Oakhurst', a home for 26 young mothers, was her first moral welfare job.

Florence has that quiet, confident authority and faith that doesn't impose itself on others. She believed her career in residential social work fulfilled her need to nurture.

When you're single, you've got to have a purpose in your life, haven't you? You have to have somebody to love, and this fulfilled me to a large extent. I'd love to have got married and had children, but I was born at the wrong time. The war came along when I was coming up to marriageable age. Half of us were left

158

single because of the war. So many men did not return.

On her own initiative, she encouraged girls who were giving up their babies for adoption to send a letter addressed to the baby and a little gift on the day it was handed over, and most of them did so. She also asked adopting parents to keep something of the clothing the baby arrived in, so that later the child would know that it was loved and well cared for by its 'other mother'. I thought of the pathetic mementoes in the glass cases in the Foundling Museum that never reached the Coram children, and hoped Oakhurst's adoptive parents, like my own, had the wisdom and sensitivity to keep these precious items for their children.

She obviously enjoyed her years at Oakhurst and it sounds as if many of the girls there appreciated her efforts. She told me about a recent reunion she'd had with a former resident and the daughter she'd had adopted.

I had a phone call and this voice said, 'I'm looking for a Miss Shepherd who used to be at Oakhurst.' I said, 'Yes, that's me.' She said, 'I don't believe it, I've got a long list of numbers and you're the first on the list!' Then she said, 'Do you remember my mother?' and she told me the name, and I said, 'Oh yes!' because she was a great girl, she really was. She was only 14 and she was with us for six months. She was a real tomboy, but she did so much for the others there. We'd got one or two grumpy ones and it was quite hard going. And she turned round one day and said, 'Well, whose fault is it we're here?' She was so matter-of-fact, she was a lovely girl and we kept in touch until she got married and moved away, then somehow we lost touch. This voice said, 'Well, I'm her daughter and we've just been reunited. We wanted to contact you to tell you.' They've been up to see me. I was just thrilled for them.

Was there a strong moral dimension to her work, I wondered?

To me, that was never the important side of things. The atmosphere of that age was very condemning, but there's no way I would ever have condemned a girl for an illegitimate pregnancy. In many cases they had been abandoned by the baby's father, even occasionally by their parents. No, I was there to help them, not to condemn them.

She admitted that others did, though. There were one or two members of Oakhurst's management committee who were more judgemental, reluctant to make life too easy for the girls.

Unmarried mothers got it in the neck from two powerful forces: religious moralisers talked about sin and punishment, and the growing body of psychologists starting to influence thinking at the time talked in pathological terms about deviant behaviour and dysfunctional relationships. The mothers have babies because of their craving for love and attention, they said, a thesis still given a regular airing in certain newspapers today.

It is hard to imagine now, but until the 1960s this area of social work was dominated by denominational voluntary organisations like the Diocesan Boards of Social and Moral Welfare. The 1948 Children Act introduced children's officers in local authorities for the first time (the Curtis Report recommended that *'she should not be under 30 at time of appointment'*). Local authorities had a supervisory role over all adoptions (except private arrangements made directly by the mother), but much of the casework was done by moral welfare workers and the adoption societies. Though local authorities could arrange adoptions themselves, few chose to do so until later in the 1960s. Specialist social work training (notably at the London School of Economics) grew slowly during the 1950s, so that by the start of the 1960s there were two kinds of social worker: a new breed of idealistic young children's and child care officer, and 'the Morals' as some of them called their older Christian colleagues.

One child care officer remembers:

I had dealings with local moral welfare officers, with one over some years. Probably typical, she was a middle-aged, well-meaning spinster, more into saving souls than casework, but kindly and with a fund of practical good sense. Her first aim was to keep mother and child together. Cynics might have said this was to punish the girls for their sins, but she held that the love and responsibility helped the young mums who, as she pointed out, so often became pregnant again almost immediately if they had to give up their babies.

Some of us high-minded trained younger workers (I was 22) grumbled that most of these women whose potential husbands had been killed in the First World War had taken up work with children to satisfy their frustrated maternal instincts. Looking back, I think

161

we were somewhat patronising and arrogant; many were kind and sensible, but I do recall some being absolutely venomous about girls who'd 'got into trouble', possibly from sexual jealousy.

A worker with the Southwell Diocese Board of Moral Welfare in the 1960s also recalls co-operation:

At local level most moral welfare workers had a mixture of friendly rivalry and positive co-operation with local authority social workers, enabling us to work in partnership on many occasions. The greatest benefit for adopters and natural parents was the durability of moral welfare workers who, like me, tended to stay in the agency for many years and could always be relied on to respond when contacted much later.

From the little statistical evidence available and from the memories of those working in adoption, it seems a high proportion—probably more than half—of unmarried mothers during these years kept their babies. Figures from Church of England Diocesan Moral and Social Welfare Councils for 1968 quoted in the 1972 Stockdale Report on adoption show that, of 19,493 mothers of illegitimate children, 54.3 per cent kept the child and 34 per cent gave them up for adoption. Presumably the remainder of the children ended up with relatives or in children's homes as paid fostering was less common then. A 1957 moral welfare study looked at 180 children kept by their mothers. After five years 82 per cent were still with them; the remainder had been adopted, were living with relatives or had been placed in children's homes. So, despite the formidable difficulties, an impressive majority of those who made the decision to keep their child succeeded in doing so.

*   *   *

With hindsight, Angie Mason believes she made the wrong decision to give up her baby for adoption in 1967. Angie and I worked together when she joined the Independent Broadcasting Authority in 1975 to replace a woman who had left to look after her new adopted baby. Almost 30 years later, I learnt that Angie had herself given up a child. She was in her second year at Leeds University and pregnant by her boyfriend Mick, her husband for more than 40 years.

I had a feeling of absolute doom. Everything I'd worked for, everything my mother had striven for, was now just going to end. Because when you were pregnant in 1966, first of all there was the shame, the humiliation on the family. Then what was going to happen to this child? And what was going to happen to me? I don't think I went to the doctors for weeks, because I wanted it to go away. Abortion wasn't on. I thought, no knitting needle job in a Leeds back street for me, thanks. I was left with either leaving university, or having the baby adopted.

Leeds University seemed to have a system in place for people such as myself, because ahead of me had been Clare Short [the Labour politician later reunited with the son she gave up for adoption]. We were referred to a private nursing home outside Leeds and on payment of, I think it was £200 which at the time was a king's ransom—I know it was a term's grant—you were given this fast track into the home as soon as the child was born and then the child was whisked away and you never saw it again, and it was placed for adoption privately with select middle-class parents. And that's what I wanted. I wanted my child to go to a doctor's home. I wanted this child to have the best possible start in life. I couldn't give it to her, so therefore, to me, going to a doctor's home in Ilkley or Otley was the sine qua non.

From Angie's description of arrangements at the nursing home, they sounded more callous than those of the worst church mother and baby homes. Posh and private it may have been, but 'Falloden' was a production line in which the aim was as swift a turnover of girls as decency would allow. The mothers were not allowed to see their babies and had to nurse and bottle-feed each other's. After giving birth in St James's Hospital at 6 a.m. after eight hours in labour in agony and alone, she was bundled back to the home by ambulance a few hours later.

As soon as I got back to Falloden, the baby was taken out of my arms. The only physical contact I had with this baby was when I went across in the ambulance, and I remember thinking, am I doing the right thing here? This little thing is mine and I'm going to give it away. There was no counselling at the time. It was an inhumane system, cold, impersonal and mechanical. Now I know, me being me, it was the wrong decision. I would have coped, because I'm a coper and I would have found a way of getting back into university. I made the wrong decision, I know that now. A few

164

years down the track I had a terrible time thinking, I could have coped, we could have managed. Mick and I got married the following year and we're still married so in fact we were a very strong unit. Mick never saw her. Not until she turned up on the doorstep more than 30 years later.

Because Angie was under 21 at the time, her mother and father had more involvement in the adoption than the father of her child. Mick says now:

Adoption was a foregone conclusion. We didn't discuss keeping the baby. I don't know when I started to feel regrets; it wasn't all that long afterwards. I kept it to myself but I kept imagining she'd turn up one day. I'm certain it wasn't the right thing to do.

The rights of the mother in the adoption process were clear, if tough. The putative father had no meaningful rights over the future of his child, even if he acknowledged paternity and was paying maintenance. A child care officer in Dorset remembers:

We didn't spend much time considering the needs of the fathers. I shall never forget one who, when I interviewed him, told me how desperately he wanted his baby girl and how upset he was that the mother would not marry him and would not change her mind about the adoption. He was in his late twenties, not the usual teenage father, and said it had always been his dream to have a baby daughter. He cried a lot, but I could give him little hope. In law his only right was to be heard, not to be given parental rights

165

over the baby. The little girl was adopted and he had to be told that this was final.

Not all putative fathers were absent or shadowy figures, and even 'the usual teenage father' sometimes showed a touching sense of responsibility. Florence Shepherd encouraged fathers, if they were in touch, to make a contribution towards their girl's keep at Oakhurst.

I had one young man, he was very sweet. He was only about 16 himself. He paid me 10 shillings a week while she was there, and I thought that was really lovely. He was doing his bit.

My most striking discovery about the realities of adoption practice at this time is the difference between the testimony of the mothers and those of the women who worked with them. Perhaps this isn't surprising. The mothers who came forward with horrific stories about this crisis time in their lives have a burning sense of injustice and a need to tell the world about a scandal they believe has been swept under the carpet. For every one who volunteered her story, there are perhaps dozens of others with similar experiences unwilling to share the humiliations of the past. On the other hand, the social workers who came forward were likely to be proud of their work and so have an investment in putting a positive case for the 'caring ministry' or professional job they were doing to the best of their ability.

Though none admit to direct experience of unorthodox practice (and I have no reason to doubt them), some hint at being aware that such things went on. Catholic mother and baby homes were most often mentioned in this context. You have to wonder whether, in a sector so dominated by different Christian interests, sectarian prejudice played some part in this. Perhaps, but what we've discovered in the recent past about cruel and sadistic practices in Catholic institutions (Magdalene laundries, industrial schools and child migrant settlements) in the UK and elsewhere in the last century, together with more recent exposure of child abuse by priests, lends credence to these stories.

What is clear is that, whatever branch of the church or organisation ran them, there was always a risk of abuse of power in these 'closed' institutions that the public took no interest in and would much rather didn't exist. The social stigma of unmarried motherhood and the punitive moral and religious climate of the time legitimised practices that would be judged intolerable now. There may be some post hoc rationalisation on both sides, but what I do know is that those at the receiving end of treatment that was at best insensitive, at worst deliberately cruel, can remember what happened to them as if it was yesterday, and they always will. It's not guilt they feel, it's anger.

Angie's timing was exquisitely unlucky. Her experience immediately pre-dated two important developments that revolutionised sexual relationships and attitudes to them, and spelt the beginning of the end for the mass adoption of illegitimate babies. Later the same year the 1967 Abortion Act legalised abortion up to 28 weeks, and in the following years increasing availability of

167

the contraceptive pill meant that for the first time women had a reliable means of avoiding unplanned pregnancies.

The peak year for adoptions in England and Wales was 1968: over 25,000, of which more than 16,000 were to non-relatives. After hearing the moving stories of women who had given up babies, I now wanted to look in another corner of the adoption triangle—the agencies and their clients, the hopeful couples who created adoption's boom years.

9

ADOPTERS AND AGENCIES

A person wanting to adopt a child today has a straight road to travel, with most of the ambiguities of the law cleared away; and the road is well-beaten. About 17,000 children are adopted each year in this country, so that the business is no longer unusual and the neighbours do not think it queer.

What the neighbours thought was still important to many potential adopters in 1952 when the authority on adoption practice, Margaret Kornitzer, wrote this. By then another Adoption Act in 1950 had consolidated the dribs and drabs of legislation since 1926. This confirmed the 'clean break' character of the arrangement, protecting adopters' anonymity from natural parents by using serial numbers instead of names on adoption records. These measures continued to encourage adopters to think of their child as having no past before it came to them.

There was by now a marked shift in public perceptions of adoption. Before the war it was seen as a response to the 'social tragedy' of illegitimacy and one met mainly by working-class adopters. Now childless couples from all social backgrounds saw it as the answer to their infertility. At the time, infertility was poorly understood, virtually untreatable and sometimes still attributed to women being 'neurotic'. Women with a history of miscarriage fared little better. No one was able to tell them why they couldn't conceive or carry a baby to full term; they were dismissed or patronised by doctors, and their failure was obvious to all. Like illegitimacy, the stigma of infertility was real; it was not something to be admitted, discussed or even shared between doctor and patient. An adoption officer with a Diocesan Moral Welfare Board remembers, 'I received one medical report on a prospective adopter saying "This man has a negative sperm count and has not been told, neither do I think he should be".'

*　　　*　　　*

After two years of marriage and no sign of a family, Ann Blatcher was initially given short shrift by a specialist:

I saw this consultant who was really most unsympathetic and unhelpful. He more or less told me, 'Go away, don't bother me for another couple of years, just give it time,' which upset me because I knew there was something not right . . . everyone assumed and always did at that time that the fault lay with the woman.

Much later a more sympathetic consultant discovered that Ann's husband Tom was infertile as a result of childhood mumps. Adoption seemed the obvious solution.

There was just never any question of 'it might be difficult', or 'it might be unwise', or 'you don't know what you're getting', it was just 'we'll adopt'.

170

The prospect of being able to adopt the 'perfect baby' must have been a lifeline for many desperate couples. And, as I discovered, they were all perfect and they were all babies.

Important advances in child development and genetic theory fuelled this new interest in adoption. In 1951, John Bowlby published his influential theories on maternal deprivation and attachment in a report to the World Health Organization. These had terrific impact. For the first time he described the importance of the physical and emotional bond between mother and child in the first months of life, suggesting that separation could have a lasting impact on the mental health of the growing child. Though on the face of it this looked like an argument against adoption, it was seen as clear evidence in favour of moving a child to its new home well before that original bond became too established. Bowlby believed that if this was broken after the age of two the child would fail to attach to new parents and adoption would be problematic. His work broke new ground and was vital to understanding children's emotional development and how they learn to relate to adults. It was also widely read. *Child Care and the Growth of Love* was the popular version of this work and the title at the top of my list of set texts when I was a trainee teacher almost 20 years later.

The other development, also part of a growing interest in the science of child development and all things psychological, was the idea that nurture could be equally, if not more, powerful than nature in determining a child's physical and intellectual potential. One of the barriers to adoption in the past had been the countervailing belief that the 'bad blood' of natural parents—especially the mother—automatically passed to their children and meant they would inevitably turn out bad too, however much good was done to them. Now the new scientific theories brought a more positive message of hope. You could cheat nature by giving your child the best physical, emotional and intellectual environment—State orange juice and school milk for his body, a loving two-parent home for his mental health, and a grammar school education for his mind.

Dr L. S. Penrose, Galton Professor of Eugenics at University College London, spelt it out to delegates at the 1953 Standing Conference of Societies Registered for Adoption, the 'trade body' of the private and voluntary agencies:

Parents transmit to their children things called genes. These are real things though you can't exactly see them . . . all we need to be sure about is that environment can alter intelligence as well as stature.

But the bad blood theory still had a strong grip on adoption workers. For example, most agencies rejected the offspring of incestuous relationships, ostensibly because of the risk of genetic abnormalities, but probably reflecting deeper fears about the hereditary transmission of immorality. Dr Penrose was quick to quash objections to these children as 'ignorant'. Citing the Pharaohs and Ptolemys who had inbred for generations, he considered *'no greater likelihood of abnormality than arising between cousins'*. But the taboo—and the ban—continued. By 1964, the NCAA was still

172

rejecting offspring of incestuous relationships and of 'promiscuous' mothers.

In the face of new-fangled theories on the propensity of nurture to overcome all, the agencies stayed wedded to the policy of 'matching'. Babies' looks, social background and even supposed intellectual potential were matched to those of their adopters as closely as possible, perpetuating the idea that the adopted child should ideally pass as a precise substitute for one born to them. I am an early example of a perfectly matched baby, and there are lots of us about. How many adopted children from the 1940s to the 1970s were told as they were growing up, 'Aren't you like your mother/father?'

Many adopters were grateful for the care with which agencies matched the babies placed with them because it helped the bonding and assimilation process. Ann Blatcher and her husband Tom adopted Richard in the mid-1960s.

He looked so much a part of my family. I have photos of my younger sister at about 18 months, and photos of Richard at about that age, and you don't know which one's which. He is so much a part of my family, and Tom's as well, he just fits us so well. I must say the Church of England Children's Society were amazing. They matched the baby to the parent so well. The natural father's interests were the same as my husband's interests, the natural mother's were the same as mine. His family's interests and his physical being were matched very closely to our family. There were other coincidences: he was born on my birthday, his names given by his birth mother were common in my family. There were so many

173

things like that, it was almost as if it was meant that he should come to us.

Matching was an art, not a science. Mary Ellison in her 1958 book, *The Adopted Child*, believed that:

General Secretaries of good adopting agencies have a natural flair for choosing the 'right child for the right adopter'. They are skilled, experienced social workers and under their guidance first-class adoptions are constantly being arranged. There are always parents available for adoptable children, however unattractive these may appear. Even the dullest, podgiest child will make an irresistible appeal to a certain father and mother.

To the dull, podgy ones presumably. Adoption workers were convinced that a good matching job was critical to the success of an adoption, but subjectivity and prejudice were inevitable, and social class crept into it too. By the late 1960s, prominent voices were wondering whether matching on this basis was really such a good thing. Leading paediatrician Professor R. S. Illingworth wondered aloud to the Standing Conference:

If we think that a baby has a rather slow developmental potential, and the father wishing to adopt is a manual worker, are we right in saying that it will be perfectly all right, whereas if the father is a barrister, we would say that the adoption is unsuitable? If a child is thought to be mentally superior, should we try to place him in a professional home? I do not think the matter is an easy one.

John Triseliotis, one of the most respected researchers in adoption practice, found this was exactly what was happening in a study he did for Edinburgh University in 1970.

Our findings suggest that adoption practice does not appear to have been significantly influenced by some of the findings of studies in child development which stress the beneficial effects of an enabling environment on the development of the personality . . . The practice at the moment is to place the children with the most favourable background history in the home with the best 'apparent' potential, and to place the children with the poorest history in homes with the less obvious potential.

Adopters, too, could be choosy. A local authority adoption worker in the 1960s remembers:

Before the [Abortion] Act some prospective adopters were extremely demanding as to the type of child they wished to have. Physical appearance, educational standards and social background of the mother were often specific requirements, and very frequently the need to keep up with their friends was mentioned as though a child was the equivalent of the latest car model. Not many persons seemed to be worried about the lack of information on the natural father.

Girls, perceived as easier to manage and more likely to be a comfort to parents in old age, were more popular than boys. Redheaded babies were notoriously difficult to place. Twins and siblings were sometimes separated in order to make a relatively scarce resource go further (though the

175

NCAA reported placing 20 sets of twins in the first two years of the decade).

On the list of 'unadoptables' along with babies born of incestuous relationships were those of 'mixed blood' (mixed meant bad until increasing numbers and more enlightened attitudes to race forced a reappraisal in the late 1960s), children over two, and babies with a health problem or physical disability. 'Disability' sometimes existed only in the eye of the beholder. A former local authority adoption worker remembers a moral welfare worker rejecting a baby because it had 'a Mongolian bottom'.

The agencies laid great stress on their ability to offer babies with a clean bill of health. An important, if archaic, part of this was the Wasserman blood test. This was the standard test for syphilis, the nastiest and most feared of the venereal diseases that finally sends you mad. It was standard practice for all mothers and babies passing through the hands of adoption agencies to undergo this test, whether it was thought there was a chance they might be infected or not. I had the Wasserman test, my mother Marjorie had it, and it was still happening well into the 1960s. Patricia Basquill remembers the humiliation, as a pregnant teenager, of being taken to a VD clinic for the test.

I spent my 16th birthday in a VD clinic. The dentist's chair moved up till I was on a level with the doctor's face, and there were six male student doctors there. That's when he took the swab and I just cried all the way through it. He said if I didn't relax it would take twice as long and they'd have to do it again. It obviously hadn't bothered me to strip off before so

176

what was the problem now? That was my birthday present.

As late as 1966 Jane Rowe, the influential writer and tutor on adoption practice, was still noting that *'it is the venereal diseases that create the greatest anxiety in adoption work'*, even though by then cases of congenital syphilis were extremely rare. The threat—and that old, lingering spectre of 'bad blood'—was more potent than any reality.

The change from finding a home for an 'unwanted' baby to finding 'the perfect baby for the perfect home' meant long queues at reputable adoption agencies. There were 55 registered adoption agencies and societies by the early 1950s. Local authorities were empowered to arrange adoptions other than of children in their care in the 1958 Adoption Act but few chose to do so in any systematic way until much later. Despite the post-war baby bulge, most agencies had many more prospective adopters than they had babies. At the start of the decade the NCAA reported 12 times as many approved adopters as they had babies available. And even 10 years later an internal Dr Barnardo's investigation found that *'something approaching 90% of all applications are rejected on no logical basis other than . . . they cannot be handled'*.

This may help explain another amazing fact: only one in 10 adoptions at the time were arranged by the agencies—half the number estimated by the Horsburgh Committee when they were reporting on agency practice in 1939. If waiting lists at agencies were so long (and potential adopters wanted to avoid the bother of their suitability

177

being properly investigated), then no wonder third party and direct placements by mothers—the other form of 'unofficial' adoption practice frowned upon by adoption workers—were so popular. I had assumed that all adoptions were handled by the voluntary agencies before local authorities started to get involved from the late 1960s, but this was far from the case. Even taking into account adoptions by relatives, which didn't need the services of an agency, the societies still dealt with a fraction of 'stranger' adoptions, contrary to the noisy impression they gave at the time of dominating the sector.

The other thing that emerges only slowly from the adoption story is that there were probably many more adoptions than the official figures, which were based on Adoption Orders granted, recorded. Apart from adoptions formalised by the issue of an Adoption Order, there were likely to have been many more that were never legalised, or even notified to the authorities as required by law. Mary Ellison claimed in 1958, for example, that *'in many cases those who receive the baby through a third party do not proceed to legalisation'*. What is intriguing and frustrating is that we'll probably never know how many. But if third party adoptions were outnumbering agency-arranged ones by five to one in 1953, as one government minister claimed, an estimate of at least double the official figure would not be wide of the mark. The official figures recorded between 10,000 and 25,000 legal adoptions a year in England and Wales during the 1950s and 1960s. On this estimate, there would have been almost 700,000 children adopted in this period (not all of them to strangers admittedly, but certainly moved from the care of the mother).

Bizarrely, the mismatch between supply and demand may have given the agencies—especially the well-known national ones—something of a cachet with middle-class adopters. Certainly, the NCAA had a reputation as 'the posh people's agency' in the 1950s, though this may have had more to do with its Knightsbridge location and the string of titled ladies on its letterhead than the social class of its adopters, or its babies.

Some of the most fascinating and emotional moments during my journey into the highways and byways of past adoption practice came when I was contacted by people who'd worked at the NCAA and knew its personnel, premises and practices intimately. I had a moving exchange of letters with a former children's nurse who'd worked at Castlebar mother and baby home in 1952, only months after Marjorie had been there with me. It was her initial description of what happened when the baby was finally given up that stopped me in my tracks.

If the baby was to be adopted one of us on the staff took it to the NCAA in Knightsbridge either on the bus, or often if she could afford it the girl would pay for a taxi, but she was left at the front door and was always waiting in the same place when I returned and asking many questions [about the adopters] *which I couldn't answer. It always bothered me when the babies were so well dressed by their mothers and given toys and mementoes and when I got to Knightsbridge everything was taken away and new clothes provided!*

The image of the mother waiting outside in the street (the offices were over shops) for news of who had taken her baby was haunting enough, but I was devastated by this new possibility that the beautiful clothes I'd arrived with weren't from Marjorie at all but provided by the good lady volunteers of the NCAA. But my correspondent was quick to reassure me by return of post:

First I must tell you that the change of clothing was not NCAA policy, it was the choice of the adopting parents. I have no doubt that your parents took you as you were, clothing included, which I think was lovely. Some adopters wished for a clean break and thus arrived in Knightsbridge with everything new. I had of course no idea you were one of the babies and I'm sorry if you were upset.

With the letter were two black and white photos— of her holding a baby on the terrace steps outside the nursery, and a view of the garden from the first floor. For the first time I was seeing Castlebar as Marjorie must have seen it. I stood in the kitchen and cried. Her description of the house, the staircase Marjorie cleaned, the gardens with their views to the Kent hills, and what she did there, all brought it home to me from half a century away.

Everything she told me confirmed what I wanted to think about Castlebar: that it was a sanctuary, not a punishment, for the girls who had their babies there. I must have been among the last babies at Castlebar; it closed in 1953 after 20 years as the NCAA's flagship hostel, a victim of the Association's parlous financial position.

Juliet is definitely posh. She was adopted from the NCAA in 1942 by a woman originally from Buenos Aires, 'a fast lady' who'd danced with the Prince of Wales in the 1930s and who was unable to conceive after a botched abortion in New York. Though she adored her adoptive father, Juliet now believes this was an unsuitable placement that wouldn't have been approved had it not been wartime. After adopting Juliet, her mother became one of the NCAA's 'Honorary Visitors', a band of leisured women volunteers who played a key part in the vetting of adopters. On the face of it, Juliet's mother didn't seem especially well qualified for the work, but she did have a typewriter.

I was an only child, so when I went off to boarding school she had nothing to do. My mother was involved in 'inspecting' potential adopters. This involved visiting their house and generally making sure that the right baby went to the right parents. By 'right' I mean in the social sense. My mother had no social work training (did it exist then?) but she had a typewriter and could type up her reports. She also involved other friends of hers in 'inspecting', providing they could type! This was all done voluntarily.

Juliet became involved with the NCAA herself as a volunteer at the age of 17 at the end of the 1950s.

I was a smart young thing in London—I wasn't a deb but I was on the periphery of it—and I found myself on a junior committee for the NCAA's annual fundraising ball held at the Dorchester. We didn't do the work—other people did the work—we just met. I remember going to all these very nice houses in London. One of the places was Lew Grade's house. He was involved very heavily; I've got a feeling he and his wife adopted a baby. They were very, very generous, and he always got the cabaret for us, people like Bruce Forsyth.

The impresario Lew Grade, champion charleston dancer, whose nephew Michael became Chairman of the BBC, was one of the founding fathers of ITV in the 1950s. His biography, *Still Dancing*, notes the many charitable causes his wife Kathie was involved in from their Cavendish Square home, though the NCAA isn't mentioned specifically.

Juliet remembers the General Secretary, Mrs Plummer (known for some reason as Mrs Rochford in the office, as Clarissa to the adoption fraternity and as Dee-Dee to her friends) as a formidable woman of strong opinions who 'was very sweet and pleasant if she liked you'. She obviously liked Juliet, as she got her her first job in the City with her solicitor son-in-law. Long after Mrs Plummer retired, Juliet went back to the NCAA seeking information about her natural parents. She discovered that, contrary to what her adoptive mother had always told her, she was even posher than she thought. But that's another story.

Even the big national agencies like the NCAA and the National Adoption Society had few paid staff and relied a great deal on volunteers. Since by law the agencies weren't allowed to charge for their services (though adopters had to pay Court fees and for the *guardian ad litem* appointed by the Court to act in the interests of the child during the process leading to an Adoption Order), money was always tight. A great deal of effort went into fundraising and recruiting and maintaining wealthy and influential patrons. This explains the begging appeals at the end of every letter to Marjorie for 'a donation, however small'. They really were operating from hand to mouth for much of the time. Mother and baby homes were invariably in big old houses and expensive to run. Adoption societies' balance sheets were always on a knife-edge: it wasn't unknown for societies to ask potential adopters for a stack of stamped addressed envelopes for replies to their letters.

At the other end of the scale, small regional—usually denominational—societies had even fewer staff, and worryingly amateur practices. After graduating from Manchester University with a degree in Social Administration at the age of 20 in 1959, Barbara Jacobs worked with the Lancaster Diocesan Protection and Rescue Society, a Catholic adoption agency in Preston which dealt mainly with girls coming over from Ireland to have their babies adopted.

The job was an unqualified social worker to assist the priest who ran the organisation. The only other member of staff was the secretary.

My job was never very well defined and I don't think he really wanted an employee, but he and his Board had been encouraged by the Home Office, after an inspection, to bring some social work knowledge into the organisation. I was never given much to do and I used to spend a lot of time trying to look occupied at my desk.

The assessment of adopters was probably fairly rudimentary in those days, and the most important criterion would have been that they were good Catholics. My most vivid memory of that time was being sent to remove a child from adopters following a critical report by the local authority about the standard of the home. No attempt was made to help the adopters. It was just decided to remove the child without giving them any warning—possibly illegally. I arrived in a taxi from the station and told the mother I was removing the child. She didn't resist, but we later had heartrending letters from her asking for its return.

Having selected all the perfect babies, how did the agencies then identify 'the perfect home'? It obviously helped that they had plenty to choose from and could afford, as Margaret Kornitzer put it in 1952, 'to divide the sheep from the goats'. Probably the most important consideration, given the number of denominational agencies, was religious belief and church attendance. For the majority of agencies, you didn't get in the door without a reference from your vicar, minister or priest. Even the non-denominational national agencies, like the NCAA, preferred some evidence of religious belief. And of course you had to be a married couple, with some agencies specifying a minimum number of years, and unable to have children of your own. The qualifying age window was narrow: no younger than 25 and no older than 40, with some agencies such as Dr Barnardo's barring couples 'with a marked difference in age'. You could also be weeded out if you had poor health, if your husband was in the armed services, or if you had previously been 'the guilty party' in a divorce.

If you met all of the above requirements, then your home would be inspected by a social worker, moral welfare worker or volunteer Honorary Visitor. Jane Rowe described this process in her 1959 'bible' for potential adopters, *Yours By Choice*.

A social worker will visit you, not, as you might imagine, to see if she can find dust under the beds or dirty cups in the kitchen sink, but to give her a better picture of your home and family life. The physical standards demanded by Adoption Societies are not unusually high and the worker will neither be unduly impressed by an ultra-modern home nor discouraged about your ability to be good parents because your furniture is shabby. She will be interested to find out if your house feels comfortably well lived in, a place where a child would feel at home and where muddy little feet and sticky little fingers will not be considered a crime.

When regular church-goers Ann and Tom Blatcher adopted two boys through the Church of England Children's Society in the mid-1960s, it was one of the major national voluntary agencies and the only one they'd heard of at the time.

A lady called Mrs Biggs came to see us—a middle-aged, large, friendly smiling lady. We had to fill in forms, and we had to give two referees: one had to be the rector of our local church to say that yes, we were church-goers and that he knew us and we were OK,

185

and another had to be a friend who could say whether she thought we'd be good with children . . . and then Mrs Biggs had to look at the whole house, all the rooms, everything. I cleaned the house from top to bottom, even the drawers. I don't know why because she wasn't going to go poking about in drawers. I think it was just to see that there was room for a child and we weren't all in one room or something like that.

Some 'home studies', as they were known, were more thorough than others. A former child care officer working in Derbyshire in the 1960s remembers hearing from a colleague about a moral welfare worker who had visited a home but found the prospective adopters out. *'She had looked round the outside of the house and decided they would be suitable without even meeting the couple concerned!'*

Ted Roadhouse and his first wife were childless and desperate to adopt at the end of the 1950s. They were not church-goers, so they approached the main non-denominational agencies who told them there was virtually no chance of success because of long waiting lists. After much agonising and discussion, Ted agreed to his wife's request that they approach a denominational agency, The Mission of Hope, run by evangelical Anglicans, who had babies available and required only that adopters attended a Protestant church of their choice. Ted, an agnostic, had a crisis of principle about having to join a church in order to get a child, but he bowed to his wife's overwhelming need and together they joined a Congregationalist church. Forty-five years later, Ted is still a

186

Christian, though he insists he is 'a flexible, not a didactic' one. If they had waited a few years until 1966, they could have gone to a new agency, the Agnostics Adoption Society, founded specifically as an antidote to the religiosity of most societies. Later this became the Independent Adoption Service, on whose adoption panel I served for three years from 1998.

The Mission of Hope's vetting process appeared to be relaxed.

Before we applied to the Mission of Hope to adopt, we'd done some fostering for the local authority, so we'd already been vetted by the children's officer. When we went to the Mission of Hope they appointed a lady deacon to check us up and come and chat to us. She was a very nice lady, the Minister's wife, and she came and sat and drank tea with us. We got on with her very well and she thought we were nice people. I can't remember her looking round the house.

At the Mission of Hope they were very religious people and they used to do a great deal of praying for guidance as to which children should be sent where and whether prospective parents were suitable and so on. I don't know whether God always got it right!

Religion wasn't an issue in my own adoption through the NCAA, though my father remembers a more rigorous vetting process in 1951.

We had several visits, a number unannounced, from a rather severe lady who didn't smile until about the third visit. She gave us a very stiff interview and I remember her looking in the larder. But we got to

187

*know her quite well—I recall we even met up for tea
in Exmouth when we were on holiday—and she gave
us a lot of helpful advice in the months after we had
you.*

My parents' application was undoubtedly helped
by the support of my father's boss at the time,
Mr Cashel, the Deputy National Assistance Officer
for Croydon, who had first encouraged them to try
the NCAA. Their other referees, my mother's
sister and brother-in-law, Megs and Norman, were
pillars of their local Baptist church.

Even though the material comforts and social
standing of the home must have weighed heavily,
as Professor Illingworth reminded delegates of the
Standing Conference in the late 1960s:

*. . . it is not so much the social class of the home that
matters, or even, up to a point, the intelligence of the
parents; it is the quality of the home, the love it
provides, the stimulus to achievement, that matters.*

He gave delegates a very long list of requirements
he would look for in good adopters, from being
able to 'inculcate good moral values, and to impart
a sensible attitude to sex', to 'being ambitious [for
the child], without being over-ambitious'.

*We want a lot from parents. If the child is to achieve
his best, it is inevitable that we should want so much.
We are not aiming at his becoming a genius; but we
do hope that he will be helped to use the talents
which he has to the full—and not only to be a clever
child, within the limits of his ability, but to be a nice
child.*

188

Mrs Hilary Halpin who had by then succeeded Clarissa Plummer as General Secretary of the NCAA agreed, even if she felt his list of requirements *'was rather like a TV commercial for Daz'*, but she still thought matching was the key.

I think that however much or little we know about matching it is important to match the background of the child and adopters, to try and match the intelligence of the two sets of parents, if only because later the adopting mother can say to the child, 'Well your mother was a girl probably very like me, we obviously shared interests, we came from the same sort of background and had I known her I hope we would have been great friends.' This could be a tremendous help to an adopted child.

Would this have helped me? I think it would. But despite being impeccably matched by Mrs Halpin's agency, my mother never felt able to say anything like this, and I doubt whether many adoptive mothers in her position would.

But the matching debate was about to become an anachronism. By now the tide had already turned. The Standing Conference certainly didn't realise it at the time, but by 1969 the age of the mass transfer of perfect, white infants from unmarried mothers into childless two-parent homes was all but over. Ann Blatcher looks back on a very special time for her and her family:

We were so fortunate, we adopted just at the right time. There were a lot of babies about, with the Flower Power of the sixties and what have you. A lot of illegitimate children were born, and a lot went for adoption I'm pleased to say, because out of that we have two sons that we wouldn't have swapped for anything. They have been a worry, a problem and an absolute delight. They have not been perfect; if they had I would worry. They've been—just sons.

The face of adoption was about to change beyond all recognition, and with it the fate of the voluntary agencies was sealed.

10

CLOSING

The following years were, I like to think, among the happiest of Marjorie's life. She had 'the good people' around her, and Syd and Eileen were more than good neighbours. Syd did her weekly shop at Sainsbury's and Eileen did her hair, with the occasional perm and colour rinse, every week.

Eileen always wanted to be a hairdresser but for some unaccountable reason went into catering instead. Her own hair was a fabulous bleach blonde confection, piled up in late forties style and topped with a nest of exquisite kiss-curls. I could hardly take my eyes off it; it always looked immaculate, whatever the time of day or the occasion. She did a weekly 'shampoo and set' in the old-fashioned way for a few of the old ladies in the block, and we joked about Gladys upstairs, who was very fussy about how Eileen did it. 'I don't know why she bothers, she's only got about five hairs,' Marjorie would say.

She had a thing about whoever lived upstairs. First it was Fred, an alcoholic who tended to bring back homeless winos for late-night revels; then, after the drink finally got him, it was Gladys. She seemed perfectly alright to me, if a little bossy for a 90-year-old. Marjorie was never vindictive but there was always someone she didn't like. With her it was Gladys Upstairs. 'Does she *have* to do her clog dancing at six o'clock every morning?' Gladys was her Edie figure.

Syd and Eileen came from Acton originally and were younger than Marjorie. 'I'm the baby of the block,' Eileen liked to say when she was in her mid-sixties, but they took to each other, and no one—including me—could have done more for her. They invited her in for fish and chip suppers of a Friday and generally waited on her hand and foot. In return, Marjorie was good company.

We always had a laugh, talked about the telly we'd seen and about what was going on in the world. She'd potter into her kitchenette and make me tea.

'D'you want a biscuit? Go on, have a biscuit. They're nice ones. Syd got them from Marks's for me.'

Marks's—Marks & Spencer—was a cut above her usual Sainsbury's so it was an honour I felt duty-bound to accept. We always sat in the same places: we'd bought her a cheap two-piece suite for £99 when she moved in and she sat on the right-hand side of the small sofa (pole position for the telly) and I sat in the single chair, facing her. She would bring the smallest table out from the nest of tables salvaged from Bungalow Road and put a coaster down on it for my tea. Considering she lived for years in complete squalor, she was surprisingly fastidious about some things.

The room was cosy without being cluttered. Her 1960s' bookcase-cum-display cabinet held a job lot of unread romantic novels—another of her mail-order bargains—ornaments, a large glass dolphin, photos of her new family, and a collection of miniature teddies Fiona and I had brought for her from places we'd visited. On the wall above the sideboard, a painting of Alfriston Church by Ron, the husband of her old childhood friend, Betty. She'd lost touch with Betty for many years but Fiona and Steve had taken her to visit them recently, and she'd been very taken by Ron's paintings. On her small sofa, she looked completely at home.

When later Bevan and I went to see Mike Leigh's film about adoption reunions and family relationships, *Secrets and Lies,* the biscuit routine came back to me like a clout round the head. It was my story, except I wasn't black, and Brenda Blethyn was 30 years younger than Marjorie. But they both said, 'D'you want a biscuit? Go on, have a biscuit,' in exactly the same south London way. We came out of the cinema crying.

The year we were reunited with Fiona, we had a summer party in the garden at home. Fiona invited some of her friends and it was a lovely follow-up to the Walker Close flat-warming we'd had earlier in the year. Marjorie was particularly taken with my friends Herb and Deb's newborn baby Herbie, and I have a photo of him in her arms. I remember thinking at the time, the last time she did that, it was probably with Fiona. She loved babies and children and always talked to them. She loved it when friends' children came round when she was with us and always remembered their names and asked after them afterwards. You could see how it might have been.

We took her on a holiday to Jersey for a week— she'd always wanted to go to Jersey and she'd never been on a plane before. And we went on little trips, to Hampton Court, for a picnic in the grounds of Trent Park, and up the Grand Union Canal on a narrowboat. She would come over to lunch and I would go to see her every couple of weeks. She was always pleased to see me, never wanted to let me go, but never made demands.

'It's always lovely to see you . . . when you can, though, 'cause I know how busy you are. When you can, my Number One Daughter.'

*   *   *

Simon and I pulled out all the stops for our parents' Golden Wedding. There were two parties in Bognor—a large one for family and a smaller one for friends and neighbours. My father made an embarrassing speech about us being 'a meaningful family unit' (he never quite shook off the social work jargon) and my mother seemed cheered by the attention of friends and family around her. We organised a surprise treat for them afterwards. Simon hired a posh limo and I borrowed a chauffeur's hat, courtesy of the Chairman's friendly PA at work. Unfortunately the Chairman's chauffeur was a slight five foot five and Simon, an ex-policeman, is a burly six foot two; it was far too small but he still looked the part as he swept up to their bungalow and held the door open for them.

We drove in convoy to a large country house hotel on the Surrey–Sussex borders where, in their wood-panelled suite, my mother marvelled at the capacious bathroom with his 'n' hers sinks, the champagne and the flower arrangements we'd ordered. We had tea outside in the August sunshine and forgot about our mother's deafness and everything else that was wrong with the world. They'd been married for 50 years; it was an inconceivable achievement for me, who'd avoided

194

getting married altogether, and for Simon, whose first marriage had ended some time ago.

Six months later in the same hotel, Simon married his girlfriend Sarah. One of the first things that struck me about her, apart from her very loud and easy laugh, was that she was adopted. Quite early on, Simon had encouraged her search for her birth mother. They made contact by phone but the woman who answered denied all knowledge. It was enough to stop Sarah's search in its tracks.

In April 1996, shortly after her 76th birthday, my dear mother died. She'd had a series of minor strokes and had been poorly for some time. I couldn't bear to see her looking so ill in those last months and neither could my father, though he would never share his burden. She'd had a suspected heart attack just before her birthday and went into hospital, where she seemed to be doing well at first. Then she was moved to a much drabber ward, where there were fewer staff and all the patients were asleep, a sure sign that things had taken a turn for the worse.

My father called from there, but he couldn't speak and handed the phone to a nurse. 'I think you should come now,' she said. The words you always dread.

It was after 10 p.m. and we drove straight down to Sussex.

We sat with her behind the screens as her breathing got irregular and stertorous, taking turns to hold her hand. I always envied my mother's hands; they were soft, delicate, with beautiful almond-shaped nails. At about 2.30 a.m. I went out into the corridor for a few minutes. When I got back she'd gone. My father was winding the wire stem of a small red fabric rosebud round the identity tag on her wrist. The heart label on it said 'With Love'. It was the saddest thing I ever saw.

I wanted to remember her when she was happiest, when we first moved to Bognor in the 1960s. When she changed her name to Anne and seemed to become a new person. She was slim, attractive and laughed more than at any time I can remember. There were Burt Bacharach LPs in the house and she came home from work one day raving about how wonderful Procol Harem's *Whiter Shade of Pale* was. She started organising parties for the first time. For these I made a lot of stuffed eggs with salad cream and curry powder; no one in Bognor had heard of mayonnaise. She laughed and danced and was very silly when she got drunk on champagne. In the few fading Polaroid photos of my 21st birthday party, there she is, at 52, looking so pretty and glamorous— unlike me, gaunt after glandular fever. She was never the same after her big operation. I felt I'd lost her then really. But there wasn't a waking moment in my life when she wasn't my mother.

*   *   *

My relationship with Marjorie was different. I might have been her Number One Daughter, but to me she was a dear, elderly friend with whom I had a special bond. We weren't instantly close; we developed a relationship over some years. Though I felt guilty about it, I saw more of her than I saw of my parents because she was nearby, and because it was so easy to share things with her.

Sunday 31 August 1997
8.35pm. An hour ago we cycled down Lynwood Road to the A40 to watch the body of Princess Diana being brought back to London from Northolt. There were small groups of people lining the road. It was an extraordinary sight . . . everyone is shocked and sad . . . She was the most famous person in the world, dead at 36. Marjorie came to lunch and we consoled ourselves with drink. What a day.

But she was getting less and less active. At first, she'd walk her shopping trolley the mile and a half into West Ealing to Sainsbury's, but that soon gave way to Syd's shopping service. He did it for all the old ladies in the block; he'd always worked and done things for other people, and he wasn't about to give up now. I tried to encourage her at least to take a walk around the patch of green at the back of Walker Close every day. 'Yes, I must,' she said and we both knew she wouldn't. Marjorie always had good intentions, but lacked the motivation to carry them through. 'Yes, I must make a start on those piles of clothes in the bedroom.' 'Yes, I must sort through those bills.' The Bungalow Road years had set the pattern; she was quite happy just to sit with the television on all day and well into the night. Snooker and horror films were her preferred late-night viewing.

Her blood pressure rose, she became breathless and was prescribed steroids. She put on weight and her legs and ankles swelled up. So she stayed inside even more. But she never asked for help, even when she needed it. 'I'm alright love,' she always said.

One oppressively hot summer Sunday when

197

Fiona and her family were with us, she came over for lunch. Bevan brought her from Hanwell and I could tell from the look on his face that something was up. As I saw them coming up the path, I was conscious of what looked like big sticking plasters on all the toes showing from her open sandals. But they weren't sticking plasters, they were her toenails. Solid and yellow, they were so long they were curling back over her toes. I had to swallow hard to stop myself feeling sick.

'Marjorie, for God's sake! Why didn't you tell me your nails needed cutting? They're revolting!'

'Oh, I know, they're horrible, but I can't get to reach them any more. I've been meaning to get something done about them.'

It was just like Bungalow Road. The need had to be absolutely self-evident; she would never ask.

There began a long and frustrating odyssey to get an appointment with an NHS chiropodist. It took 10 weeks, by which time the toenails had grown even longer and Marjorie was having difficulty walking. After several cockups and cancellations we finally got in to see the young woman chiropodist. Marjorie started apologising as soon as I bent down to take off the only shoes she could get on at that point—a pair of bright green canvas sandals, one of her many catalogue purchases, with the straps undone.

'I'm really sorry Doctor, they're in a bit of a state.'

I could have forgiven the NHS anything when, quite unfazed, the chiropodist set to with the hacksaw and pliers and said cheerfully to Marjorie, 'Don't worry Miss Heppelthwaite, I've seen a lot worse than this. We'll soon have you sorted out.'

After that I started washing Marjorie's feet for her. It was a strangely soothing task. I tried to put the religious symbolism out of my mind.

Though the steroids eased her breathing, they really slowed her down physically and mentally and put a dampener on that lovely life-spark she had. We spent hours in the chest clinic 'next door' at Ealing Hospital, and the dose went up and down according to how bad things were. Even though it was only the other side of the River Brent from Walker Close, it felt like another planet, it was such a major expedition. It always took at least four hours door-to-door, for what was usually no more than 10 minutes with the specialist. The journey itself took three minutes. Getting her in and out of the car, finding her an empty chair in Outpatients, finding a parking space, waiting for a wheelchair, waiting for the specialist, waiting for the X-ray, waiting for the pharmacy, just plain waiting, took up the rest of the time. When we got back to Walker Close she was exhausted and so was I, and I'd make her a bit of scrambled egg on toast, her post-hospital pick-me-up.

It was me pottering into the kitchen to make the tea by now.

'I want to make it to my 80th you know.'

' 'Course you'll make it—we'll have a special party. You'll be a millennium birthday girl.'

The increasingly rare crinkly smile.

'Would Stephen come, do you think?'

'He wouldn't miss it for the world.'

*   *   *

11 August 1999. Solar Eclipse 11.11am.

Monica coming for lunch tomorrow. We'll visit Marjorie in the afternoon. Worried about her; she seems to be losing it a bit.

From the autumn of 1999 she started to go downhill. Where once the steroids had blown her up, she now looked thin and sucked-out. I'd got a cleaner in to tidy the place up once a week, but she seemed to resent the intrusion.

A series of panic calls from Eileen. We went over there this morning. She looks such a pathetic little thing, all shrunk and falling over on the sofa. Maybe a home is the inevitable next step. An Xmas card from Steve Leahy was the one thing that cheered her up today.

The flat started to smell of urine and we suspected that on some nights she wasn't bothering to go to bed. Eileen would check on her last thing at night and first thing in the morning and sometimes found her exactly where she had left her the previous night. She now had difficulty sitting upright and was obviously not getting to the toilet in time.

Over the next few weeks I learnt a lot about what happens when old people get ill. Her GP wouldn't come out to visit her, but without him we couldn't get access to any other help. I had several difficult conversations with him on the phone where he made me feel I was taking up his precious time. 'I've got patients waiting,' he said, as if I was ringing to chat about the weather. Eventually, in desperation, I rang the geriatric specialist at Ealing Hospital direct. A minor flu epidemic had just started and he was harassed, but he was also sympathetic and agreed to come and see her. By this time she was in bed and doubly incontinent.

She looked shrivelled and small in the bed. I held her hand.

'Is he coming, Mr Evans?'

'Yes, don't worry, he said he'd come tonight.'

'I don't want to leave here, Sue.'

'No, I know. But you might need to go to hospital for a bit, while they find out what's wrong and get you better, then you'll be home. You've got to be fit for that 80th birthday party.'

The kinds of things you say, pecker up, even as your heart is sinking.

He came about 10 p.m. and arranged for her to be admitted the following day.

I followed the ambulance and waited with her while they did the admission procedure. Normally, this would have been the cue for Marjorie to laugh and say, 'Goodness, they want to know the ins and outs of a pig's ear!' But she was quiet and compliant.

'Next of kin?'

'I am.'

I suppose that's when she stopped being a dear, elderly friend and became something much closer.

*　　　*　　　*

Initially, she was in a side ward where they put her on a drip and gave her big doses of antibiotics. She rallied immediately. She was almost back to her old self, sitting up, taking notice, eating a little, and allowing us to have a go at her nails which had become long and dirty. Fiona and I cleaned them

201

up and painted them her favourite pink, and she was much brighter. The ward was on the ninth floor and from her window you could just pick out Walker Close on the other side of the Brent. 'There you are,' I said, 'you're practically home already.'

As soon as the infection cleared, she was moved to the general geriatric ward. I tried not to see this as a negative sign. She grumbled about losing her nice private space but still seemed fairly cheerful. Fiona came just before Christmas to bring her presents before they went off for the holidays to their home on the Isle of Wight. We took her Christmas presents in on Christmas Day. She'd said some time ago that she wanted a new watch and I'd got her a nice one from Marks's. I strapped it on her pathetic little wrist, where it hung. 'Bevan'll get some extra holes put in it for you for when you come home.'

But she knew she wasn't coming home. I spoke to the ward sister.

'Marjorie must make the effort to get herself up and about now. Otherwise . . . well, hospitals aren't healthy places you know.' There's a lot that goes unsaid in those wards. But she wasn't making the effort and she slowly sank. Almost sadder than anything was her hair, always so beautifully done by Eileen, now so wild and matted I could hardly get a comb through it.

Friday 31 December 1999
The last light of the second millennium as I write this. A drab December day to end the 20th century. Xmas lights look warm opposite. We've just had lunch (it's 4.15pm) after chores and visiting Marjorie. They say

202

she's now medically fit but she has that haunted, hollow look that Bevan's Mum had latterly. She hardly does or says anything except manage the odd, increasingly rare 'crinkly' smile of hers, and to sigh 'Oh Sue'. I have to start thinking about nursing homes but can't help wondering if she'll last that long. They'd like her out as she's blocking a bed for someone with a better prognosis, but they make every appearance of being kind. She never wants me to leave and is now frightened, I think.

Now pitch, apart from Xmas tree and room lights. Still quiet. No birds now.

I went in on New Year's Day. The ward cleaner had given all the patients a small Christmas gift and Marjorie's was a little photo album. I filled it with the photos she'd brought to show me when we first met, and which she'd given me to keep: Marjorie at 15 in sunglasses with her Mum and Auntie on the beach at West Mersea; her father in borrowed Flying Corps uniform; Marjorie at a wedding in her twenties, smart in high heels, hat and fox fur; Marjorie in her Fire Service uniform. She was barely conscious but I went through the photos with her. I wanted her to look at her life and take some happy memories from it. And I wanted her to know.

'Finding you is the best thing I've done in my life.'

'Oh Sue . . .'

It seemed for a moment as if something else was about to come out on the wings of that sigh. But no, just the sigh as she sank back down into the pillows.

I kissed her, disengaged my hand from hers, her

nails still neat and polished, and crept away. That night I couldn't sleep for thinking about angels and willing them to come and take her. When the phone rang at 5 a.m., it was almost a relief. 'I think you should come straight away.'

*   *   *

Rolling down from the heights of Horsenden Hill, the empty beech wood lies ahead like a wide brown cathedral with its vaulted ceiling of bare branches. I run through its open doors and on to a rug of leaf mould and desiccated leaves. Slow, stop. Birdsong high in the branches. January sun. I am light-headed from lack of sleep, but feel safe, enclosed, uplifted. Whole.

*   *   *

Sunday 2 January 2000
Marjorie died between 5 and 6 this morning. She was gone by the time we got there. Yes, she did look at peace, but she was also unrecognisable—wasted, yellow, hair uncharacteristically wild. Now 2pm and I've just sorted through her hospital things. The smell lingers, sad smell. Curious, this juxtaposition of finality and new beginning. Joy and optimism, heaviness. Dear Marjorie. It's all over now. I'll miss you so much.

I rang Fiona in the Isle of Wight to tell her the sad news. It was particularly difficult for her: her mother and mother-in-law were staying with them so she could say very little on the phone and could share her grief only with Steve in their few private moments.

Because of the flu epidemic we couldn't have Marjorie's funeral for almost three weeks. Fiona wanted to see her, so we plucked up courage and went together to the back parlour of the Co-op on Pitshanger Lane, where she'd been laid out for us. It was the right thing to do, but it wasn't pleasant. Behind the mortician's thick make-up, there was even less of the Marjorie we knew than when I'd last seen her. We said our goodbyes then.

The funeral at Ruislip was held in perfect, brilliant sunshine and all the good people were there. Monica read the eulogy.

For most of us here, Marjorie came into our lives less than 10 years ago when Sue, and shortly afterwards Fiona, made contact with her. By then she was already in her seventies.

Yet she had a big impact on all of us because in her quiet way she was that special sort of person it was easy to know and easy to love.

She in turn loved people, was interested in them, and was always ready to reach out to them with a word and a smile. She wasn't a demanding person, yet we were all happy to do things for her, because she was very giving in return. Her great loves were clothes (it was always difficult to tear her away from a mail-order catalogue!) and dogs. Her canine calendars reminded her of her beloved Benny—she was distraught that he couldn't make the move with her to Walker Close.

In life Marjorie had more than her fair share of difficulties. Unlike many of us, she never had a loving lifetime partner, or the comfort and support of a family of her own. And it's hard to imagine now how

205

painful it must have been for her to give up the two children she loved, because she was unable to provide all that she would wish for them.

Adversity should have diminished Marjorie. Instead it made her strong, independent and especially sensitive to the needs and feelings of others.

She kept her optimism, her infectious good humour, and her enviable ability to talk to anyone, anywhere.

Her time at Walker Close was undoubtedly the happiest and most settled.

She loved her flat and the river, trees and birds around her. Syd and Eileen were exceptional neighbours—and good friends. She was living the independent, secure life she'd always wanted. Perhaps most importantly, Sue and Fiona were in close contact with her and they were able to spend a few precious years knowing each other. As I and all her friends will know, that contact brought her unceasing wonder, joy and happiness. I personally know how exceptionally proud she was of their talents, how she loved their partners and their families, how protective she was of them in a quiet, sensitive way.

Marjorie, we will miss you very much.

We are very glad to have known you.

Thank you for showing us how to love and give unconditionally.

We will try and remember to do the same.

We left the crematorium chapel to the gospel anthem *Oh Happy Day*. Despite the wildly inappropriate title, Fiona and I chose it carefully: it starts quietly, reverently, and then gathers pace and tempo in a glorious affirmation of life and

206

faith. It was how we felt about Marjorie and the day we all met; we wouldn't be parted again. We went out to see the flowers and I noticed a man standing at the back of the small crowd. It was Martin Runchman.

*　　　*　　　*

Fiona and I cleared Walker Close. Eileen had the glass dolphin and Liz the cleaner had the smiling puppy. The housing association came to pick up all the usable furniture and we paid the driver to take the soiled bed and the sofa to the dump. We found about 60 pounds' worth of loose change in drawers, some old papers, and a few bits of old jewellery, probably her mother's, including a small Edwardian brooch with 'Baby' engraved on it that made us cry. And clothes, lots of clothes. Six or seven large bags went to the charity shop. Just like Bungalow Road, I felt I should clear the kitchen but there were only two small cups of fat at the back of a cupboard.

Small things set us off. Fiona wept when she found the hot water bottle, still in its wrapping with gift tag, that she'd given Marjorie several Christmases ago. And in the sideboard drawer, every letter, postcard and greetings card we'd ever sent her; those first letters from Monica, the first one from me, all there. We half expected to find some further clue to her past—a letter, a photograph—but there was nothing that changed anything.

Clearing the flat confirmed all I thought I knew about Marjorie. She was a human being—full of small failings but big gifts. She hoarded everything (including old fat) but was generous and loving. She avoided cleaning but had spirit and a joyful sense of humour. In the end she lived her last years as she would have wanted—pleasing herself, with people she loved and who loved her, around her. What more could anyone want?

When I ran into Horsenden Wood the morning after Marjorie's death, I felt an emotion guiltily close to euphoria. It was the end of something difficult but good; there was a sense of completeness that overwhelmed grief. I knew I'd made a difference to her life. I could never wash away her years of unhappiness and regret but our time together was rich in laughter, intimacy and mutual support. Balm for old wounds.

It was over, complete. I thought the book on Marjorie Phyllis Heppelthwaite was closed.

11

CHANGING TIMES

Mark, a former Barnardo's boy, was one of a new kind of adopted child for the 1970s.

He was illegitimate, but he was 11 before he was adopted. He had been in institutional and foster care before that and he was, in the terminology of the time, 'coloured' or mixed-race. Mark symbolised the new face of adoption in Britain in the final decades of the 20th century—one of the 'children who wait', as they were called in an influential 1972 report of the same title carried out by the British Association of Adoption Agencies. This had identified hundreds of children 'stuck' in residential care because they didn't fit the old 1950s' model of an adoptable child. They weren't perfect, white or babies.

Mass immigration from Commonwealth countries to meet Britain's post-war employment needs meant that, from the 1950s, the major cities became home to a much wider racial and cultural mix. During the 1960s, social workers noticed a slow but steady increase in the number of black and mixed-race children coming into voluntary and local authority care who were, on the face of it, available for adoption. Ignorance, racial prejudice and sheer lack of experience in this kind of adoption work meant that these children were automatically excluded from the adoption pool. It was assumed that adopters, who were almost without exception white, wouldn't want them. As early as 1953, a children's officer in Liverpool reported to the Standing Conference of Agencies Registered for Adoption 'a marked colour problem', with 'near-white' babies being rejected by adopters because of fears they would produce dark offspring.

Dr Barnardo's, who had always taken mixed-race children into their homes but had never placed them directly for adoption, reviewed its policy from 1961 (*'where every other condition is good, coloured babies should be placed direct for adoption'*). But they were anxious to have prospective adopters waiting before accepting any children: *'the right course is to receive applications to adopt a coloured child before we receive the children themselves'.*

Mark was born in Bradford in 1964 to a Northern Irish mother and Pakistani father. His mother placed him in Barnardo's care almost immediately. Although he eventually found a loving adoptive family after being fostered by them from the age of seven, Mark feels bitter that he was denied the chance of a secure family life from the start. Much later, in the course of tracing his mother, he uncovered a letter on his Barnardo's file that recommended adoption. But it seemed not everyone agreed.

*What really got to me about this letter was that above [the recommendation], there's a handwritten note that says, 'I think **not**. Half-caste Pakistani.' And that hit me very, very hard at the time. To think that somebody in, I presume, a senior position had handwritten this. Because of the colour of my skin, I wasn't going to be given the same opportunities as* *anybody else. That was quite unacceptable.*

At the time, of course, no one knew that files were later to be open for inspection by the subjects of these decisions. The unseen hand had long gone, leaving others to justify and explain.

By the time Mark was born, the agencies were in fact already starting to ask adopters to consider a mixed-race child. In a publicity leaflet from the early 1960s, Dr Barnardo's advises potential adopters that *'we also have a few children with a mixed racial background and a small number who may have a handicap. We are always pleased to hear from people able to take a child who needs special and sensitive care and understanding'*. Ann Blatcher remembers being asked by the Church of England Children's Society in the mid-1960s *'whether we wanted a wholly British child, or a foreign child, or a mixture'*. But this was always left for adopters to decide. Unsurprisingly, adopters usually wanted children as much like themselves as possible, and the younger the better. But those available for adoption now were increasingly mixed-race like Mark, older children who'd spent time in children's homes, and babies and children with physical disabilities or disturbed backgrounds.

A social worker for a local authority in the 1960s remembers:

I did not find any couples who were willing to consider a coloured or mixed-race child despite advertising in both the local and national press. The same applied to a handicapped child, although there were occasional exceptions, but these were few and far between and did not usually result in legal

211

adoption, rather long-term fostering.

Increasing numbers prompted a more radical approach. In 1966 the British Adoption Project advertised for married couples to adopt mixed-race infants under 12 months, promising as a reward *'the knowledge that they are helping to solve the wider problem of integration of a large number of non-white children into the Community'*. As a result, 53 black and mixed-race babies were placed with 51 mostly middle-class white adopters. Follow-up studies of the children in 1969, 1974 and 1983 found them well-adjusted, but with the important caveat that the children were still not old enough to test how easily they would relate to their own communities as they grew into adulthood. Now that mixed-race children adopted into white families in the 1960s and 1970s are adults, they can reflect on their experience.

David and his first wife always planned to have four children, and adoption was part of the plan from the start.

Right at the beginning of the 1970s, population size was a big issue. If you had more than two or three children you were socially irresponsible—the population explosion was very serious. So we said, why don't we have two of our own and adopt two? This was the grand plan. I suppose we also felt that it was socially a very noble thing to do to adopt a child who needed a good loving family. So we had two of our own and then set about trying to adopt two more. We started the process with our local authority, soon after our second child was born. It was pointed out to us that if we insisted on adopting a white baby, we could forget it; we'd be waiting for ever. But if we took a mixed-race child that could be very quick, and we said, yes, fine, that's absolutely alright. It wasn't an issue for us. And so we adopted Amanda in 1976.

The local authority gave them a letter about Amanda's birth parents to show her when she was older, but offered no advice that David can remember about any special challenges in adopting a mixed-race child. Ten years later, he was bringing up the three children as a single parent, though the children regularly saw their mother.

Amanda was a very different personality from the other two but bringing her up was absolutely no different. The only problem I had was managing her hair. We lived in a mainly white neighbourhood and almost all Amanda's friends at primary school were white. Years later, she told me how often she'd wished she was white, like her friends. My feeling now, looking back on it, is that I'm not so sure it was a good idea for a black child to be adopted into an entirely white family. There are cultural differences that affect a child . . . it would have been better if she could have been adopted into a black family, but the point is there weren't black couples to adopt kids then. If I had my time over again, I would perhaps think about that more carefully than I did at the time.

Amanda remembers a loving family, but a difficult time.

I always knew I was adopted, but I suppose I was about seven or eight when I first became aware I was a different colour. It was extremely painful when

213

someone new to the situation made reference to it and then it would all go away again till someone else brought it back out of its box.

It was a very close-knit middle-class neighbourhood and everybody knew everybody else. It was predominantly white and there were times when I did feel very different—obviously I was a different colour and my hair didn't move. My hair was always such a huge issue. As a child I had no sense of wanting to be proud of being black. I just remember wanting to be the same as everyone else; being a little girl to me was being like my friends and I wasn't like any of them. I hated my hair so very much because it wasn't what I wanted to be, and it was so difficult to maintain—or at least it seemed difficult because it was such a problem for everyone around me who was white. I'd scream and hide under the table when the comb came out. Mum and Dad didn't have much idea what to do with my hair, how to stop it getting tangled, how to grow it, and so of course they cut it off and I always had really short hair, so that was another way in which I felt really unfeminine.

By the time I became a teenager I was so, so lost, I had a huge identity crisis. Whereas at primary school it was small and close-knit and I was accepted, when I got to secondary school and there were other black children there, they immediately hated me. They couldn't understand me and they called me Coconut all the time. I was in absolute turmoil with myself. I remember vividly at 15 or 16 having to walk down the High Street with my Dad shopping, being painfully, acutely aware of myself and thinking, I really don't want to be out with my family, then in a horrendous temper, shouting at Dad that he was not to walk with

214

me in case everyone realised I was a half-breed. I had it pretty bad. It's taken me a very long time to resolve—more than 10 years.

Perhaps it would have been easier if I had been adopted into a black family. Black people wouldn't have been such a mystery to me and I wouldn't have felt like I was missing out on so much. But then I just can't imagine life without my family—I can't imagine not being part of them. We are close; we're so very different but we find our own ways of communicating and getting along, it's lovely.

Mark had a different, though no less painful, experience. After seven years with black and mixed-race friends in the closed community of a Barnardo's home in North Yorkshire, he faced racism for the first time when he moved to live in rural Cumbria with the foster parents who later adopted him.

Children would refuse to play with me on the grounds that I was coloured. They'd call me Sambo, Darkie, and obviously as I got older, moving to secondary school, it was Nigger and Coon. Particularly at seven and eight that would have had a big, big effect on me. I certainly don't have any recollections of being able to speak to anybody about this, which is why I think I ended up sitting in the bath scrubbing myself with a hard nailbrush. I can remember my foster mother telling me just to ignore it and it would go away, but of course it didn't. It was six years of sheer torture from about seven until I was 13, and it only got better because I broke into the under-13 rugby squad at secondary school, so I became one of the lads then.

215

In fact, Mark was one of the luckier ones. From the age of about 18 months he had been taken home for the holidays, as was the practice at Barnardo's homes at the time, by a care worker who introduced him to the family who later fostered and then adopted him. Otherwise he may have had to stay in the children's home. If so, he would have been among the last groups of children looked after in homes. By the 1970s, after more than 100 years of championing institutional care, Dr Barnardo's was closing its homes (it had dropped 'Homes' from its title in 1966) and was turning increasingly to foster care and other ways of supporting children and their families.

*   *   *

There are no formal records of how many transracial adoptions were arranged in the late 1960s and 1970s, but this was a new feature of adoption. These were almost exclusively black and mixed-race children into white homes as non-white adopters were not being specifically targeted. Many middle-class adopters sympathetic to the American civil rights movement considered it a socially and politically admirable thing to do, and the mood and social policies of the time favoured assimilation rather than recognition and celebration of difference. But casework experience, research studies, and the growing influence of black social workers and lobbyists led to an awareness that cutting a child off from its cultural roots in this way was likely to set up identity and attachment problems in adolescence and adulthood.

From the 1980s, increasing efforts were put into campaigns to recruit black and mixed-race adopters who could provide cultural role models and reference points for the child. In a sense, matching had come full circle. A decade or so on from the mid-1960s when it was considered that any approved adopter should accept any child, regardless of race or background, it was recognised that matching cultural and racial background was likely to be critical to the healthy development of the child.

There were other fundamental changes afoot. The supply of perfect white babies had started to dry up in the late 1960s as abortion was legalised and the new oral contraceptive pill became widely available. Paradoxically, the number of illegitimate babies increased—by 1979 they were nearly 11 per cent of all live births. But as economic conditions and State benefits improved, and the permissiveness that had liberated the Flower Power generation in the 1960s permeated a new generation in the 1970s, it became acceptable for the first time since the 18th century to have a child outside marriage—and want to keep it.

*　　　*　　　*

In 1969, the Labour government appointed a Royal Commission to investigate the needs of one-parent families, and the 1974 Finer Report recommended improved benefits and an end to discriminatory housing policies. Like many radical social documents, few of its recommendations were taken up (four years later, only 38 of 230 had been implemented), but things were improving for the single mother. In 1976, Family Allowance was extended to the first child, and by 1977 local councils had a duty to house all but those who'd made themselves intentionally homeless. In theory this was a giant step forward, as lack of housing was one of the main practical barriers to unmarried mothers keeping their babies.

In practice, though, it meant more unsatisfactory temporary accommodation in bed and breakfast 'hotels' and old workhouses rapidly converted into bleak bedsits. I saw how one of these might have looked at Southwell Workhouse in Nottinghamshire, now a National Trust property. The final and most moving exhibit on the tour of the massive 1824 'model' workhouse is a second-floor room, once one of the women's dormitories. This is re-created as a 1970s' temporary 'flat' for a homeless family: five hospital beds lined up cheek-by-jowl against a wall, an ancient gas stove with slot meter above, a stained china sink with its wooden draining board and a Formica-topped table. Even in the last decades of the 20th century, the workhouse was still there in every community as the cold comfort option of last resort.

The mother and baby homes—a sanctuary for some, a prison for others—were facing hard times themselves. By the end of the 1960s, many homes were closing through lack of demand and lack of funds. A National Council for the Unmarried Mother and Her Child report in 1968 found a variety of unsatisfactory conditions and practices in homes, and noted that many were closing because of staffing problems. Many of the dedicated single women for whom the homes had been their life's work were starting to retire. And

218

mothers' needs were changing too. By 1972, the NCUMC reported that fewer than 6 per cent of pregnant women coming to them now wanted this kind of facility: *'An increasing number of mothers are now able to stay with their parents or friends during their pregnancy.'*

The old Diocesan Moral Welfare Boards were having to reassess their role and their nomenclature as the care of unmarried mothers and their children became fully integrated into the new 'generic' social services departments from 1971 and this branch of social work finally lost its old voluntary image. Moral welfare workers disappeared into retirement and Josephine Butler House, which had trained most of them, finally closed in 1972. The Moral Welfare Boards regrouped and assumed the more client-friendly name 'Family Care', and the other denominational agencies finally abandoned their banner-waving 19th-century names: the Mission of Hope became Christian Family Concern and the Crusade of Rescue became the Catholic Children's Society. The Edinburgh Guild of Service, which originally grew out of the National Vigilance Association of Scotland founded in 1911, and which changed its name again to Family Care in 1978, identified some of the challenges it faced on the brink of the 1970s:

What new demands are already emerging? In the short term there is home-finding for children with special needs . . . Perhaps we should be experimenting with ways of helping adoptive parents and adopted children and adults, now that it is generally recognised that adoption is a more complicated thing

219

than was previously thought . . . What about counselling for the childless couples who may not be able to adopt because there are fewer babies needing homes? And what about a return to preventive work—helping to avoid unwanted pregnancies instead of coping with them?

Home-finding for children with special needs turned out to be a much longer-term project than anyone at the time imagined, and post-adoption work—in its infancy then—was about to become much bigger still.

The adoption agencies, too, were struggling. With the supply of babies all but cut off, they had to decide whether to adapt to meet the new needs of older, 'hard-to-place' children, perhaps with disabilities or mixed parentage, or to close. Those that specialised only in baby adoptions were left with a problem; ironically the old voluntary denominational childcare organisations— Barnardo's, the Church of England Children's Society, the National Children's Home—survived because they had a wider range of activities and funding sources, and were ultimately more adaptable. One of the last social workers at the NCAA in the 1970s recalls:

I think we were all aware that the Pill and the Abortion Act would affect us and tried to take this into account. When the supply of babies dried up, the prospective adopters applying were told that we already had too many waiting and unless they were willing to consider a 'hard to place' child or children we could not deal with their application.

Jenny Lumley was a social worker with Charing Cross Hospital, and later for a local authority, who had regular dealings with adoption agencies in the 1970s. She had both professional and personal contact with the NCAA.

It was a very nice, very middle-class agency, but they were very caring. They were an organisation I felt I could work with.

So Jenny felt comfortable approaching the NCAA to adopt her first child in 1977. She was fortunate to be offered a baby within months.

When we went to collect Ali from the office in Knightsbridge, we had the carrycot with us and we decided to treat ourselves—it was our ninth wedding anniversary—so we went to Harrods for lunch, just round the corner. We were in the lift coming away from the restaurant and this woman looked in the carrycot and said, 'Oh, it's empty!' My husband said, 'Yes, we're going shopping!' She looked horrified and we just fell about laughing, and after that, we always called it the adopt-shop.

When they returned to the NCAA for another child a couple of years later they were devastated to find that it had closed down in 1978. After 60 years of bringing illegitimate babies together with adopters, in the face of changing times, straightened finances and a new raft of regulations in the 1976 Adoption Act, it had finally thrown in the towel. They went to another national agency thinking that, as proven adopters, their application would be straightforward.

In those days there was quite a lot of pressure to adopt a child of a different race. And if you said you didn't want to, you were regarded as being racist. And I remember thinking, but I don't know many people of different cultures and ethnic backgrounds. I felt it was enough to take on board adopting a child, without the extra cultural issues. The interview was ghastly. I remember they asked strange questions like, how would we cope with a child with red hair? I remember thinking, well, so what? I did not like their attitude at all, but I thought, OK, I'll swallow hard, we want a baby, we'll play the game. Then one morning a little letter came through the post, 'We're not pursuing your application.' Just a couple of lines. No reason. I was just beside myself, absolutely gutted, the way it was done. So we had to start all over again. Finally we were taken on by Barnet Social Services and within a very short time we had Tom.

Jenny realises that their late-1970s' adoptions were unusual: *'We are profoundly lucky to have been able to adopt two such young children.'*

By the 1980s the adoption of illegitimate babies by strangers had become a relative rarity. Public policy now assumed that the best place for a child was in its own family and resources were channelled into support for families in difficulty, rather than to adoption services. And because the children available for adoption tended to be older, there was more emphasis on maintaining contact with birth parents and siblings and preparing adopters to accept and explain the child's past through the preparation of a 'life story' book for them to read as they grew up. This was a far cry

222

from previous practice where adopters could take a young baby and be confident that they would never again have to think about where it had come from once it was in their own home.

*   *   *

Childless couples desperate for a baby now turned to other countries to provide what Britain could not. After the fall of Ceausescu in 1989, pitiful scenes from Romanian orphanages sparked a new interest in inter-country adoption, and each political revolution and humanitarian disaster inspired a trail of hopeful adopters.

Initially procedures were lax or non-existent, there was no legal framework and social services departments had no formal responsibility for overseas adoptions. There was ample scope for abuse of adopters, children and birth parents by unscrupulous individuals and commercial organisations quick to exploit the poverty of parents and the desperation of would-be adopting couples. The baby-farming business had become internationalised. UK and European law was slow to catch up with the increasing popularity of inter-country adoption, itself fuelled by dozens of websites 'advertising' babies.

At the start of 2001, Alan and Judith Kilshaw were dubbed 'Britain's most hated couple' by the press after they paid over £8,000 via the Internet for US-born six-month-old twins. But Beverley and Kimberley were already the subject of claims, both by a Californian couple that *they* had paid the 'Caring Heart' broking agency £4,000 for them and so had prior claim, and by their natural mother,

Tranda Wecker, who now wanted them back. Social services and the US and UK courts quickly became involved, and the publicity-seeking Kilshaws daily demonstrated to the world their lack of suitability as adoptive parents. Finally the twins were returned to the US. It was a complex and distressing case that dominated the headlines for weeks and seemed to prove that international adoption was still a fraught and very murky business.

By 2003 there were increasing numbers of inter-country agreements, and UK regulation, including local authority supervision and thorough home studies, was just as strict as for domestic adoptions. Since 1996, inter-country applications processed by the Department of Health (and now by the Department for Education) have been running at several hundred a year, forming a small but significant part of the modern face of adoption.

Like inter-racial adoption, inter-country adoption brings additional challenges, and it is still controversial. Should affluent people be able to pluck the children of the poor from other countries and cultures to satisfy their desire for a baby when there are needy children available and desperate to be adopted at home? Or is it perfectly acceptable, given the stringent safeguards now in place? Is it just a straightforward matter of supply and demand? Like other aspects of adoption, we may not know the answers, if there are any, until everyone involved is a lot older and the 'babies' are themselves able to assess the impact of adoption on their lives.

Official adoption figures, though sometimes hard to interpret, tell the story of change and decline in the last decades of the 20th century. Ten years after the 1968 peak for 'stranger' adoptions, the 1978 figure had dropped by more than two-thirds to less than 5,000. Figures stayed around this level for much of the 1980s and fell further in the 1990s, so that by 1998 little more than 4,000 Adoption Orders a year were being granted, including to relatives. This, too, was significant: the proportion of adoptions by relatives, a result of increasing divorce and remarriage, was also rising.

In 1998, adoptions were at their lowest level since 1929, partly because the process was perceived by potential adopters—with a little help from the tabloid press—as hamstrung by bureaucracy, busybody social workers and political correctness. Worried about the lack of effort local authorities seemed to be investing in this area, the government set new targets for the adoption of children in local authority care, or 'looked after' children as they are known. As a result of the Quality Protects initiative begun in that year, adoption levels rose initially. By 2010, 10 per cent of adoptions were of children from the care system.

The 'permanency movement' which gathered momentum in the 1990s was a response to concerns that many looked after children spent their young lives drifting from one foster placement to another without proper planning and with little prospect of a permanent home. Adoption, out of favour for a decade, was rediscovered, not least by the then Prime Minister, as a means of giving disadvantaged children the benefits and opportunities of a permanent family. There were good economic arguments, too, for

225

making adoption easier: it is a cheaper and longer-term solution than either foster or institutional care, and 'permanency' also means that responsibility for these children shifts from governments and hard-pressed local authorities to adopting parents.

Tony Blair personally championed the change and the White Paper that later became the 2002 Adoption and Children Act, and he had good reason to take such a personal interest. His father Leo was the subject of an early *de facto* adoption in the 1920s when his unmarried travelling entertainer parents handed him over to Clydesdale shipworker James Blair and his wife Mary after they'd met on tour in Glasgow. The Blairs brought him up as their own, and Leo obviously instilled the importance of a secure family life in *his* son:

I know how much difference a loving and caring family made to me. No matter how good a care home is, it isn't as good as having a loving family. The whole purpose of this [draft legislation] is to clear away the clutter of rules that stop children having a decent home. We have got to get some common sense back in the system.

There is a revival of interest in adoption—not as a solution to illegitimacy or infertility, but as a means of rebuilding the lives of children damaged by disability, family breakdown, physical and sexual abuse and the effects of the care system. But it is a much taller order for adopters than taking on a babe-in-arms. These children have a real, tangible and usually complex past. They may still be in regular contact with their birth family, and they will test their adopter's love and resolve to the limit. As one adopter told Tony Blair in 2000, *'Adoption is a very long road. It's that commitment beyond normal parenting. It will take [my son] a whole lifetime to overcome what he experienced in the first three years of his life.'*

In 1998 I joined the Adoption Panel of the Independent Adoption Service, a small national agency, originally the Agnostics Adoption Society, in the business of recruiting adopters mainly for local authorities. I never met any adopters: just as I ended my three-year stint in 2001 the IAS was about to change its policy and admit them to Panel meetings. But I must have studied and commented on the best part of 100 adopter applications during that time. They were all kinds of people: couples—married or not, single people, gay men and lesbians, old and young, from all classes and racial backgrounds. They had had their homes and their private lives minutely investigated, their motives exhaustively explored and their own baggage painfully worked through over a period of perhaps two or more years in order to reach the stage where a social worker was recommending them to the Panel. Almost always convinced, we in turn recommended their approval. I found it a humbling experience. These people were totally committed; they were going into adoption with their eyes open. Despite the difficulties and the challenges of parenting a damaged child, they wanted to do it. They'd come through a long and intrusive assessment process, and they were as prepared as they could be. I had the greatest admiration for them.

Major changes to social attitudes, economic

conditions and to the needs of the children themselves had transformed the face of adoption in the last quarter of the 20th century. But in my view, the most significant development came right at the start of that period with the passing of the 1975 Children Act. Like the Abortion Act almost a decade earlier, it marked a watershed in the history of adoption, but this was different. This had more direct impact on adopters, adopted people and their birth parents than any other single piece of legislation or any other development in the history of adoption in Britain in the 20th century. This impact is still being felt, and probably will be for at least another generation.

For the first time, legislation allowed adopted people over 18 in England and Wales [In Scotland those over 17 had had this right since 1930.] access to their birth and adoption records, giving them the information necessary to trace birth relatives. This revolutionary provision in the 1975 Children Act was enshrined in the 1976 Adoption Act and overturned at a stroke the carefully preserved culture of secrecy begun by the first Adoption Act in 1926 and buttressed by subsequent legislation.

It gave birth mothers renewed hope of being reunited with the children they'd had to give up a generation or more before. It gave adopted people the opportunity for the first time to find out about a past that had been hidden from them. And it struck fear into the hearts of those adopters who saw it as a betrayal of all they had been promised about this most significant and emotional of life decisions being a new beginning and a clean break with the past.

It changed everything.

12

SEARCH AND REUNION

*Was u giving the name Richard Gary Smith at birth
and born at the Chiswick Hospital for Unmarried
Mothers around 1963–1965 to Eileen Hazel Smith
then if so or if you have any info please please
contact me I am his half sister. Thank u..*

Like car crashes and horror films, once you're
logged on to one of the dozens of Internet contact
sites it's almost impossible to look away. You move
from one pathetic appeal to the next, in search of a
familiar name or a more uplifting story. Instead
there is only dull misery and longing for the
elusive family member who remains detached,
unknowable, till that glorious day when reunion
will mend all. Most of these sad messages are from
mothers looking for the children they gave up for
adoption and from adopted children looking for
their birth mothers or siblings. There are hundreds
of them.

Adoption wasn't meant to be like this. Reunion
was never part of the plan. Until the late 1970s,
records were closed to all parties. If adoptive
parents didn't wish to disclose what information
they had about their child's background, they
didn't have to. And the birth mother wouldn't
know anything about her child's adopters unless
she'd arranged the adoption herself, or been given
information by a third party who'd arranged it for
her. All 'proper' adoptions—those arranged by

agencies—were conducted in strict secrecy on the absolute understanding that there would be no further contact between mother and child. As Labour MP Leah Manning said during the debate on the 1950 Adoption Act, *'the most important thing with regard to adoption is that the book should be closed and the curtain come down absolutely'*.

Of course this didn't stop those who had managed to garner a little information by stealth, subterfuge or accident, but agencies and local authorities couldn't offer help so this had to be a do-it-yourself project, with all the risks and pitfalls that entailed. That changed after the 1975 Children Act, and the advent of the Internet in the 1990s meant that whereas once those who searched had little or no information at all, they now have more than they can handle—'a maze of madness' as one searcher describes it.

The radical provision in the 1975 legislation, confirmed in the 1976 Adoption Act, that opened up birth records to adopted people for the first time, didn't just come out of the blue. As early as 1954, the Hurst Committee recommended access to those over 21, because *'it is not in the interests of adopted children to be permanently precluded from satisfying their natural curiosity'*. This conclusion seemed to be based entirely on gut feeling rather than empirical evidence, which was puzzling given that access to adoption records had been available in Scotland since 1930. But no one had bothered to find out how widely this had been taken up, or with what results. Nevertheless, the Hurst proposal caused much anxiety among adoption specialists. Mary Ellison warned of dire consequences:

This is a most startling proposal, and one that seems to undermine the main purpose of the Act of 1950, which seeks . . . to separate the adopted child for ever from its natural parents, and to ensure that . . . it shall stand for the rest of its life in relation to its adoptive parents as if it were a child of their marriage . . . If this recommendation is accepted, it will certainly deal a deathly blow to the security of many adoptions; there will undoubtedly be a dramatic increase in private irregular placings; and many good potential parents will abandon their idea of applying to adoption agencies for children.

They needn't have worried: Hurst's recommendation was completely ignored in the 1958 Adoption Act. The Houghton Committee had another crack at access issues in 1972. This was far more authoritative because it was able to use the findings of John Triseliotis's influential research on the Scottish experience, *In Search of Origins*, which was published the following year.

To put it at its simplest, Triseliotis found that *'adopted people have to establish who they are if they are to become whole and complete people'*. For the first time, he demonstrated that knowledge and understanding of origins—including the circumstances of their adoption, their ethnicity and cultural heritage—contributed very significantly to an adopted person's sense of identity and self-worth. On the other hand, evasion, secrecy and lies were damaging to the development of the growing personality and to the child's relationship with its adoptive parents and others.

[Adopted people] need to have answers to questions

231

such as: Why was I put up for adoption? Who were my birth parents and what kind of people were they? . . . Was I wanted and loved before I was given up? . . . Finally they must find their own answers to the question of 'Who am I?'

He identified the jumble of difficult feelings associated with being adopted: anger, rejection, grief for lost or missing relatives or a past unacknowledged and unvalued. This was the first breakthrough research on the experience and impact of adoption, generations after it first became common in Britain. Its findings contradicted long-established policy but confirmed what many adoption workers now knew from experience: that openness, though not without its own problems, was better in the long run than secrecy. This convinced the policy-makers, who overturned the central premise of 50 years of adoption legislation.

The press sniffed a promising Pandora's Box. There were stories with headlines like *'The knock on the door that mothers dread'*, stirring fears of families disrupted by the arrival on the doorstep of a long-concealed illegitimate child. Adoptive parents told of their fear of 'losing' their children to 'the other mother', or of children finding out horrific things about their past. There was much fear and dread in the air.

There was a certain amount of trepidation among social workers too. The 1976 Adoption Act required local authorities to set up post-adoption services, and counselling became a prerequisite for access to birth records (although anyone who had their original birth name could get round this fairly easily). But they had no idea whether the new legislation, which came into force in November 1976, would prompt a trickle or a deluge of enquiries, and they'd had little experience of how to help and prepare people undertaking a search for birth relatives. In fact, the expected flood didn't happen—fewer than 2 per cent of those eligible to apply for their original birth certificates did so initially. Adopted people appeared hesitant to seek information at first and often justified it as a purely practical exercise to check out medical histories. Loyalty to adoptive parents and the newness of the idea of access to information as a right held many back, though numbers steadily increased. By 1999, over 70,000 adopted people had exercised their right to obtain their birth records and today it is estimated that at least half of adopted adults set out on a search at some time in their lives.

A former adoption worker with Hereford and Worcester County Council sent me a report of her experience with her first 27 'counsellees', written a couple of years after the new law was implemented. Some searches she helped with were successful, even if they stopped far short of reunion:

Mr W in his twenties. Long Lartin Prison. Had not been told of his adoption until 11 years of age. Appeared greatly helped by very full letters from both the Adoption Agency involved and the GAL [guardian ad litem]. *Both confirmed he had been a loved child.*

The report recorded successful reunions, rejections, distressing discoveries, continuing and

233

abandoned searches and everything in between—the whole spectrum of search experience. Women outnumbered men by 4:1 in her caseload. One of her abiding memories of this early counselling experience is of talking to birth mothers who never forgot their children; some even showed her diary entries secretly recording their birthdays. She was surprised at the number of mothers who later married the child's father and also the number who never told their husbands they'd had an illegitimate child. Though now retired, she is still involved in counselling and thinks, on balance, the change in the law has had good consequences, *'because even when the news is bad, it can help people to understand why adoptions were like they were'.*

This conclusion, however painful it may sometimes be, seems to be borne out by the experience of the people directly involved.

Adopters are understandably apprehensive about the idea of uncovering the past. However sensible and rational they may be, it is hard not to see this as an emotional blow and implied criticism as well as a risk to the security of the relationship with their son or daughter. Ann Blatcher remembers her anxieties on hearing about the change in the law.

I was worried because we had two sons. I wouldn't have stood in their way if they'd wanted to find their birth mother, I would have given them all the information we have—but I know I would have been worried, because they were my children by then. They were mine, nobody else's . . . I felt that the adoptive parents were pushed to one side in a way. Nobody seemed to be worried about how much emotion there is involved, how much you give to a baby. Whether you've given birth to it or not, your whole life is devoted to these little ones, and they are yours. I was afraid for a while—not for very long—and it doesn't worry me now because I know nothing can break the tie between my sons and me.

Some adopters explain their children's lack of interest in searching in terms of there being 'no need' because they already have a full and loving family life. That's a natural response, but I think it misunderstands the nature of the searcher's needs. Secure adopted adults who love their parents search, not to find something better (they know and value what they already have, which is why so many hesitate before initiating a search), but to fulfil a need to find out more about *themselves*. Motivations—and the way they are articulated—vary, but starting a search rarely has anything to do with adoptive parents.

Mothers perhaps have more reason to be apprehensive than fathers. Ted Roadhouse took a positive interest when his daughter told him she wanted to search for her birth mother.

I think I was generally encouraging and not in the least afraid or resentful. Clearly she had thought about it long and hard and it was definitely what she wanted to do. It was very much her decision. We are friends now and I hope we have got out of the parent–child relationship. Also, I must confess I was very curious to find out more about her mother, because of the good write-up she'd had from the agency. At the same time, I did sound a warning note.

Some adopted children find that their mothers are not interested in them and do not want to see them. This must be a massive put-down for the adopted daughter or son. A great disappointment. And then there's a well-known novel by P. D. James about an adopted child that found her mother was a murderess . . . well, I suppose that doesn't happen very often, but it does give emphasis to the reality that you never know what you are going to discover—good or bad.

Anne Houghton is quiet, determined and very proud of her family and her comfortable home. She has a satisfying career in education and a strong sense of her own worth. But she is haunted by the thought that her birth mother doesn't want to know her.

Anne had a very happy childhood and a good relationship with her parents, but felt strongly motivated to meet her birth mother, partly because of the circumstances of her adoption and what her mother had told her about it. Anne's was a private adoption arranged by her birth mother's father, an inspector at the bus depot where her adoptive father worked. But after giving her up, her birth mother continued to visit, coming round every Saturday afternoon to play with her. After some weeks her mother, worried that the girl would change her mind about the adoption, didn't open the door and after that she stopped coming.

When I was told that, it really coloured my whole view of my Mum. It meant that I hadn't just been cast aside like some other babies. My Mum was different, my Mum wasn't like that; she really didn't want to let me go, but she had to. And I'm like that, we're the same. I thought she was like me because she'd tried to keep in touch with me. I was convinced in my mind that this woman was an older version of me completely, right the way through. I thought, she's just sat there waiting for me to make the first move and as soon as I do . . .

Counselling prepared Anne for the possibility of a less positive outcome, but she was still devastated by the response when a tracing agency finally made contact with her mother. After a cautious initial response, the tracer had a call the following day from the woman's husband. He dismissed Anne as *'just an incident that happened years ago'* and made it clear the approach was unwelcome. This is very hard for Anne to accept.

I won't let it go. I will contact her one way or another. I would love to know my Dad's name. I'd like to know about health things, for my own sake, for my children's sake. The idea of meeting her wasn't to have a new Mum because my adoptive Mum and Dad are dead now, it wasn't that at all. I just wanted some answers.

She deserves to get them, and I hope her mother eventually finds the courage to give them. Despite Ted Roadhouse's fears, Anne's experience is relatively unusual. In the biggest UK study of adoption searches, conducted for the Children's Society by David Howe and Julia Feast in 2000, only 19 of a sample of 274 adopted people were rejected outright by a birth parent. Like Anne, these people felt frustrated, hurt and upset by the experience, but after time, understanding and acceptance replaced the hurt feelings. Frustration lingers because they never discover the reasons why their birth parent rejected them, and that must be hard to bear.

There is frustration, too, for the adopted person whose search stalls because information cannot be found, or appears to be blocked. Sylvia Sheridan floated her media company after starting the business from scratch in 1989. For a former television researcher on *This Is Your Life* who grew up in a poor single-parent family in the north-east, this is a huge achievement but no one who knows Sylvie is the least bit surprised. 'Focused' might have been coined to describe her. So it makes it all the more disappointing for her that she can't progress her adoption search because of lack of information.

She was born in 1948 to an Irish mother, adopted from a Catholic convent mother and baby home in Manchester and taken to join her two older adopted sisters in Newcastle. Soon after, her adoptive parents separated and she was brought up very happily with her mother and sisters, while remaining in touch with her father.

In 1991 I approached my local social services to try and find my birth mother. The social worker came to see me a couple of times and took all the details. The adoption had been handled by solicitors in Consett, County Durham. When she called on them, she said that all my adoption papers had disappeared, which was very unusual. I contacted the local Catholic church and said to the priest, 'Do you remember this adoption? Will you give me some information about it?' And he said, 'Well, all I can say is, while your

238

adoptive father is still alive, I really don't want to go into the details.' I sent a couple of letters subsequently but they were just ignored. Last year my adoptive father died. The priest came back to the wake and I said, 'Would you be prepared to help me now?' He said, 'Send me another letter and I'll do what I can.' I haven't heard anything since. The social worker said it was very unusual in her experience that my records had gone astray. 'The only thing I can think of,' she said, 'is that you must have been a priest's baby . . . it's almost as if you don't exist.'

Knowing Sylvie, she'll get to the bottom of it, but in the meantime she lives with uncertainty, conjecture and obfuscation. The Catholic Church and its clergy still seem to exercise considerable sway over what information is made available and what decades-old secrets are to be kept hidden. Sylvie's experience thus far bears out Ted Roadhouse's advice—that you have no idea what you're going to find when you set out on a search—but long-suppressed secrets have a habit of wriggling their way out into the light, sooner or later.

Sometimes these can come as a shock. As a mixed-race adoptee, Amanda wanted to trace her birth parents to find out more about her black heritage. The information given to her adoptive parents—that her white mother had had a relationship with a Nigerian medical student—turned out not to be true. She traced her birth mother easily but was upset to be told, via an intermediary, that she wanted no contact. Finally, Amanda's mother admitted she'd been violently

239

raped after a party and had no idea who the father was; she'd deliberately given the adoption authorities misleading information. This seems to compound Amanda's problems: her mother doesn't want to know her, she has discovered she is probably the product of rape, and she is further away than ever from knowing anything about her black origins. She was angry with her birth mother for withholding information and for rejecting her, but she has now managed to extract as much information as she feels she is ever going to get about the circumstances of her conception and adoption. As a result, she is more reconciled to what must be one of the worst situations an adopted person can find when tracing their origins. Importantly, she has not been bowed by the search experience.

All I wanted was the truth. I needed a sense of closure. I feel incredibly strong about it now. I'm very, very lucky in that I've got really good friends around me, and also Mum and Dad. I've had the support of Mum and Dad the whole way through—they've been brilliant.

Juliet, adopted from the NCAA in 1942, discovered from her search that everything she had been told about her birth parents by her adoptive mother was untrue.

I was told a whole load of codswallop about my background. I was told I was the daughter of an Irish maid and that my father came from Yorkshire. My adoptive mother told my [adoptive] cousins that, and they treated me like shit, there's no other word for it.

240

They all treated me like some lower form of humanity.

Juliet's search was unorthodox. In the early 1970s, her 18-month-old son was having unexplained convulsions and she was desperate to find out more about her medical history. The press was full of stories about the pros and cons of opening up birth records in the wake of Dr David Owen's failed Private Member's Bill that finally led to the access provisions of the 1975 Children Act. Juliet wrote to the *Daily Telegraph* about her need to search for her birth family and had dozens of replies from adopted people with widely different experiences of search and reunion. All encouraged her not to give up. She went back to the NCAA, and because her adoptive mother had been one of their Honorary Visitors, the General Secretary Hilary Halpin agreed to provide her with her birth mother's name—an unusual but strangely familiar one.

With the help of *Who's Who* and *Debrett's*, she discovered that her birth mother's family were aristocratic landowners, well known in the social circles her adoptive family moved in. Juliet had been the result of a 10-year affair. Her mother and father were both 29, but her maternal grandmother had threatened to cut her daughter off from the family completely if she kept the baby. Her mother had Juliet adopted, stayed part of the family and never married.

Juliet turned up on her mother's doorstep and was invited in. An affectionate relationship was established over the years, though her mother chose never to reveal Juliet's identity to other members of the family. Since her mother's death, though, Juliet has been welcomed by her many cousins and now feels she has found her 'real' family.

What of her father? She would love to know and has tried tracing him through a private tracing agency, but he has a common name and she knows nothing about him. She only has a photo of him and her mother together, outside the family estate in Sussex.

They look absolutely so in love and so happy in each other's company. We can only guess that Granny intervened because he probably wasn't good enough, which is very sad. The only person who I'm told would know is the butler, because the butler knew everything.

Juliet hasn't given up. She first attempted to find out more about her origins when she was 17. Over 40 years later, she still feels there is more she needs to know.

Life-changing events—the birth of a child, marriage, death—are often triggers to a search. For Paul Brotherton the trigger event was life-threatening. He had made half-hearted efforts to find his birth mother before, but a serious car accident made up his mind.

I remember lying there in the crash room with the nurses running round, probes all over me. All kinds of things go through your mind. Stupid things like never flown on Concorde, never been to America, never rode a Harley Davidson, and of course out of it comes, I wonder if my mother's still alive? I wonder what she'd be thinking now if she knew I was here in hospital like this? Once it's in your mind you start really thinking about it. That was a turning point and I thought I must put some real effort into tracing my mother. She might not want to know me—she's most probably got her own family—but if I trace her at least I can let her know who I am and then it's up to her whether she wants to take it any further.

Paul's experience is close to my own.

I contacted social services and they eventually found my file . . . and in the file was a letter from my grandmother, two or three letters from my mother, and when I read the letters, the way they were written, I was quite upset. There was this lady wondering what had happened to her son, even though it was just after she'd had me—1952, 1953—so I decided that I must find this lady, my mother, and let her know what had happened to me.

Social services made contact with Paul's mother, June, in Hove. After some hesitation on June's part and a period of letter-writing and exchanging photos, Paul and June finally met in a Brighton hotel. Paul laid on champagne, a huge bouquet and a bag full of small gifts—all in June's favourite pink.

The meeting was so special in a lot of ways. It filled an area that I didn't even know was empty. All of a sudden questions could be asked about me, about my life. The full story about why she had to have me adopted. I don't feel any malice about it, but I just wanted to know the details from her side . . . It started

243

to fill things up—things there that I didn't know, strange feelings. They talk about this word completeness, or closing the book. I don't know whether it closes the book, but it certainly fills a gap.

For June, it was her 'miracle'. For 50 years, she'd kept a photo of herself as a 1950s' teenager (bobby socks, ponytail) holding Paul as a tiny baby, covertly taken by another girl's boyfriend at the mother and baby home where she'd been banished by her mother. She was an 18-year-old professional ice-skater who'd fallen in love with a saxophone player—they met in the Tower Ballroom in Blackpool—but the young lovers' mothers got together and decided that this was not to be. June still isn't sure whether her boyfriend even knew she was pregnant.

Well it was, it was a miracle. I can see it all in my mind every day, him standing at that hotel and coming to greet me out the car, and how we hugged and kissed and cried. It's been about 18 months I think now, but to be quite truthful for the first six months after it happened, I used to wake up in the morning and I thought I'd dreamt it. Then I'd look at all my photographs all round my room and all his letters I've got in a pink folder, and I sit and read all his letters and I know it was true, but when you've waited 50 years, it's a long time . . .

Paul is tall and large and chatty and dominates the room; June is short and petite and chatty and dominates the room. They've spent the past 18 months getting used to each other and their new relationship, meeting other members of their

244

respective families. There have been ups and downs and, as in any lively extended family, there will be more. Reunions, as those who have successfully searched and found know, are not the end; they're the beginning.

*   *   *

Thus far, the legislation allowed one-way access only: adopted person to birth relative, not the other way round. So it was both more unusual and more difficult for mothers to trace the children they gave up for adoption. But there were exceptions.

When his first book was published I saw it in the library and I thought, that name rings a bell! I opened up the back cover, 'Born in London, raised in Essex', and of course the face. As soon as I saw his picture I knew it was him.

Bernard Cornwell's mother Dorothy 'found' the son she'd given up for adoption in 1944 when he first became an author of historical novels, a genre she loved. She wondered for years about trying to make contact with him, but doubts held her back.

Time was getting on and I thought, shall I write to him? And I thought, you write and you say, ooh, by the way, were you illegitimate and adopted at birth? If so, I may be your mother. OK, that puts it in a nutshell, but supposing you're not the one, and again perhaps you are and he doesn't want to know?

So she didn't take the initiative, but Bernard did.

As a child, he'd found the names and addresses of his birth parents in his father's open safe one day, but did nothing with the information for years.

I had known my real parents' names since I was 11, but had no particular desire to find them. I liked the idea of being unattached. I felt myself to be a clean slate, no family expectations, no ties—and, as a result of my upbringing, I had no particular fondness for family life either. I waited until I was nearly 60 before looking for them, and then only because, if they were still alive, it would probably prove to be my last chance. And by then, I was curious. I was not particularly curious before that. I wanted nothing from them, needed nothing from them and also suspected that they felt the same about me.

Bernard, who lives in America, found his father first.

Visiting Vancouver, which is close to where my real father lives, I decided to see if he was still alive. I wrote to him, promising that if he ignored my letter then I would make no further effort to meet him, but he answered and so we met. It was, of course, a revelation . . . I found two half-brothers and a half-sister. The biggest revelation was simply being among people who were like me. They snort when they laugh, as I do. I look like them. I felt immediately at home. The overwhelming thing is the sense of being among your own people, and that was extraordinary after 57 years. For most folk it's normal, but for adoptees it's a strange experience.

It took longer to find Dorothy; his original

information was almost useless as she'd married and moved several times. A newspaper appeal drew a blank, then the *Mail on Sunday* took on the search and two journalists turned up on Dorothy's doorstep. *'The penny dropped, straight away,'* she says. Their reunion, at a discreet London hotel, was arranged and attended by the newspaper. These are not ideal conditions for such an emotionally charged occasion, but mother and son share a reserve, a stoicism, about such things. Dorothy describes the reunion as *'strange, but no restraints . . . it was lovely'*. Bernard describes it as 'interesting'.

I know that's an inadequate word, but by waiting so long, and because perhaps I'm not aware of any emotional holes that needed plugging, and because I've been happily married for a long time and because I'm not unsuccessful, both reunions were bereft of emotional freight. The dominating sensations for both were humour and generosity. There was immediate acceptance—on both sides I hope. There was probably more emotion meeting Dorothy, though looking back I see she was determined not to show it, and my childhood taught me to be wary of expressing emotion, so I always disappoint people by telling them, truthfully, that neither meeting was marked by tears of excessive joy. They were, nevertheless, deeply satisfying, and the more we see of each other, the deeper the satisfaction.

The hardest thing about his search, Bernard says, was wondering whether he really wanted to go through with it. But he's glad he did and, though it happened later in his life, he believes the timing

247

was right.

I met my parents when I was an adult, almost a pensioner. We met as grown-ups. What is delicious is that I like them both, very much, and feel far more strongly about them (is this love?) than I ever felt about my adoptive parents. I feel comfortable with them, admire them, and look forward to their company. Above all I'm hugely grateful that they had a disastrous affair so long ago and gave me life! A happy ending? Yes.

*   *   *

Doreen Larsen and Patricia Basquill both managed, against the odds, to track down the children they gave up, unwillingly, for adoption. But the longed-for reunions have not translated into happy endings for them.

With some difficulty, Doreen traced her son Michael, whose adoptive parents had told him his mother had died soon after he was born. After an uneasy reunion (Doreen believes in retrospect they should have had a mediator to help prepare them) and a correspondence, the letters suddenly stopped.

The last letter I got from Michael was on my 64th birthday and I answered it. After that I never heard any more, not a word, and that's over eight years since. The longer I go on, the more the hope diminishes. I don't know what Michael thinks; I can only express what I think, and I can't understand why the sudden stop. Have his parents had any influence, did his new girlfriend have any influence? I miss him.

I can't tell you how much; nobody can say how much they miss their own, not when they love them.

Because her daughter was adopted in Scotland, Patricia Basquill found her somewhat easier to trace. With the help of a Scottish researcher, she made contact with her daughter Elaine. The joy of their first telephone conversation was tempered by the realisation for both that everything Elaine had been told about her original background was untrue. She believed her birth father had been Jewish when he was in fact Catholic; that she'd been named Helen not Elaine; even the birth weight was wrong. And given Patricia's past experience of and antipathy to social workers, it didn't help that this was the profession her daughter had chosen. It was not an auspicious start, and after a couple more phone conversations, contact ceased.

My feelings now are very different to what they were when I began. I've learnt an awful lot in the past 25 years. I've reunited three and a half thousand adoptees and natural parents, so I know what the reality is. Whether I'd actually want to meet her now . . . it would be interesting to be able to tell her the truth. Up to this point she doesn't want to know the truth. Her file, all the paperwork is waiting for her in Scotland. It's in a box. I wrote and told Elaine, Pandora's Box is waiting in Scotland. You've got instant access to it any time you want. So far she doesn't want to open Pandora's Box and she's leaving it closed, and I think she possibly will until her adoptive parents are dead. And that might be the first time that she actually faces the reality about her own past, the truth.

Truth is a valuable and sometimes disputed property in adoption stories. On Elaine's side all is silence. Meanwhile Patricia's pain is evident in all she says and does in her quest to avenge what she sees as a great evil and injustice.

*   *   *

Liz McCabe comes from a large Belfast Catholic family. When she became pregnant at 21 in 1969, her parents were horrified and adoption was a foregone conclusion. But Liz never got over the loss of her baby daughter, whom she named Anne Marie.

I had seven sons, but she was always missing. I just needed to put my arms around her; I needed to see her face. I used to pray for that, night and day: please God, let me hold her before I die.

Anne Marie was adopted by a Protestant–Catholic couple who decided to emigrate to Queensland, Australia in 1972 as the Troubles in Northern Ireland escalated. Her parents had made a pact never to reveal that she was adopted, but it all came out when she was 16 and doing a school project on family trees. She was puzzled and upset, but there was no discussion and it was all 'brushed under the carpet'. It wasn't until she had her first child that she started to think seriously about her birth mother.

I thought, there just has to be a story. I'd really love to know why she gave me up and what happened. When I gave birth I remember holding this baby in my arms, sitting in this chair, thinking: 'I've just got to know.' I thought, how can someone give this away. You know there has to be a really, really good reason for it, and that's when I started to think I needed to find out why. Did she love me or was it—could it have been—a rape? It could have been a one-night stand, it could have been anything. You have all these things in your mind. But I still felt as though it wasn't something I could broach with my parents because I still wasn't able to talk to them about it and I didn't want to hurt them either. And I just thought no, it's not the right thing to do, so I left it.

She waited until she was 30 and her mother had died before starting her search. Her father told her everything he could remember about what they knew (though crucially, he got Liz's maiden name wrong) and she set off with the help of a genealogist. After a number of setbacks, she finally spoke to Liz on the phone.

I remember thinking, oh my God, she sounds just like my Aunt Dorothy . . . she had the West Belfast accent the same as my Dad had, the same as all my Aunties had. I just felt like it was so normal. I think we were on the phone for three-and-a-half hours or something that night, just firing questions at each other. My heart was beating 100 miles an hour, but it was very, very natural and very easy and there wasn't anything I was afraid to tell her, and she was happy to answer all my questions.

Six months and many three-hour phone calls later,

251

Anne Marie flew to Belfast to meet Liz and her family. Mother and daughter both talk about the sense of completeness the reunion experience gave them.

I can remember her walking up and I was looking into her eyes and saying, they're my eyes, you know. It just all made sense, it all fitted into place then.

It's not easy to lose a baby. Then, all of a sudden this 34-year-old woman appears in front of you—that's your baby, handed back to you again. It was just a whole loss of years and it was terrible, but I have to thank God for being able to see her face again, and being able to hold her again.

The reunion was such a success, Anne Marie and her family left Australia for Belfast in 2003 for a minimum of two years. Developing relationships with a new family in a new country while dealing with the doubts and fears of her adoptive family on the other side of the world has not been easy. Adopted people always feel they are in the middle of a tug-of-war in these situations, however sensitive and caring the parties are, and the extreme distance in this case must make things particularly difficult for Anne Marie. But the joy of finding another extended family where she has been made so welcome and where she feels so comfortable has made it unquestionably worthwhile.

*   *   *

In all these stories, things are much more

complicated than they appear from a brief synopsis. The people involved have to reconcile their own conflicting feelings and deal with the emotional needs, jealousies, anxieties and fears of the loved ones around them. Searching is a high-risk business that can bring huge rewards, but it also has costs. Some searches have frustrating, disappointing or painful outcomes, but the 2000 Children's Society study found that a large majority of the adopted people who had a reunion with a birth relative, whether they had initiated the search or not, found the experience positive and worthwhile.

Tracing facilities in the UK are no longer a one-way street. After much discussion in the 1990s, the Adoption and Children Act 2002 finally made provision for mothers to have limited statutory access to the children they gave up. From 2006, new intermediary agencies ('Adoption Support Agencies') came on stream to make contact with adopted people on their behalf. If contact is not wanted then, in theory at least, the search ends. As with previous radical changes to the law, there are concerns about how it will work in practice. Some adoption workers are concerned that an approach on behalf of a birth relative may be distressing and would compromise an adopted person's freedom to decide whether and when to search. On the other hand, there are still many thousands of mothers who relinquished children in the last 60 years because of social, moral and parental pressures, for whom information and contact would help close a painful episode in their lives.

Bernard Cornwell's mother Dorothy had no doubts.

I think it's great, I really do. You never forget a child you've given birth to. Never ever. It's always there. I was fortunate that I knew Bernard had made a success of his life. If you're in a position where you never know, that must be awful.

But a 93-year-old former Barnardo's adoption worker rang me specially to say she'd been giving it a lot of thought and had decided it was not a good thing. She was worried that greater access could be abused.

People are too keen on their own rights these days, and tend to forget their responsibilities to others.

Balancing conflicting rights—in this case the right to know against another's right to privacy—is always difficult. Similar debates went on in the run-up to the legislation change in the 1970s. As with every other aspect of adoption policy, we won't really know whether it's the right thing to do until at least a generation hence, but that's not a good reason for doing nothing. As we learn more about the effects and outcomes of adoption policy during the last century, we have a duty to act on that knowledge to do better in future. It took 75 years to discover that secrecy doesn't work and that separated families usually benefit from shared information and the opportunity of contact. After listening to the testimony of so many mothers, I believe extending that opportunity to birth parents is a form of natural justice denied for far too long.

254

13

ENDING?

A quiet close in Hanwell in spring. The trees are in leaf and everything looks swollen with new growth. Fiona and I park the car a discreet distance from the sheltered flats and look for the start of the rough river path that leads down to the Brent. I know it's there: I came for a recce on a particularly bleak January afternoon. Now there is a solid bank of thigh-high undergrowth, the kind of mildly menacing weedage that grows on untended urban riverbanks.

We dither and giggle a bit, then hack our way through where I guess the path might be, the Co-op carrier bag weighing me down. The path, such as it is, comes to a natural stop after 100 yards or so. We are lower now, at the foot of a steep bank of vegetation that separates the back of the flats from the river. We're surrounded by giant gunnera, dwarfed by nature. To the right the traffic on the Uxbridge Road seems more distant than usual. On the far bank and above us, the blue bulk of the hospital. But down here just the squabbling ducks, the birds, the Brent—not really a river but a sprawling stream—and us.

More nervous giggling, then the serious business of the Co-op bag. Inside, a cheap cardboard box. Inside the box a plastic urn. Inside the urn our mother's ashes.

'Will you do it or shall I?'

'You do it.'

'Oh God. Here goes then.'

I turn out the contents. Some settle on the gunnera leaves, and a fine mist flies off on the breeze to the right of us. It is secluded, green and peaceful.

'You're home,' we say to the wind.

Afterwards we go back up the bank and call on Syd and Eileen for milky Nescafé in china cups. There we talk about Marjorie and how we all miss her.

*   *   *

In the months after Marjorie's death, I felt a strong need to write about her and the story of our reunion, and I took a short sabbatical from work to do some research. I was conscious of the big gaps in her life that I knew nothing about. The only person with a direct link to her past was her old friend, Betty. They were at school together but had lost touch for a long period between the 1950s and the late 1980s. I'd spoken to Betty on the phone but we'd never met; she and Ron weren't able to come to the funeral at the last minute. I was sure she could tell me more about Marjorie's early life that would perhaps explain why she ended up having two illegitimate children. I asked if I could come and see them.

Marjorie was always telling me how Betty and Ron went on a lot of long holidays to distant places, so I expected them to be rather comfortably off. Their address certainly sounded large and rural, but when I got there it was a small semi-detached bungalow on a sprawling estate on the edge of a Sussex country town. They were welcoming and kind, and I felt at home as soon as I recognised Ron's landscapes on the walls. We settled down with cups of tea.

'There was me, Marjorie, Vera Paxton from over the corn chandlers, and Peter from the cycle shop. We all went round together. I think it was because we were all only children.'

She'd looked out an old photo album to show me.

'Here we are in a school play. We were at Gipsy Road School then. Marjorie went to Salters Hill Elementary School on Norwood Hill and left at 14. I think her first job was at Eyre and Spottiswood, the publishers. I went on to the grammar school and we lost touch a bit after that. We met again later though.'

What was Marjorie like?

'Thin, like her father. When she was younger she had long hair in ringlets done with rags like they used to in those days. Fair, mousy hair. Nice hair. Her mother was quite often poorly and so we used to take Marjorie with us on trips, me and my Mum and Dad. We'd get the tram or the bus into Brixton, you know, to the shops, or into the country sometimes. She was very close to her mother and used to nurse her when she was ill. I think Marjorie was lost when she died. Here she is at our wedding.'

Smart, coat open, standing by the happy couple.

'Did you know about me and what happened?'

'Yes, we knew about you.'

Then she seemed to start talking about something completely different.

'We've got so much stuff up in the attic. Ron was up there the other day sorting some of it out. Tons

257

of stuff up there. I hate to throw anything away, don't I Ron?'

She made to get up.

'Anyway, I found a couple of letters Marjorie wrote me years ago. I thought you might like to have them.'

She went into the next room and came back with two small envelopes, one stamped and on black-edged mourning stationery, and a smaller, hand-delivered note. I put my cup down to take them. They looked and handled like museum pieces. I opened the smaller of the two and took out the single sheet inside. There was Marjorie's round, careful hand.

13 January 1952
My Dear Betty,

I am so very pleased with your news of a son, did you want a boy? Anyway, you will love it just the same, whether boy or girl. I am very pleased for you. Hope you are feeling a little stronger now. When you are about again I would like to come & see you, there is so much to say, I cannot write it all on paper. Am feeling more myself now, and have just started a new job, but it has been a real fight & I just long to have my Baby, but I know at the moment that is just impossible, anyway I know she is being well cared for & loved. It has been a terrible chapter in my life, but I must do the best I can, and start afresh. George has been very good & decent to me. I do not know what I should have done without him.

Am giving this letter to your Mum as I do not know what hospital you are in. Remember me to Ron, I bet he is thrilled to have a son.

Will say bye-bye for this time, lots of love & a big

kiss for the 'Babe'.
  Yours
  Marjorie xxxx

Oh God. I opened the second, on mourning stationery.

24 February 1952
My Dearest Betty,
  Firstly I must say how very sorry I am to learn of your Dear Dad's passing, it is terribly sad, & such a shock to us, I only learnt of it yesterday.
  There is nothing very much Betty, I can say, but try & be brave, you still have your Mum, & I know she will be a great comfort to you Dear.
  Thank you for your nice letter, I will ring you as soon as I can & have a chat to you, there is such a lot to say. I am longing to see Michael, I know he is a Darling.
  I am not feeling too bad, but I shall never be the same again Dear, & there is that terrible emptiness, which I shall never fill, I just long to have my Babe, but that is just not possible, so must just be content with a memory.
  Please excuse more now Betty. Lots of love to you & keep your chin up.
  Yours Marjorie
  xxxx

I couldn't speak for tears. Even after 50 years in an attic they reeked of her desperation. Clinging on to the proprieties of social intercourse. Sending warm congratulations to Betty on the birth of her first child, even as weeks before she'd had to give hers up. No one congratulated *her*. Conveying

259

condolences just as she was coming to terms with the fact that her baby wasn't ever coming back to her. Impossible, incomprehensible cruelty.

Such a lot to say. And no one to say it to. She was obviously so full of pain she longed to talk to someone about it. Who? Her father didn't want to know. *You've made your bed.* It would be unfair to impose such a burden on Betty, recently bereaved and with a new baby. So she kept it inside.

George knew. Who was George? Betty didn't know (or couldn't remember, or didn't want to say). I assumed it was the same George Marjorie spoke of from Fire Service days, the older man and father figure. It would fit. It didn't sound as if George was my father. *Very good & decent to me* didn't sound like 'Peter White'.

I had no stomach for further interrogation. I apologised for crying and we chatted about neutral topics like Michael and their travels. It was enough that Betty had given me these precious, terrible letters. I took them home and put them carefully with the others.

*   *   *

I frittered away my sabbatical and wrote nothing, but I did spend some time in south London, finding out more about Castlebar or, to call it by its proper name, The Princess Alice Emergency Hostel for Mothers and Babies, where I spent the first six weeks of my life with Marjorie.

First, I went to have a look at 217 Gipsy Road. Yes, there was the old Board school, just as Betty had said. A row of shops: perhaps this was where

260

Vera Paxton's corn chandlers was and, later, the tobacconist where Fiona's putative father worked. Along the road 217 was the right-hand part of a four-storey mid-Victorian pair, originally substantial villas but divided now, as in Marjorie's day, into flats. She'd spent the first 40 years of her life in the ground floor flat. In the basement below lived a postman where, she said, sacks of stolen mail were subsequently discovered. Though the accommodation wouldn't have been large, and they probably had to share a bathroom with other families, the house was still a cut above Bungalow Road. Once imposing, it now looked worn down from generations of multiple occupation. But I could see her there, in her rag ringlets.

On, up to Castlebar.

Close to Crystal Palace, Sydenham Hill is one of the highest points in London, with far views out to the Kentish Weald and the Surrey hills. Developed in the late 19th century for City gentry, its houses are large and ugly, with self-important towers and turrets, and extensive grounds with their views to the rear. Many have already gone, destroyed by Hitler's bombs and 1960s' developers, replaced by blocks of flats. Sydenham Hill is a quiet, wide, sweeping road and you can easily imagine cabs and carriages clattering along its length and caped servants going about their masters' business. And 50 years later, young women with big Silver Cross prams taking the high south London air.

I didn't expect to find anything left of Castlebar, but it was all still there, down to the engraved name in Gothic lettering on the gatepost. Easily the ugliest building in the road, it had the *de rigueur* towers and turrets but presented a flat, grey, institutional face to the street. It was now a private nursing home for the elderly infirm. I tried to picture her there but it looked cold and unwelcoming, unlike the place she had described with some warmth and affection. It didn't look much like a sanctuary.

The local studies section of Lewisham library was overseen by a fierce woman who demanded quiet, no bags on desks, no phones, strict discipline at all times. Then she went off to lunch and was replaced by a much more sympathetic man who led me to their cuttings file.

Lewisham Journal 17 March 1933

QUEEN MARY'S VISIT TO SYDENHAM.
-
NURSERY TRAINING CENTRE OPENED.
-
BEAUTIFUL BUILDING AT SYDENHAM HILL.
-
Loyal Greetings from Residents.

These were expansive times when newsprint was cheap, circulation booming, and no self-respecting sub-editor used one headline where four would do.

Sydenham gave Queen Mary a right royal welcome on Wednesday afternoon . . .

So some clichés don't change then.

. . . when Her Majesty visited Sydenham-hill to open Castlebar, which is now a nursery training centre and hostel for children under the auspices of the National

Children Adoption Association.

On it went for 29 column inches, in the florid prose of the time, detailing all 127 dignitaries present, their designations and their wives. Mrs Stanley Baldwin was there, along with the gloriously named Loveday and Garland Bullivant, Mrs J. Peppercorn and Miss Violet Dalgleish (Bedford College of Dancing).

. . . After a tour of the hostel, which seemed to give Her Majesty intense satisfaction, she partook of tea in the matron's sitting-room, at the close of which she said Good-bye to those around her and, as she left the building, she passed through a guard of honour formed by the students of the Princess Alice Training Schools, the band in the meantime playing the National Anthem . . .

And there she was, coming down the steps, Queen Mary, stately as the ship, dead animal round her shoulders to ward off the March winds, fresh corsage on her ample chest—a living testament to the benefits of good living and Spirella corsetry.

*   *   *

Fiona and I had grown closer since Marjorie's death. When she and Steve moved to Surrey to be teacher–houseparents in a State boarding school, it meant we could see a bit more of each other. They now had two girls, and with my brother's two, I had two pairs of nieces of similar ages. I quite liked being an Auntie, and it was a special pleasure to be able to give Fiona occasional treats. We went to a

263

sponsors' evening at Ballet Rambert where she could see and meet dancers she'd always admired, to Matthew Bourne productions and girlie lunch and shopping trips. It was something neither of us had had the opportunity to share before so we appreciated it all the more; it was a novelty we never tired of.

'Supposing we'd grown up together. What would our relationship be like now?' Fiona asked at lunch one day.

'Terrible probably. We'd have fought like cat and dog and then stopped speaking in our twenties.'

She agreed, laughing, but then looked wistful.

'I wish we had, though.'

Fiona, in my view, had a rather romanticised idea of family life borne out of the loneliness of the only-child experience, but I knew what she meant. We felt the loss of years together. But if we had stayed together, it would have meant growing up with Marjorie, and that raised all kinds of other questions. We'd have had a much more difficult time and might even have risked being taken away from her at any moment. Would she have been a good Mum under those conditions? Would we have had the same opportunities and turned out different people? Might we have turned against her? We agreed we didn't really want to think too much about that.

*   *   *

In September 2002 I was halfway out of the door to work one morning when Bevan remembered there had been an answerphone message for me the day before from someone he didn't recognise, but he

264

thought they said they were from Walker Close. Probably Eileen, though I couldn't think why she'd be ringing me. Bevan said it didn't sound urgent, so I left it till the evening to play the message back. It was from the warden at Walker Close. Would I ring her?

Things had changed since Marjorie's day. There was no longer a live-in warden—she came in during office hours only, so it was the following day at work before I got to speak to her.

'A Recorded Delivery letter has come addressed to Marjorie. The new tenant at 54 thought it looked important so he brought it to me. Do you want me to open it?'

Well yes, of course. It was a bit late for outstanding bills; Marjorie had been dead 18 months. Probably sent in error.

'It's from East Midlands Social Services . . .'

*　　　*　　　*

I'm ashamed to say I laughed. It might have been a mild hysterical reaction.

'. . . shall I read it to you?'

Absolutely no need, my dear, but yes, go ahead anyway.

Dear Ms Heppelthwaite,

I have been asked by a third party to try and trace Marjorie Phyllis HEPPELTHWAITE, who was approximately 35 years old in June 1960. At that time she lived at 217 Gipsy Road, West Norwood, London SE27, and worked as a telephonist/receptionist.

I have some information that may be of interest, if you are able to identify with the above information.

265

Well, the age was wrong but there was no question it was Marjorie.

'OK,' I said, trying to stop myself shaking, 'that's really helpful, thank you for taking the trouble to ring me. I think I know what it might be about. Can you give me the contact number and then just pop the letter in the post to me? Thanks.'

No solid walls in my office this time. I was a part-time consultant now and only warranted a glass-fronted cubbyhole. I hated the way a bank of filing cabinets outside blocked me off from everyone else on the floor but now I was glad of them. I put my head in my hands. Three times. Oh you poor, poor woman. Then I rang the number. Sorry, they said, Linda Beaumont is away on a course till Thursday.

*   *   *

I went to lunch with an ex-colleague, a plain-speaking Yorkshireman, and shared my morning's news. 'Well of course, there could be more. Many more,' he said, and I had to agree there was a chance he could be right. She hadn't told me about Fiona; she hadn't told either of us about number three. There could be numbers four or more out there. Or perhaps we weren't numbers one and two after all.

I was desperate to tell Fiona, but decided to try to think it through before breaking the news. It was possible she'd have the same angry reaction I had when I first learnt about her. Once again I had

266

privileged access to incendiary information that, sooner or later, I'd have to impart to the person it would be most likely to upset. There was so much to think about, I had to write it down to try and make some sense of it.

There is the distinct possibility of a third child. And as Peter put it in that straight-out-with-it way of his, there could be many more. Which there could. We used to joke about eight (how we laughed). We found nothing among her things to give anything away— about any of us. Did I find a baby picture when we cleared Bungalow Road? I can't remember. I may have imagined it. Maybe there were pictures, documents and letters that just got thrown away with all the rotting remains of her old life.

Like the children we still are, we need the certainty of knowing who our family are. My Number One Daughter. She said it constantly and I believed it. There was me, Gillian, and then as I soon discovered, there was Linda five years later. But what if I wasn't Number One? There could have been others before me. Where are they? Do they know? What more is there that we don't know about our mother?

The really interesting thing, putting our emotional feelings to one side for a moment, is how someone— not someone, Marjorie—could live with that past, all the turmoil and unhappiness, and cope. She coped by part-forgetting, part-suppressing, part-willing things to be better. And she shared that so rarely with me. Gave hardly anything away.

1960 I think the letter said. That would figure. Just before she moved to Bungalow Road. But she would have been almost 40. No time to have your third illegitimate child. Was it the same agency? They would have been building up quite a file on Miss Heppelthwaite. How did single women have a sex life before easy contraception without having babies and then giving them away? It's all unimaginably bleak and horrible. Then she moved in with Bill and there were no more babies. I presume.

Tomorrow I'll speak to the social worker and find out more. Chances are it will be another girl. Except she will be a girl of 42. And a new dimension to our family history opens.

I tell Fiona. In the back garden, on the phone.

'Are you sitting down? I've got some news.'

'Oooh, exciting! What?'

'I think we may have another sibling.'

She immediately gets the wrong end of the stick.

'What . . .? You mean you're pregnant?'

'Er, I don't think so. I'm 50, remember?'

'Yes, sorry, I'm being stupid. A sibling. You mean a brother or sister?'

'Exactly.'

'Oh my Lord! How do you know?'

'A letter came for Marjorie from their social worker. I haven't been able to get hold of her yet but she's back tomorrow. I'll find out more then.'

Silence.

'Fiona? Are you still there?'

'You won't go off me, will you?'

'Don't be ridiculous, you're my Sis.'

'Why didn't Marge tell us? How could she not tell us?'

I know exactly how she feels at that moment.

So much for the carefully thought-through, measured approach. I couldn't do it because I didn't feel measured myself. There were too many disturbing questions. I could accept another younger sibling—I'd been through the pain barrier already with Fiona—but I was haunted by the idea that there might be others. What if I wasn't the first, as I'd always thought? Marjorie was 31 when she had me, plenty of scope for an earlier child. Or children. What if there *were* eight? Oh, for God's sake woman, get a grip. Concentrate on the matter in hand. What if it's a brother? That *would* be a novelty. It wasn't likely, as I knew only half as many men trace as women.

But the horror of what Marjorie went through undercut everything else. She'd obviously lied about her age: the shame of a third illegitimate child in her 40th year would have been almost too much to bear. In the mother and baby home with the 18-year-olds. How could she have gone through it all again? But that was the price you paid for any kind of grown-up relationship with a man before the 1970s if you weren't married. If your primitive contraception failed (assuming either of you used any) and you got pregnant, your choices were all cruel: an illegal or a self-induced abortion; giving up your babies for adoption; or battling to bring up the product of your shame for all to see, in the face of towering social and practical difficulties. No wonder there were so many old maids.

*　　　*　　　*

Linda Beaumont was very apologetic that she hadn't been available for several days. I told her not to worry. I wanted to avoid another round-the-

269

houses conversation with a distant social worker so I dived straight in.

'This may sound a bit strange, but I've been here before,' I said. 'I'm Marjorie Heppelthwaite's daughter and there are already two of us. I've got a feeling you're about to tell me there's a third.'

Not a beat missed.

'Yes, that's right. Your mother didn't tell you?'

No, she didn't, but no matter, I was getting used to it by now.

'Yes, you have another sister, born in April 1960 and named Elizabeth. She's called Hazel now and she's a lovely person. I'm sure she'll be thrilled to know she has two sisters. I know she'd very much like contact with you both and your mother.'

Oh dear.

'I'm really sorry. Our mother died nearly two years ago.'

If only shame and vanity hadn't made Marjorie take five years off her age, Hazel might have started her search earlier and got to her in time.

*   *   *

A week later Fiona and I are pacing up and down my living room like a couple of nervous teenagers, waiting for Hazel to arrive with Linda Beaumont. The photos we've already had from her show definite echoes of Marjorie in a large, jolly young woman with masses of dark curls, different again in colouring from either of us. We already know a little about each other's families, including the amazing fact that Fiona and Hazel both have 12-year-old daughters born within days of each other and with the same name. Now, here we

270

are, after agonies about what to wear. ('*Nothing ostentatious, no flashy jewellery.*' '*Speak for yourself, I don't own any flashy jewellery.*' '*Alright then, we'll dress for comfort.*' '*God no, we don't want to look like a couple of drabbies . . .*')

I've banished Bevan till lunchtime. He's rather hurt, and I'm not sure my rationale is entirely sound. We'll be a houseful of weeping women and we need to do this on our own, initially at least. I'd much rather he's not there for the weepy bits.

There's a lot of nervous giggling.

'What if we don't like her?'

'More to the point, what if she doesn't like *us*?'

'Have we got plenty of tissues handy?'

We've already had enough coffee to be completely wired and I'm thinking of looking out the cooking brandy. Fiona is at the window.

'Oh my God, a taxi.'

We hug each other quickly. Whatever happens now, we say, we've got each other.

I'm first to the door. Linda Beaumont comes in as Hazel pays the taxi.

'Hello, new sister!' We stand in the hall and embrace for what seems like 20 minutes, while Fiona exchanges pleasantries about the journey with Linda. Hazel is crying already. I feel happy but conscious of the lack of space in our tiny hall, where the four of us are packed round the front door. If this were a film, the camera would be circling round us in that irritating way, but luckily there's no room for a camera. Finally we move into the living room where Fiona too gets the chance to welcome Hazel, who is still crying. She seems entirely overwhelmed, hardly able to speak. Our hearts and our tissues go out to her.

271

Then we sit down and talk at the poor girl for about two hours. About Marjorie. About Bill Russell and Bungalow Road and the rolls of dust and the saucepans of fat. About how she loved Walker Close and the birds and squirrels, and Syd and Eileen. About the funeral. The stories of our own searches and how we felt when we found one another. And how Marjorie would have loved Hazel because, of the three of us, she is most like her.

Hazel composes herself and tells the story of her own search. Just like Fiona's, it is a series of tantalising chances and 'what-ifs'. Her husband Dave finds the Walker Close address on an electoral roll website even though Marjorie has been dead for nearly two years; a week later, her name has gone. What if the tenant at 54 had just binned the letter instead of giving it to the warden? What if the warden hadn't still got my details on file?

And, intriguingly, what if Hazel had known Marjorie's true age—would she have started the search earlier?

'I really don't know about that. Would I have felt ready? You search when you feel ready, don't you?'

Her Mum and Dad are supportive and interested and she tells us that she too arrived with an expensive trousseau. She knows even less about her father than we know about ours. Another dubious name—Paddy Jacobs—who lived 'somewhere in Scotland'. It sounds desperately sad. Her adoption society is different—the grim-sounding Mission of Hope in Croydon—and she is distraught to hear about the letters from Marjorie

272

we both have on our files.

'But I haven't got anything like that . . . why haven't I?'

I put forward my thesis, not just because I want to console her, but because I believe it.

'She couldn't risk it. Immediately after she'd given you up, she left Gipsy Road and moved in with Bill Russell. She didn't want him to know about her past; he probably would've thrown her out. So she couldn't afford to have letters about babies coming to Bungalow Road from the Mission of Hope. She just had to pull the shutters down. But I bet she thought about you constantly.'

We hand the tissues round again. Bevan comes back from his exile and greets Hazel warmly.

'There's no mistaking whose daughter *you* are! Come on, let's see all the little Heppelthwaites together.'

We giggle and pose like children. If only Marjorie could see us. Hazel gives us both little presents. We give her one of Marjorie's prized teddies and one of her rings, probably originally her mother's, an Edwardian setting with tiny diamond chips. She seems very affected by the gesture.

'Are you sure?'

'Absolutely. She would have wanted you to have it.'

We're not at all surprised when it fits her perfectly and looks right.

The champagne comes out. 'To the Heppelthwaites!' The lunch I've made hardly gets touched; high emotion has taken away our appetite. This is a source of regret to the three of us, as we all enjoy food rather too much. We go outside for photographs.

'This must be a nice change from your usual social work routine?' I say to Linda. She laughs. 'I should say. I love this bit of the work. I've just come from three years in child protection—you don't get happy endings like this.'

I nod sympathetically into my tiramisu. Happy it undoubtedly is, but I don't believe for a moment that it's an ending. Adoption stories aren't like that.

*   *   *

In October 2003 Hazel came to stay with me for a few days and we went on an odyssey to Marjorie's old south London haunts. We saw 217 Gipsy Road, which must have changed very little since she played in the street in her rag ringlets in the 1920s. We accosted a tenant outside the building. He was hesitant to talk about the flat and who lived there until we assured him we weren't from the council. We saw Bungalow Road, which was just as shabby as when I first clapped eyes on it more than 10 years before. The terraces were now dominated by 57 different varieties of uPVC window, and the front curtains at number 13 looked suspiciously like the ones we'd left there in 1992.

And we went up to Sydenham Hill. We wanted to see Castlebar, but there was another big house on the Hill that had a new significance. We'd been looking at Hazel's adoption file the night before and noticed that her medical report had been written from 'Belt Wood', Sydenham Hill. It seemed likely that this was the Mission of Hope's mother and baby home where Marjorie had stayed

274

until Hazel's adoption, and it was literally down the road from Castlebar. Gracious houses on Sydenham Hill had a curious attraction for Marjorie.

We rang the bell at Castlebar, and an unseen care assistant pushed the buzzer that let us in. It was lunchtime and the elderly residents were being fed in the large lounge looking out over the grounds and the Kentish views at the back. We walked in; no one stopped us or asked who or what we wanted. We looked into the lounge, wandered up and down the hall and went up the wide staircase that Marjorie polished with pride in 1951. I looked for a plaque to commemorate that March day in 1933 when Queen Mary had opened the National Children Adoption Association training nursery and babies' home, but it must have gone long ago. Where once were babies, now there were only old people in chairs, in bed, incapable. We spoke to no one, no one spoke to us, and after about 10 minutes we left. I couldn't see her there, not even old and in a chair.

Then down the road to Belt Wood, well hidden in wooded gardens with its own gatehouse at the top of the drive. It was once a fine house with unusual bow windows at the front, now neglected, though there was a car in the drive and signs of habitation—humans and horses—round the back. Again we rang (security camera over the front door) but there was no response. When you ring doorbells you can usually sense whether there's anyone in: you feel the vibrations somehow. There was no one in this big house. We walked round and admired its splendid garden front, now faded and peeling, and Hazel took photographs of the place where she'd started life with Marjorie. Intrigued, we asked about it at the pub next door, but all they could tell us was they had a terrible problem with rats coming in from there.

Then we went to Croydon to the address Hazel had for the Mission of Hope from her file. We weren't sure we had the right place: an anonymous building in a suburban road that looked as if it could once have been a residential institution of some kind, but time was getting on. We needed to get back round the M25 so we didn't venture in.

It was a strange, sad journey. We were glad we did it, and I think Hazel found it a comfort, but it didn't tell us anything about Marjorie that we didn't already know. The ghosts still lingered around Gipsy and Bungalow Roads, but all visible signs of a once bustling adoption industry had long since gone.

*   *   *

I now know a lot more about adoption than I do about Marjorie. There are parts of her that will remain forever private, unknowable. In social work terms, she was something of a phenomenon, a 'multiparous' mother, a serial producer of illegitimate children, a 'repeater' as the moral welfare workers called them, condemned to further pregnancies in a subconscious attempt to replace the child she'd lost before. Women who 'fell' more than once were not unknown (a former social worker remembered a 26-year-old client with her sixth unsupported pregnancy) but they were unusual. Apart from anything else, until the late 1960s when babies for adoption started to

276

become scarce, mothers of second illegitimate children were turned away by many agencies, particularly the denominational ones, for fear of being seen to encourage immorality.

Marjorie was untypical in another important respect. She wasn't young. Most of the 'girls' in mother and baby homes in the 1950s to the 1970s really were girls, or young women in their early twenties. As one child care officer remembers:

The typical unwed mum I came across was about 18–25, working in a factory, shop or office. She wasn't promiscuous. Her object in life was marriage and a family; she saw herself as being let down by the boyfriend she'd hoped would marry her, described herself as having 'slipped up', and where nowadays she could seek abortion, she saw adoption as her only chance of achieving marriage. She accepted, maybe reluctantly, permanent separation from her baby and a chance to put her 'trouble' behind her and start a new life.

Marjorie might have fitted this profile 10 or even five years before she had me at the age of 30. But by then, she seems to have established a pattern of doomed relationships with older, married men, looking for the attentive father figure she never had. A 1966 survey of unmarried mothers found that only 18 per cent were 30 or over, and only 2 per cent were 40 or over. She was unusual to have had three of us; to have us all when she was over 30 must have been exceptional.

What made her do it? I was telling Marjorie's story to a 90-year-old who'd worked with unmarried mothers in the 1950s. 'Poor woman,' she said, 'she must desperately have wanted a family.' I hadn't thought of it like that before. Marjorie loved children and she did what young women have always done: she had sex and she produced babies. It was her misfortune to do it at a time when this was considered immoral if you weren't married, and you faced a living Purgatory as a result.

Family life is organised differently now. Marriages are ended by divorce rather than death. People have serial marriages and serial relationships because they live longer, and the old nuclear family of two parents and two children has given way to new extended families of step-relatives. Single-parent families still struggle financially but coping with benefits discrimination and neighbours' whispers no longer makes things worse. Couples choose to start families without marrying and no one turns a hair because so few people still subscribe to the religious and moral codes that once outlawed such arrangements as 'living in sin'.

Having a child outside marriage is now entirely unexceptional: by 2010 nearly half of all births were out of wedlock, the majority to cohabiting couples. And since the 1987 Family Law Reform Act, 'illegitimacy' has ceased to have any legal—or indeed social—meaning. After 70 years of campaigning by the National Council for the Unmarried Mother and Her Child and its successor, the National Council for One Parent Families, the stigma, the discrimination, the name-calling, the legacy of the old Bastardy Acts are finally vanquished.

Shotgun weddings ('pre-marital pregnancies' to

278

give them their official name), which traditionally masked the true level of illegitimacy, have also become a sociological curiosity. Friends of ours—two married couples—make no secret of the fact that their 1960s' marriages were precipitated by pregnancy. But it came out in conversation recently that their respective parents married in exactly the same circumstances, and they went to great lengths to conceal the fact. One even celebrated their wedding anniversary—including their Golden Wedding—on an entirely fictitious date. It seems extraordinary today, but people of their generation felt compelled to lie about such significant dates in their lives in order to avoid gossip and moralising.

Family relationships have changed too. Parental control is less absolute than it was. As much as Marjorie hated her father, she couldn't bring herself to cross him and she didn't leave home until she was nearly 40, which seems inconceivable now. For the first 60 or so years of the last century young women depended on their parents for a roof over their heads until (and often after) they got married, and were rarely financially independent. Since then, young people have become economically active and far less dependent on their parents, unless they are unemployed or in full-time education. Parental pressure, once so critical in determining behaviour and life decisions, has been replaced by peer group pressure. Never mind what your Mum and Dad think, what would your mates say?

The family never was the universal haven of love and social respectability the moralists claimed, but the flip side of greater independence from the family and the rejection of moral and social inhibitions is 190,000 abortions a year, big increases in venereal disease and the highest teenage pregnancy rate in Western Europe. Some things get better as others get worse.

I now understand how constrained Marjorie's options were, once she found herself pregnant. But how could it have happened again and again? In my search for explanations, I have to consider the possibility that there was some pre-existing history of depression, mental illness or other psychological problem that caused her, in her own words, to 'go off the rails'. She felt bereft after her mother died but we won't ever know if there was a more pathological reason. The fact that she'd come through the experience of giving up three babies and endured a life of poverty and disappointment without losing her sense of proportion or her sense of humour points to an essentially strong human being who never had any difficulty relating to other people. Her fatal weakness was wanting to love and be loved. The men she chose for the purpose were unavailable, unsuitable or just plain bastards. In the figurative sense, of course.

Perhaps I don't need to look for anything more extreme than the conditions prevailing at the time. It wouldn't have happened today: she would have had access to financial help, housing—or an abortion. In which case I would not be here struggling to make sense of what I have discovered on my adoption journey, and my sisters and their families would not exist. Instead, we are what we are and we're grateful for everything we have. All three of us found secure and loving adoptive homes and our parents are among the most important people in our lives. We know we've brought them mostly happiness and they will always be our Mums and Dads.

My fury with adoption is that it was such an unequal, loaded and secretive arrangement for so much of the 20th century and that, in the words of Doreen Larsen to her child's adoptive mother when they first met, 'Your happiness was built on my heartache'. Histrionic perhaps, but it happens to be true. As many of the adoption specialists at the time recognised, if birth mothers had had more financial, housing and parental support, they would never have given their babies up. But I can see now how it happened: Britain was in the economic doldrums following two world wars, the welfare state either didn't exist or was in its infancy, and inflexible moral attitudes prescribed a very narrow range of choices for unmarried mothers, especially those under 21 whose parents often made the decisions for them. Birth parents were considered the least important participants in the adoption triangle, and many suffered inhumane treatment that caused a lifetime's unhappiness and sometimes worse. They paid the price for the mid-20th century adoption experiment.

The secrecy built into adoption legislation and agency practice after 1926 was designed to protect adopters, but we now know that the long-term effects of this did more harm than good to all concerned. First, it cut birth parents off from the possibility of ever knowing what happened to their children, much less knowing them; for the children it removed a crucial part of their identity jigsaw; and it allowed weak, misguided or selfish adopters to lie, conceal and prevaricate about their children's past with impunity. Ultimately, though, it proved a false security, because the secrecy law was finally overturned and children were able to find out about their origins for themselves. And now birth mothers have the chance to find out what happened to the children they gave up.

Adopters often claim that they are now the forgotten partners in the triangle, and there's some truth in this. Adoption legislation until 1975 favoured and protected adopters—taking precedence over even the child's interests—in order to encourage recruitment. Since then adopting has become a much more complex and demanding task and they deserve more public recognition than they get. But what of the adopters whose children are now well into adulthood, parents and grandparents themselves? Are they to be despised because they were willing participants in a mass transfer of infants in the middle years of the last century that we now look on as a regrettable aberration? They adopted to fulfil their own needs but the majority did a good job and raised happy, well-balanced people with life opportunities that they probably wouldn't otherwise have had. In this respect—and it is an unavoidable one—the 20th century adoption project worked brilliantly.

The other, even more neglected, participants in the adoption story are the adoption workers and agency staff who made it all happen. Their story is rarely told outside social work textbooks and it has been illuminating to hear their testimony. They believed in what they were doing; they did their best, as they saw it, principally for the child and for adopters but also for mothers, often against the odds and the moral tenor of the times. Many were pragmatic about accepted practice and adapted it to suit particular situations; many were sympathetic and went out of their way to help mothers in need. A few admitted that they didn't like the work, but being committed to a Church organisation meant they had little choice in the matter. One confessed that she struggled to reconcile her adoption work with her own grieving for the child she, as a single woman, knew she would never have. Some of the workers I heard from were pioneers in local authority childcare at a time of post-war expansion and great optimism for the future. A surprising number said they had welcomed the opportunity to look back on their careers with affection and some satisfaction.

I have to own up here. Because my father worked in social services all his life, I have a predisposition to think that social workers are misunderstood and undervalued. They sometimes make horrible mistakes but they work in a profession where even the smallest misjudgement can have human consequences. We expect too much of them, and then pillory them when parents neglect, torture or murder their children. Social workers are a handy target in a blame culture.

So I'm torn, compromised, by being able to see adoption from everyone else's point of view. It is the adopted child's burden. In one of his early outcome studies, John Triseliotis found that we were *more than usually sensitive to the attitudes and feelings of others*.

I was adopted at the mid-point of the last century, just as the big adoption experiment was

283

getting into its stride. No one then thought of it as an experiment; it was a major social intervention to improve the lives of children and childless couples and relieve unmarried mothers of an economic and moral burden. Everyone who mattered assumed it was a jolly good thing, though Margaret Kornitzer wisely warned in 1952 that *'as a long term social measure adoption still has to be fully assessed'*. It is still being assessed as far as I can see. Though we now know that some of the policies and practices between the end of the Second World War and the mid-1970s produced damaging outcomes that could have been avoided, we still don't know whether current adoption practice—ostensibly based on the lessons of the past—will produce anything better. We should have a few clues in another 30 years.

Adoption today is very different from the boom years of the 1950s and 1960s, and it's still changing: developments like surrogacy and sperm donation present new questions. The issues, though, are still tantalisingly similar: the need for openness balanced against the individual's right to privacy; parents' motivations and attitudes and their ability to cope with difference; the child's need to know where it comes from; and that mysterious, often indestructible link between biological parent and child.

The great mid-20th century adoption project *was* an aberration; we'd never do it like that again. It was a product of its time and the conjunction of a particular set of conditions and circumstances that won't be repeated. Changing times bring changing needs. Adoption is still a viable and valuable way of creating families and helping children, but it is not the simple solution we once thought. For those directly involved it's a complex and on-going business that is still not fully understood. Making sense of it all goes on.

There are large, unresolved gaps in my own story. Who were our fathers? It's probably too late to find out. Even if the names Marjorie gave were correct, and they are still alive, they'd be very old by now. More to the point, are there other siblings out there whom we don't know about, and who don't know about us? Almost certainly, as our respective fathers probably had families of their own before, during or after their relationships with Marjorie.

But did Marjorie herself have other children? For me that is the most intriguing question. Until we decide to try and find out or they—if they exist—make contact, it remains open. Either way, the story continues.

POSTSCRIPT

The day before Mother's Day 2012. I am in Coventry Cathedral taking part in a special service for adopted people and their families. They are here to celebrate the joy of reunion and help heal the pain of separation and loss. This inspiring modern landmark, rising from the blitzed ruins of its medieval predecessor, is dedicated to the cause of reconciliation and rebirth. We are in the right place.

Spring sun breaks through the stained glass as I read a short extract from *Love Child* about my last days with my birth mother Marjorie, my reflections on our relationship and the difference it made to both our lives. It takes all the self-control I can muster to get through it without faltering. I am almost overwhelmed with emotion, but reading the words brings back the strange sense of euphoria I felt at the time. Something difficult had been resolved, leaving only good things behind.

It is now more than a decade since Marjorie died but she is still with me. She smiles at me from photographs, her funny south London sayings come to me at the most unexpected moments, and the memories of good times still resonate. Best of all I have her two other daughters, my sisters Fiona and Hazel, to share those memories with and to remind me that Marjorie gave us the greatest and most permanent of gifts, the opportunity to know and love each other.

*   *   *

Before it fell silent in October 2007, its contents digitised and consigned to a distant bunker, the Family Records Centre in London crackled with concentration and the sound of turning pages. Here on the ground floor people searching for family members ancient and modern pored over indexes recording every significant 'life event' in England and Wales since 1837, the volumes symbolically bound in red for Births, green for Marriages and black for Deaths.

Earlier that year I found myself among the page-turners, hands shaking a little with apprehension, looking for Marjorie's lost children. Were they real or were they just phantoms of a romantic imagination? It was time to find out. Starting with the 1934 Births I worked my way through the Heppelthwaites (there weren't many) in every volume until 1970, covering the likely duration of her childbearing years. I found Gillian in August 1951, Linda in July 1956 and Elizabeth in April 1960. And in the 1948 index under the Elliotts I found Susan Mary, whose tragic death a few months later led to me being 'chosen' by my new Mum and Dad.

Though no surprise, each discovery brought its own pang of sadness. Here we all were. There were no others. Marjorie's little joke about there being eight of us was just that. Relief was tinged with disappointment: relief for her sake, disappointment that such a significant question in our lives had been answered so finally in this big anonymous room of books.

When I told them, my sisters had mixed feelings too, but we all agreed on one thing. Whatever the disappointment at being denied a new search and reunion adventure, we were very happy with what we already had. But if the answer to the sibling question had been unexpectedly swift and conclusive, it now opened up a new and much more problematic possibility.

We'd never given our respective birth fathers much thought. After all, the focus of the adoptee's search is usually the mother; siblings come as an added extra and fathers as an afterthought or not at all. But a perceptive review by an adoption expert and comments by a male friend suggested that I had missed something important in writing *Love Child*. They pointed out that I'd dismissed our respective putative fathers in a couple of sentences as chancers who had passed through Marjorie's life without thought to the consequences of their (probably extramarital) flings. I had assumed the worst, not because Marjorie told me so—in fact she was always careful to speak well of them—but because I couldn't bear to imagine what it must have been like to be serially abandoned by lovers in such cruel circumstances.

My sympathies were so entirely with her and against them that it was easy to dismiss these men as incidental to the whole business of our arrival in the world. But now I was forced to consider that the circumstances might have been more complex than they first appeared, and that they might have had feelings too. More important perhaps was the belated realisation that two people had made me and that half my genetic heritage was still missing. It had taken a long time before I felt compelled to look for Marjorie; it had taken longer still to feel ready to know more about my birth father.

All over again I experienced that familiar conflict adopted people have about their adoptive parents. I'd gone through it with my Mum when I was looking for Marjorie and though my dear Dad was nothing but supportive throughout that time, now I held back from telling him about this new search. Something had changed in his attitude that warned me off. He was now well into his eighties, a widower for a decade, and the walls of his world were closing in. He was less interested in and less tolerant of others. I loved him dearly and didn't want to cause unnecessary pain. There was no imminent reunion and there might never be, so I said nothing.

Fiona, Hazel and I started talking about how to tackle a search. Or rather three searches. Though no fathers were named on our birth certificates it seemed obvious that we were talking about three different men. We share characteristic features but we look very different. Despite our advancing grey, Fiona is a delicate fair-skinned blond, I'm originally a mousy brown but tan easily, and Hazel's tightly curled raven hair and olive complexion give her a distinctly Mediterranean look.

The available facts about our fathers were sketchy, and we didn't even know if they were true. Mothers sometimes gave adoption agencies false names or misleading information to protect the identity of their married lovers. I had always suspected that the father's name on my adoption papers, Peter White, was made up. Other details sounded plausible but somehow the name didn't ring true. I was also haunted by the fact that

Marjorie used a completely different Christian name on the rare occasions when we talked about him. At the time I didn't question this because I didn't want her to know that I had my adoption file with all her heartbreaking letters in it.

With hindsight, this was a mistake. I should have been more open with her, and it would have given me the chance to establish the real facts while she was still alive. But how can you interrogate an elderly woman about the love affairs of her youth, especially if it was an episode of which she was still deeply ashamed? I just couldn't bring myself to do it. I let her tell me what she wanted to, which was precious little. They'd met at work. He was nearly 20 years older than her and married with a family.

We knew even less about Hazel's putative father: 'Paddy Jacobs? An Irish Jew? Is it made up, or what?' Poor Hazel didn't know whether to laugh or cry, the sketch was so unconvincing.

Of the three, Fiona's father seemed the most credible and therefore the most promising prospect. Stanley Page at least sounded as if he might have been a real person, and we knew he ran a shop near Marjorie's home in Gipsy Road at the time of the affair.

This new search couldn't be more different from the one we'd all undertaken to find Marjorie. She'd made things easy for us by having such an unusual name and by staying single. She was on the Electoral Roll and in the phone book. Like many unmarried mothers, she'd left a paper trail. By contrast, our fathers appeared in only shadowy form on our adoption files, with nothing as concrete as an address.

We felt ill-equipped to set out on such a stony

path without professional help, so in the spring of 2007 with scant information and a large health warning attached, we approached a tracer with a 90 per cent success rate for reuniting families separated by adoption. She was the best in the business. If she couldn't find our fathers, no one could. We began our new joint mission with mixed feelings but, as Hazel wisely reminded us, 'whatever happens, we'll still have each other'.

*   *   *

Fiona came into my life almost 20 years ago. Hazel, the second surprise sister, turned up nine years later. We were still getting to know her when *Love Child* was written. What seems a lifetime later, we find it impossible to imagine our lives without each other. But there were painful adjustments to be made along the way, especially for Fiona. I had an inkling of this at the time, but it was only much more recently that she revealed to me the depths of her struggle to accept our third sister.

It was difficult for me, I don't mind admitting it. Because I'd been brought up an only child, I had a different outlook on life because I was the sole focus of my parents. But I do remember thinking, I wish I had an older brother or sister, somebody else to share things with. And when I found you, you fulfilled everything. I know that sounds like I'm putting you on a pedestal, I'm not, it was just . . . I don't know if we were just very lucky, but I immediately felt a bond . . . I immediately thought, that's my sister, that's who I wish I could have been with, growing up. So

291

everything was in a nice little bubble, I was on cloud nine, everything was lovely.

I remember so exactly . . . you rang up and said 'I think there's another one'. And my world at that point—I know it sounds dramatic—but I felt as if I'd been knocked. Because suddenly, from having a nice little relationship with my big Sis, there was a third person. When it emerged that it was a younger sister I thought, Oh! I don't like that. I feel a bit threatened. Am I now going to be elbow-nudged out of the way?

The only three-sister relationship Fiona knew was that of her adoptive mother and two aunts which had always been fiercely competitive. So she associated three with conflict.

Then we came to meet Hazel and I wanted to be as supportive as possible. And when she came to your house, I hope I was. But at the same time I had this inner turmoil thinking, Shit! Shit! Shit! I don't want to say hello, and I was being like a little girl, which was ridiculous. But this is the first time I'd experienced sibling jealousy, rivalry, I don't know, trying to work through my feelings. Because to me everything had come to a halt with finding you. I'd never thought, what if somebody else comes along? It didn't even occur to me.

Of the three of us, Hazel is most like Marjorie: open and optimistic. She was completely unaware of Fiona's jealousy and took the news with characteristic empathy:

I didn't know that. I understand it, because the thought was in my head that I didn't want to come between your relationship. I can understand those feelings, and they might be the kind of feelings that would have been sorted out if we'd grown up together—all of a sudden we're three adults. I do feel it's brilliant that she can say that. I think it's brave of her. I completely understand it, because if I'd been in her position, I'd probably feel the same way.

Fiona took a couple of years to understand that having a second sister was a benefit, not a threat.

I had to come round to my feelings for her my own way in my own time. And I can honestly say, hand on heart now, she's a bonus to us, I love having her as a three. I remember once when she and I were giggling so much and we were laughing and being girly together and you were saying 'Honestly you two, just behave!' It was great, it was brilliant, and I was thinking, oh God, this is lovely, this is fantastic. But I had to arrive at that point myself . . . Now I wouldn't be without either of you.

*   *   *

Joy and pain go hand-in-hand in any post-reunion relationship and no adoption story stands still. What of the other searches and reunions that helped me paint the bigger picture of 20th-century adoption in the UK? Where are they now?

Perhaps the most heartbreaking testimony came from Doreen Larsen who, against all odds, traced the son she was coerced to give up as an unmarried teenager in 1951. They met but he broke off contact soon after. She is now 80 and hasn't heard from Michael for 16 years, yet he is no further from her thoughts than when she lost him as a baby. Her mothering instincts, once denied, never found an outlet. She subsequently married but couldn't have any more children.

It is unlikely that Michael will return to her now, but there is another much more hopeful development. Michael had children, and those children now have children of their own. Doreen is a great-grandmother. Though her grandchildren are long estranged from their father, they have welcomed Doreen into the family. Finally, and not a moment too soon, she has the chance to fulfil her dearest wish, to be recognised and valued as a mother, grandmother and great-grandmother.

When we left Juliet in 2004, she was still longing to know more about her father after tracing her birth mother in the 1970s. With the help of the same tracer we commissioned to look for our fathers, she learnt that he had died a sad and lonely death at about the same time she was reunited with her mother. Rather than 'not being good enough', it transpired that he was more than a match for her aristocratic mother, and their families had neighbouring estates. He had married and the search discovered two half-siblings.

Unfortunately, my story doesn't have a happy ending. My two half-brothers didn't want to know, and certainly didn't want to meet me. Considering they both went to Eton and Oxbridge, it really irritates me that the younger one doesn't know the difference between 'step' and 'half' sister as he referred to me as the former! Petty I know. Every now and then, especially around New Year, I think of making contact, but don't.

Juliet wonders whether things might have been different if they'd been half-sisters rather than half-brothers, but she has no regrets about tracing her father, even if the hoped-for happy ending didn't follow. She is sustained by an excellent relationship with cousins on her mother's side and she is content with that.

Annie Haggerty travelled a long way to be reunited with her birth mother Liz McCabe in Belfast and made the momentous decision to move her home and family there from Australia to be closer to her birth family. Though now back in Australia, that relationship is stronger than ever and Annie is looking forward to her next visit to Northern Ireland for the wedding of one of her seven brothers ('we're not allowed to use the word 'half').

We become closer with every visit. Thank God for Facebook and Skype—we stay in contact all the time. Liz and I are as close as ever and miss each other so much. Wish the two countries were closer! I love every single thing it has brought to my life and I love them all with all my heart. I think I've been blessed to find my family.

*   *   *

In the years since *Love Child* first appeared, Facebook has transformed the business of search and reunion. Social media not only enable people to stay in touch, they short-circuit the process of making that vital first contact. This has dangers for those separated by adoption. It is now possible for birth parents to circumvent official channels and make direct contact with their children placed for adoption, even before they are 18 and old enough to understand the implications of reunion. The spectre of 'Facebook stalking' is a concern because adoption today is very different from the times described in this book. Now the majority of children are adopted from the care system and have been removed from their parents because of neglect or abuse. At best, premature and unmediated contact is disruptive and distressing; at worst, the child could be in danger.

Since 2006 birth relatives are legally entitled to seek contact with their adopted children, but only via an intermediary agency, only once the adoptee is 18 and only if they want contact. For the thousands of unmarried mothers who gave up their babies during the years of the old 'closed' adoptions, this offered a new avenue of hope at last and intermediary agencies were inundated as soon as the law changed. But this service is not funded by local authorities and has to be paid for by the searcher. With going rates of up to £800, many elderly women may still be effectively prevented from seeking that longed-for reunion with a lost child.

Through media exposure, we now know more about the pain and discrimination experienced by mothers separated from their children over the past 60 years for no better reason than they weren't married. But for some, this small progress isn't nearly enough recognition of past wrongs.

Hazel and I recently met a small but determined group of mothers now in their sixties and seventies who are campaigning for a government apology for the treatment they suffered as a result of past adoption practice. Their individual stories of loss, regret and anger at the way they were dismissed as unsuitable for motherhood are passionately and persuasively told. Inspired by recent public apologies in Australia, their Movement for an Adoption Apology (MAA) is looking to build support from birth mothers and present day policy-makers. They have a hard road ahead. Britain's institutions are conservative and governments hate apologising for past mistakes. More enlightened countries recognise that the policies and moral conventions of a very different age still don't excuse inhuman treatment.

Perversely perhaps, not all birth mothers are rushing to support their cause. Some don't want to relive the pain and shame of past events. Others feel an apology is irrelevant to them. As Doreen Larsen told me: 'Not in a million years will an apology compensate me for losing Michael.' But they are brave women and they have started something important.

In the wider world of adoption, policy seems to be going round in circles. Like Tony Blair in 1998, Prime Minister David Cameron rediscovered adoption in 2011 as the obvious solution to the more than 65,000 children languishing in the care system in England alone. Despite local authority targets set by previous Labour governments adoption rates were stagnant or declining (just over 3,000 from care in 2010–11); over-zealous social workers were turning away potential adopters because of their class, race, weight or smoking habits; and for those who were approved, it was taking far too long to match them to waiting children. An Adopters' Charter, an Action Plan and a proposed new Adoption Bill followed in swift succession to give substance to the Prime Minister's promise of 'faster, fairer' adoptions.

Policies come and go but public perceptions haven't changed much since 1945, when a *Good Housekeeping* article asked: *'Why is it so difficult to adopt a child?'* It's difficult because adopting is a hugely demanding job, and much more so now than in 1945. Adoption breakdowns are estimated at one in five: the older the child when it goes to a new family, the greater the likelihood of breakdown. Adopters will be severely tested, so their assessment must be testing. But unacceptable delays and an undue emphasis on ethnicity exasperate prospective adopters and give the assessment process a bad name. It must be tough but it must also be fair on adopters and progressed promptly for the sake of the child. Only time will tell whether the latest round of policy initiatives will achieve that elusive balance between rigour and realism.

*   *   *

By the Spring of 2012 we'd all but given up hope of learning anything more about our birth fathers. My dear Dad had died two years before in his 88th year, relieving me of that lingering burden of guilt but reminding me that I'd never lacked a father. He was always there, a constant loving presence till the end.

The tracer was reluctant to throw in the towel but so far she'd drawn a blank on all three men, dismally confirming my suspicion that the names we had were false. We were disappointed but philosophical. We knew it was a long shot. I arranged to meet her for a kind of post-mortem: we would go through what she called her 'workings' to show what her time and our money had been spent on over the past five years, and that would be it.

Except it wasn't. When I got there, she had some surprising news. Digitisation, that boon to genealogists, means that new information is coming online all the time. Very recently, London Electoral Rolls for a sample period had been made available online for the first time by name rather than by street, making a search much simpler.

'And then suddenly, there's a Stanley Page in Gipsy Road! Which is pretty amazing actually, as he's there for one year only on the Electoral Roll, in 1953!'

This small but significant breakthrough completely vindicated her determination not to abandon our case. We now had cause for hope.

The details as yet are scant. He would have been 47 when Fiona was born and he died of a heart attack at 60. It seems he never married or had other children. A living relative, if found, could put flesh on these bare bones. For Fiona, 'even just to see a photo' would help 'to put him into reality, because at the moment he's some shady figure in the background. Are there any facial similarities or character traits?'

At least her questions have a chance of being answered. Hazel and I are still in limbo. The search for Paddy Jacobs goes on. Every possible Patrick Jacobs in England, Scotland, Ireland and Wales has now been eliminated. So Paddy must have been a nickname, which means the net must be cast wider still. And Peter White? By bizarre coincidence, the same Electoral Roll threw up one living just round the corner from Marjorie. But that's all it is, coincidence. However, there's one positive outcome to the discovery of Stanley Page that we can all share: it seems I was wrong about the false names after all. It is a comfort to know that Marjorie didn't lie, even for her own good reasons.

I hope Fiona will find some answers. The story is still unfolding. But however much or little we may discover in the future, we'll cope because we are sustained by the strength of the relationship we have with each other. Knowing my sisters has brought unexpected richness into my life and has helped me understand myself better—and I know that they feel the same. Marjorie gave us this gift and it grows with us as we get older. As Hazel says:

To me it's an ongoing thing and it gets better, firmer. It's the best thing I've ever done. It evolves, doesn't it? It's just normal, and that's what's good about it.

FINDING OUT MORE

Tracing Birth Parents

You can apply for a copy of your birth certificate and start tracing your birth parents and relatives when you reach 18 (16 in Scotland).

The **Adoption Contact Register** is for adopted people, birth parents and other relatives who would welcome contact from members of their birth family separated by adoption. You can join the register once you are 18 (16 in Scotland) and stipulate any conditions under which you want to be contacted.

Adoption Contact Register for England and Wales Go to www.direct.gov.uk and search for 'using the adoption contact register'.

Adoption Contact Register for Northern Ireland www.nidirect.gov.uk/gro

Adoption Contact Register for Scotland is run by BirthLink at www.birthlink.org.uk.

AAA-NORCAP runs its own non-statutory adoption register and support for people wanting to trace birth relatives. www.norcap.org.uk

Adoption Search and Reunion www.adoptionsearchreunion.org.uk

BAAF is an online advice and search directory for

adopted people and birth relatives.
www.baaf.org.uk

Directgov Go to www.direct.gov.uk and put
'tracing birth parents' in the search box. The
government website has an overview and links on
tracing and contacting birth relatives and adopted
adults.

General Register Offices hold birth, marriage,
death and adoption certificates. You need to apply
to the local Register Office where your birth and
adoption was recorded.

For **England and Wales** you can order copies of
certificates online at www.gro.gov.uk/gro/content/
certificates or go to www.direct.gov.uk and search
for 'general register office'.

If you were adopted in **Scotland** contact the
Scottish Register Office. Go to www.gro-
scotland.gov.uk/regscot/adoption.html for
information.

If you were adopted in **Northern Ireland**, the
nidirect website has information and links on
tracing and contacting birth relatives and adopted
adults. Go to www.nidirect.gov.uk and look for the
Adoption link in the Parents section.

Adoption and Social Media

Social media sites have made it easier for birth
relatives and adoptees to trace each other without
going through the official channels, often without
adequate preparation. This carries risks. If you are

thinking of tracing birth relatives through social media sites read the advice on staying safe at www.adoptionsearchreunion.org.uk/contact/social networking.

Adoption Blogs and Forums

AdoptionUK—go to www.adoptionuk.org and look under the 'blogs' and 'message boards' tabs on the top navigation or search by topic.

iVillage—go to www.ivillage.co.uk and put 'adoption' into the search box.

Mumsnet—go to www.mumsnet.com and put key words like 'adoption' and 'tracing birth parents' into the search box.

Netmums—go to www.netmums.com and put key words like 'adoption' and 'tracing birth parents' into the search box.

Adoption Support Groups

Tracing birth parents and relatives can be a difficult emotional experience. If you were adopted before 12 November 1975 you are required by law to use a registered adoption support agency. If you were adopted later, there is no legal obligation but you may find this service helpful. To read more and find agencies near you, go to www.adoptionsearchreunion.org.uk/help/database.

The following groups also support adopted people and birth relatives and can give guidance on tracing and contacting birth families:

After Adoption www.afteradoption.org.uk

Birthlink Services for people separated by adoption in Scotland. www.birthlink.org.uk

British Association for Adoption and Fostering (BAAF) www.baaf.org.uk

Intercountry Adoption Centre Information and advice on intercountry adoption issues for adopters and adoptees. www.icacentre.org.uk

Natural Parents Network Self-help group for birth parents whose children have been adopted. www.n-p-n.co.uk

New Family Social Information, advice and support for lesbian, gay, bisexual and transgender adopters and their adoptees. www.newfamilysocial.co.uk

TheSite.org Information on adoption and tracing birth parents written for young people. Put 'adopted' in the search box. www.thesite.org

Transnational and Transracial Adoption Group A self-help group for people adopted into families whose racial and cultural heritage is different from their own. www.ttag.org.uk

Further reading

A Child for Keeps: the History of Adoption in

England 1918–45 by Jenny Keating (Palgrave 2009)

Adoption Reunion—Ecstasy or Agony? by Evelyn Robinson (CLOVA 2009)

The Adoption Reunion Handbook by Elizabeth Trinder, Julia Feast and David Howe (Wiley-Blackwell 2004)

Bubble Wrapped Children: How social networking is transforming the face of 21st century adoption by Helen Oakwater (MX Publishing 2012)

Facing Up To Facebook: a Survival Guide for Adoptive Families by Eileen Fursland (BAAF 2010)

ACKNOWLEDGEMENTS

Many people helped make this book. I am particularly grateful to all those who shared their experience of adoption with me, some of whom originally responded to appeals in the national and regional press by Testimony Films for interviewees for their television documentaries. Mary Parsons, Assistant Producer of the *Love Child* programmes, generously shared a number of her recruits with me, provided access to interview transcripts and helped in many other ways. *Saga Magazine* kindly published my request for former adoption workers' experiences, and as a result I had over 30 fascinating responses that informed my understanding of the professional aspects of adoption over the past 50 years. My father, a retired social worker, called on former colleagues to talk to me and provided an invaluable source of support and informal research assistance. I shamelessly made use of friends and colleagues who I knew (or discovered) had unique adoption stories of their own, and I thank them for sharing what has until now been private family history. Bernard Cornwell provided unstinting and timely help from across the Atlantic, and John Byrne and Jenny Glenton gave professional and personal support when it was most needed.

Vera Butterworth's story first appeared in *A Labour of Love* and Ada Haskins' and Rose Crompton's stories first appeared in *A Secret World of Sex*, both by Steve Humphries, published by Sidgwick and Jackson. The extract from *Orphans of the Living, A Study in Bastardy* by Diana Dewar, published by Hutchinson, is used by permission of The Random House Group Ltd. The extract from *Yours By Choice* by Jane Rowe, published by Mills and Boon in 1959, is used by permission of Taylor and Francis Group. The extracts from *Adoption: Theory, Policy and Practice* by John Triseliotis, Joan Shireman and Marion Humbleby, published by Cassell, are used by permission of Continuum International Publishing Group. The extracts from *Rescue Work* by Edward Trenholme, published in 1927 by the Society for Promoting Christian Knowledge, are used by permission of SPCK. The quotes by Margaret Kornitzer are from her book *Child Adoption in the Modern World*, published by Putnam in 1952. The quotes by Mary Ellison are from her 1958 book *The Adopted Child*, published by Victor Gollancz (a division of the Orion Publishing Group).

This is not a work of academic research. I set out to find out as much as I could about the history of adoption from books and libraries accessible to the general reader, and from material published on the Internet. I am indebted to Jenny Keating for her article on the campaign for the first adoption legislation, 'Struggle for Identity: Issues Underlying the Enactment of the 1926 Adoption of Children Act', published in the *University of Sussex Journal of Contemporary History* in September 2001. The writings of John Triseliotis, Professor Emeritus, University of Edinburgh also contributed substantially to my understanding of the sometimes puzzling development of adoption policy and practice. Katrina Wilson, Information Officer at BAAF, and Christopher Reeve, Head of

Library and Information Services at Barnardo's, both steered me to relevant material from their extensive collections. I am grateful to Barnardo's for permission to quote from their 1961 review document on adoption policy and the adopters' recruitment leaflet from the 1960s. Natasha Roe of Red Pencil Projects researched and wrote the Finding Out More section.

This book would not have happened without the television documentaries, so I am most grateful to Steve Anderson and Nigel Pickard, who commissioned them for ITV despite my constant nagging. Amanda Hemmings at Random House and Jane Turnbull encouraged me to think I could do it. Most of all, Steve Humphries of Testimony Films first got me fired up about the need to tell the adoption story: he has been supporter, collaborator, critic and friend throughout.